Beyond Belief

Beyond Belief

Faith, Science, and the Value of Unknowing

Robert P. Vande Kappelle

WIPF & STOCK · Eugene, Oregon

BEYOND BELIEF
Faith, Science, and the Value of Unknowing

Copyright © 2012 Robert P. Vande Kappelle. All rights reserved. Except for brief quotations in critical publications or reviews, no part of this book may be reproduced in any manner without prior written permission from the publisher. Write: Permissions, Wipf and Stock Publishers, 199 W. 8th Ave., Suite 3, Eugene, OR 97401.

Wipf & Stock
An Imprint of Wipf and Stock Publishers
199 W. 8th Ave., Suite 3
Eugene, OR 97401
www.wipfandstock.com

ISBN 13: 978-1-62032-474-5

Manufactured in the U.S.A.

Bible quotations are from the *New Revised Standard Version of the Bible*, copyright © 1989 by the Division of Christian Education of the National Council of the Churches of Christ in the United States of America. Used by permission.

To Dr. Dan, Rabbi Dave, and Professor Walt
friends, colleagues,
and companions on the Way

Enlarge the site of your tent,
Extend the size of your dwelling;
Do not hold back;
Lengthen the ropes, and strengthen your stakes.
—Isaiah 54:2
(blended NRSV and TANAKH translations)

> If you want to look at the stars
> …darkness is required.
>
> —Annie Dillard, author

> The key to lost spirituality and numbing materialism
> is not merely to intensify our quest for spirituality,
> but to reimagine it.
>
> —Thomas Moore, psychotherapist

> What would religious people think about their central teachings,
> about the existence of a transcendent principle of meaning,
> or about the authority of their moral codes, if they were to become
> fully cognizant of evolution and the puzzling story of life that it narrates?
>
> —John F. Haught, professor of theology

> The evolutionary epic is probably
> the best myth we will ever have.
>
> —E. O. Wilson, sociobiologist

Contents

Preface ix
Acknowledgments xv
Introduction xvii

Part One: Beyond Belief 1

1 Autobiographical Sketch 3
2 Embracing the Critical Phase of the Journey 12
3 Two Ways of Knowing 35

Part Two: The Circle and the Ellipse 55

4 Understanding Religious Thought Elliptically 57
5 Understanding God Panentheistically 74
6 Understanding God's Relationship with an Evolving Creation 90

Part Three: A New Understanding of Jesus and the Gospels 103

7 Understanding the Sacredness of Scripture 105
8 Understanding the Jewishness of Jesus 117
9 Understanding the Resurrection and Eternal Life 136

Part Four: Reconciling Science and Religion 147

10 Science and Religion: Three Views 149
11 Nonreductive Physicality: The Hierarchy of the Sciences 164
12 The Theory of Evolution: A Brief Overview 181
13 Evolution and Human Nature 193
14 Darwinism and Design 213

Contents

Conclusion 235
Epilogue 241
Appendix A: Key Tenets of Process Theology 244
Appendix B: Stages of Knowing God 247
Bibliography 249
Index 255

Preface

BEYOND BELIEF DESCRIBES ONE of life's greatest adventures: the quest for God and for authentic faith in a postmodern age. It is intended for an educated Christian audience, including pastors, college and seminary students, and lay people. The target audience includes (1) those who may have reached a "critical place" in their faith journey—prompted by academia, science, reason, culture, and their own experience—and feel compelled to choose between two alternatives, their faith or the claims of science and reason, and (2) progressive Christians who may find here a framework that addresses their current theological understanding and provides impetus for their spiritual journey.

This book forms a sequel to my "Adventures in Spirituality" trilogy, for it brings that account to a close. The first volume in that series, *Love Never Fails*, introduces readers to my parents, career missionaries to Latin America during a turbulent period in that region's history (1935–1968), when democracy and Marxism contended for allegiance. The book also describes the faith of my parents, a faith early implanted in me. The second volume, *The Invisible Mountain*, narrates my 1989 solo bicycle ride across North America on behalf of Habitat for Humanity. That journey, taken during my physical prime, is told from the vantage point of a mature faith, a faith that willingly undertakes risks and is prepared to divest itself of "excess baggage" to give freely of itself in service to others. The book examines the cycling trek as adventure, spiritual odyssey, and metaphor for the journey of life.

Into Thin Places, the final volume in the trilogy, invites readers to join me as I explore fabled places across the Mediterranean world, traveling from Amsterdam to Cairo in search of cultural and spiritual roots. The book's first chapter, titled "The Sacred Journey," describes "The Hero's Adventure," a myth of human quest found in all time periods and across the globe. This particular type of myth involves a twofold venture: an inward journey to a spiritual center—a place of healing, vision, and transformation—and an outward journey toward others.

Preface

Beyond Belief describes a different sort of adventure—my search for an understanding of God in an age of science. Despite the multitude of topics addressed in this book, there is one overriding concern: my experience and understanding of God. My colleague Dan Stinson made this abundantly clear when, after reading the manuscript, he declared: "This work is written by a man who has experienced God in so many ways that he is discovering he can never experience all of God." Upon hearing that statement I was honored, for no words, then or since, better capture what is in my heart.

Years ago J. B. Phillips, translator of the celebrated *New Testament in Modern English* (1958), wrote a small volume titled *Your God is Too Small*. If, in describing my understanding of God in this book, I am found to be heterodox in my view, I trust it will be because my God is too big rather than too small. If my views are not in the mainstream of current Christian orthodoxy, it is because they belong to that tradition of Christian orthodoxy described in chapter 3 as apophatic,[1] rather than in the prevalent Western theological tradition characterized as kataphatic.[2]

My understanding of God builds on a mystical yet deeply intellectual tradition in Christianity, represented biblically in the Wisdom literature of the Old Testament (primarily in Job and Ecclesiastes), but also in the prophets and in the spirituality of Jesus and the apostle Paul. It is also found represented in Christian thinkers of all ages, including Origen, Cyril of Jerusalem, Evagrius of Pontus, Maximus the Confessor, Denys the Areopagite (Pseudo-Dionysius), Hildegard of Bingen, Francis of Assisi, Meister Eckhart, Julian of Norwich, Jacob Boehme, Blaise Pascal, George Fox, John Wesley, John Woolman, Friedrich Schleiermacher, Søren Kierkegaard, Albert Schweitzer, Teilhard de Chardin, Paul Tillich, Thomas Merton, Karl Rahner, Henri Nouwen, Thomas Berry, and more recently, Matthew Fox, Annie Dillard, Karen Armstrong, and Marcus Borg.

My God-centeredness is based primarily on the experience of love in the universe, love demonstrated most supremely in Jesus Christ, my

---

1. The term "apophatic" refers to ways of knowing God that are direct and not mediated. Apophatic Christians reflect an intuitive form of spirituality, which views God as ineffable and indescribable. Apophatics are comfortable with ambiguity and, when speaking of God, they prefer terms such as Mystery or Spirit. They prefer to worship God in silence or by striving for justice and peace in the world.

2. The term "kataphatic" refers to ways of knowing God that are indirect and mediated. Kataphatic Christians reflect a sensate form of spirituality, which prefers concrete images of God. Kataphatics are often divided into two groups: those who prefer to worship verbally and sacramentally and those who prefer to worship spontaneously and whole-heartedly, with the senses and the emotions.

exemplar not only of love but of justice, integrity, compassion, and forgiveness. I value the scriptures of the Old and New Testaments as foundation and guide for life and I continue to be instructed by the historic Confessions of Christianity, by the Book of Order of the Presbyterian Church (U.S.A.), and by my ordination vows in that church, while affirming that "God alone is Lord of the conscience."

The perspective found in this book should not be construed to mean that I have arrived at theological closure or at some pinnacle in my understanding. Rather it represents another stage in my spiritual journey. I look forward to additional steps—even leaps—ahead.

It took me forty years—most of my adult life—to understand what enlightened theologians, mystics, philosophers, biologists, cosmologists, geologists, literary figures, psychologists, anthropologists, artists, and a host of others had been saying for centuries. To quote John Shelby Spong, retired Episcopal Bishop of Newark:

> There is no supernatural God who lives above the sky or beyond the universe. There is no supernatural God who can be understood as animating spirit, Earth Mother, masculine tribal deity or external monotheistic being. There is no parental deity watching over us from whom we can expect help. There is no deity whom we can flatter into acting favorably or manipulate by being good. There are no record books and no heavenly judge keeping them to serve as the basis on which human beings will be rewarded or punished. There is also no way that life can be made to be fair or that a divine figure can be blamed for its unfairness. Heaven and hell are human constructs designed to make fair in some ultimate way the unfairness of life. The idea that in an afterlife the unfairness of this world will be rectified is a pious dream, a toe dip into unreality. Life is lived at the whim of luck and chance, and no one can earn the good fortune of luck and chance.[3]

With Spong, I too recoil to write these words, for the traditional understanding of God has been my guide from the beginning. Unlike some who have concluded that God is no more, I do not mean to say that God once existed but has since died. Nor do I mean to say that there is no God. What I call "God" is real, only not as popularly conceived.[4]

---

3. Spong, *Eternal Life*, 121–22.

4. The conventional understanding of God, based in part on medieval debates and the language of certain classical theologians, attributes to deity such qualities as impassibility (that God cannot experience pain and suffering), transcendence (that God is eternal and unchanging and largely unrelated to this world), and omnipotence

Preface

I recall reading Bishop John A. T. Robinson's best-seller, *Honest to God*, during my first year at Princeton Theological Seminary. The book, published four years earlier, sent shock waves around the Christian world. Robinson, the English Bishop of Woolwich, had taken the writings of three seminal Christian thinkers—Rudolph Bultmann, the leading New Testament scholar in his generation; Dietrich Bonhoeffer, the German Lutheran pastor who had participated in the underground anti-Nazi resistance movement and who had been hanged at a German prison camp in 1945; and Paul Tillich, the most widely read theologian in the twentieth century—and made their thought accessible to the population at large. Bultmann referred to the biblical scripture as "mythology" that needed to be "demythologized," since its message had been framed in the presuppositions of an ancient world that no longer existed. Tillich, who suggested that God could no longer be conceptualized through the analogy of a person, developed a transpersonal theology in which God was perceived as "the Ground of All Being." Bonhoeffer called for the development of "religionless Christianity," arguing that just as Christianity in the first century could not be contained within Judaism, so in our day Christianity could no longer be contained within religion. *Honest to God* sold more copies than any religious book since John Bunyan's *Pilgrim's Progress*, for the masses of people recognized in Robinson's words the articulation of things which they had long felt, but did not know how to express.

Like other seminarians, I studied Bultmann, Bonhoeffer, and Tillich and found their ideas intriguing and perceptive. Although Robinson's book and others like it were conceptually exciting, they did not square with my Christian upbringing or current "belief system." I eventually set them aside as contextual to my divinity training and continued preparing for ministry within the church. Such thinking was "modern" and I remained guarded.

Later, at Chautauqua Institution, I heard lectures by cutting-edge scholar Karen Armstrong and "Jesus scholars" Marcus Borg and John Dominic Crossan. I purchased their books and read them thoroughly, incorporating some of their ideas into my lectures. I read books on comparative religions and grappled with John Hick's notion of "religious pluralism" and Brian McLaren's concepts of "a new kind of Christian" and "a generous orthodoxy." Although these writers tilled the soil of my spirit

---

(unlimited in power and capable of doing all things). On the whole, such views are unbiblical and, with regard to the concept of "omnipotence," philosophically indefensible. For further elucidation consult chapter 5 and appendix A.

Preface

and sowed transformative seeds, none prompted the wake-up call that I experienced during the first week of the 2010 Chautauqua season, when I attended a weeklong series of lectures delivered by Bishop Spong, who was promoting *Eternal Life: A New Vision*, the final volume in his controversial writing career.

For that series of talks, which included a panel discussion and five public lectures, a crowd of over one thousand people gathered to listen, to question, and to interact with key concepts from Spong's writings. In keeping with my customary response to such presentations, I took copious notes, purchasing and then reading several of the speaker's books. During the ensuing academic year, while transcribing notes from that experience, I recognized the effect cosmic and human evolution had upon Spong's theology, and my outlook changed dramatically. Shortly thereafter, while watching a videotaped lecture series by evolutionary biologist Richard Dawkins titled *Growing Up in the Universe*,[5] the defensive walls of my worldview were breached as I accepted the evolutionary teachings of Charles Darwin as foundational for my worldview. That decision forced me to re-examine my belief system and its assumptions. No concept, however sacred, was exempt from scrutiny.

As a result, I arrived at nine realizations that inform my belief and behavior:

1. the certainty of human evolution;
2. the compatibility of science with religion (Christianity);
3. the harmony of faith (*mythos*) and reason (*logos*);
4. the inherent limitations of dogmatism;
5. the need to read scripture metaphorically;
6. the multivalency of scriptural texts;
7. the Jewishness of original Christianity;
8. the fallibility of supernatural theism; and
9. the experience of love in the universe.

Of these, the most significant is evolution, but the greatest is love.

5. *Growing Up in the Universe* was a series of lectures given by Richard Dawkins as part of the Royal Institution Christmas Lectures, in which he discussed the evolution of life in the universe. The lectures were first broadcast in 1991, in the form of five one-hour episodes, on the BBC in the UK. The Richard Dawkins Foundation for Reason and Science was granted the rights to the televised lectures, and a DVD version was released by the foundation in 2007.

Acknowledgments

It is impossible to acknowledge theological indebtedness, although specific ideas and exact wording can be recognized. While the organization of the material in this book is mine, I cannot claim originality for every idea. Where an argument is based on the discussion in a scholarly source, I reference the material in the footnotes. In cases of deeper indebtedness, I indicate that the material is "adapted" from that particular source.

As with most of us, my biblical and theological perspective began at home. Though I spent much of my intellectual life modifying that foundation, eventually rejecting its literal underpinnings, it is a tradition I received as a gift and continue to cherish.

Having been mentored by numerous individuals since the age of thirteen, when circumstances led me to leave my missionary parents to further my studies at a college preparatory school, I acknowledge with gratitude teachers and additional scholars who encouraged me to grow, emotionally, spiritually and intellectually, nudging and sometimes pushing me away from safe and traditional understandings of scripture and faith into more authentic encounters with God and matters of faith. The following played decisive roles in that journey: Bruce Metzger, Bernhard Anderson, Huston Smith, John Hick, Matthew Fox, Karen Armstrong, Marcus Borg, Brian McLaren, Rabbi Harold Schulweis, and most profoundly, Bishop John Shelby Spong. Two other individuals, representing non-Christian traditions, have provided interpretive lenses that enabled me to grow in my understanding of Jesus and to move forward in my journey with God: Vietnamese Buddhist monk Thich Nhat Hanh and renowned physician and author Deepak Chopra.

In examining the relationship between science and religion, specifically regarding evolution and its implications for the Christian doctrines of God, revelation, creation, and human nature, I am indebted to the following scholars: Ian G. Barbour, the magisterial thinker in the field; John F. Haught, longtime professor of theology at Georgetown University and now Senior Fellow in Science and Religion at the Woodstock Theological

Acknowledgments

Center at Georgetown; Robert J. Schneider, retired professor of general studies and of classical languages at Berea College; Nancey Murphy, Professor of Christian Philosophy at Fuller Theological Center; Michael Ruse, Professor of Philosophy at the Florida State University and the author of many books on Darwin and evolutionary biology; and George S. Hendry, Professor Emeritus of Systematic Theology at Princeton Theological Seminary, with whom I studied in the 1960s and whose book, *Theology of Nature*, based on his 1978 Warfield Lectures at Princeton, was my valued companion when I offered the initial version of my "Religion and Nature" January Intersession course at Washington & Jefferson College (W&J). I am also grateful to Bill McKibben, author, educator, and environmentalist, whose consciousness-raising book, *The End of Nature* (1989), awakened me from my complacency and shook me to the core.[6]

As always, my wife Susan provided constructive comment and unwavering support, particularly from her perspective as a cleric. I am grateful to Mary Ann Johnson and Dr. Linda V. Troost for carefully reading my manuscript and for editorial erudition. I am indebted to the staff of the U. Grant Memorial Library at W&J for generous use of resources and to Dr. Joel W. Cannon for reading the text and offering valuable perspective. I treasure memorable conversation and heartfelt companionship with colleagues in the Religious Studies Department at W&J, to whom I dedicate this book: Rabbi David C. Novitsky, Dr. Daniel A. Stinson, and summer school instructor Walter C. Weaver.

---

6. For a partial list of scholarly titles published by these individuals, consult the bibliography.

Introduction

From time immemorial, in every age, a set of questions has persisted, perplexing human beings. What's going on in the universe? Is there any point to it all? Why are we here? Is there any purpose to our lives? How should we live? Does God exist? Where did the universe come from? Why does anything exist at all? Why is there so much suffering? Why do we die? Do we live on after death? How can we find release from suffering and sadness? What can we hope for? These have been called life's "big questions"; philosophers speak of them as "ultimate questions." They are the ones that never go away.

It is the main business of religion to answer the big questions. And this is why, even when we try to distance ourselves from it, we remain intrigued by religion. Religion responds to the preoccupations that arise when life comes up against barriers beyond which ordinary—including scientific—ways of coping cannot take us. For our purposes, therefore, religions may be understood very simply as pathways or "route-findings" through the ultimate limits on our lives. These limits include not only death and meaninglessness but anything that threatens our wellbeing, anything that stands between us and lasting peace or happiness.

To accomplish this task, every generation of believers benefits by re-examining its theology, thereby providing society with vision. A theology that is stagnant reflects a religion that is limited in both usefulness and in effectiveness. The Reformation project has done its work, as has much of nineteenth-century liberalism and twentieth-century modernism, and there are more critical issues now at stake. Fundamentalist claims (inerrancy, young earth, literalism, dispensationalism, premillenial rapture eschatology) have long set themselves up for attack by critical scholars, producing individuals bent on discarding the baby with the bath water when they encounter evidence that their strict upbringing may not be up to the task of explaining itself in the post-reformation, postmodern world. We can do better than that.

Introduction

Since the emergence of human consciousness, one question underlies all theological discussion and continues to be the burning theological issue of the day: is there purpose to life? The Westminster Shorter Catechism utilizes traditional language to frame the question as follows: "What is the chief end of man?" The answer is clear-cut: "The chief end of man is to glorify God and enjoy God forever."

Building on the preceding, I propose: *The purpose of life is to experience Life*. According to this perspective, living life is its own reward, for those who experience life fully experience God, who is Life. Biblical support for this notion may be found in John 10:10, where Jesus is quoted as saying: "I came that they may have life, and have it abundantly." Elsewhere in John's gospel Jesus declares: "Very truly, I tell you, the one who believes in me will also do the works that I do, and, in fact, will do greater works than these." (John 14:12). Central to the understanding of this declaration is the phrase "believe in me." We will examine the meaning of the word "believe" in chapter 3, but for now I suggest the following interpretation: as Jesus' purpose was to experience who Jesus was, so my purpose is to experience who I am, and your purpose is to experience all you are. We are here—at this time and in this place—to experience God, who is Life.

Several years ago nine students, all seniors, joined me around a large old table in a seminar room for a course titled "The Development of Western Christianity." The topic was "The Sources of Authority for Modern Christians." The assigned reading featured the well-known epistemological approach called the Wesleyan Quadrilateral, which enumerates four sources of theology within the Christian tradition—scripture, tradition, reason, and religious experience—and the students were asked to prioritize them.

One fellow, preparing for the Christian ministry, began the discussion by suggesting that scripture should be given top priority. The books of the Bible, he stated, are the basis of all Christian belief and practice, since all were inspired directly by God and therefore provide the highest degree of authority. All sources of authority should defer to biblical revelation.

The next student questioned that conclusion. Admitting that scripture is central to Christianity, she noted that the biblical canon was produced by the church and therefore should be included under the category of tradition. In her estimation, tradition, understood as comprising scripture, should have priority for Christian belief and practice.

Another person brought up an equally valid point: tradition, including scripture, comes bound in cultural and historical context and requires interpretation in order to be applied meaningfully to contemporary life.

Introduction

Since interpretation must be filtered through a variety of lenses, including human reason, one could argue that reason stands as the final and foremost source of authority for modern Christians. Several students found this to be persuasive, while recognizing that not all aspects of faith derive from human reason or can be subjected to the authority of reason.

The last person to speak, while agreeing that reason should be held in high esteem, particularly where theological beliefs might be shown to contradict logic or scientific conclusions, noted that logic and reason are not exclusively objective phenomena. Rational people, after all, disagree, and in a global and pluralistic world, it is increasingly conceded that there are—and always have been—many different "rationalities." So, while affirming the centrality of reason, she concluded that reason cannot claim the final word. In all cases, experience has the first and final word.

We left class pondering that final insight. Does reason, together with scripture and tradition, derive ultimately from experience? Our exercise seemed to support that conclusion, for none of the students had prioritized or substantiated their organization of the four categories in the same way. Subjective experience, it seems, lies at the heart of human consciousness and fashions reality as we know it. What we experience, we are. What we are, we think. What we think, we create. What we create, we become. What we become, we express. And what we express, we experience.

Spiritual and theological understanding, particularly in Western Christianity, can be said to have evolved in a similar fashion, progressing through the following stages:

1. Primal spirituality (primarily focused on cosmic and holistic spiritual experience, corporately and individually applied). This stage is pre-Christian;

2. Organized religion (primarily focused on scriptures, rituals, dogmas, and clerical intermediaries and on the spiritual experiences they engender). This stage includes classical Judaism and Christianity.

3. Enlightened religious movements (primarily focused on individuals who value rationality and the scientific method). This phase occurred to some extent in medieval scholasticism and flourished during the Enlightenment;

4. Fundamentalist religious movements (primarily a reactionary approach to the rationalistic and scientific advances of the

xix

Introduction

Enlightenment, while valuing its own perceived rationality). This phase flourished in the nineteenth and twentieth centuries;

5. Postmodern spirituality (primarily focused on holistic spiritual experience, corporately and individually applied, based on global and pluralistic values). This stage began in the twentieth century and will be a predominant Western form of spirituality in the twenty-first century.

This progression can be summarized in the following manner: In the beginning a form of spirituality existed that was natural, holistic, and focused on achieving harmony with the universe. That primal spirituality became formalized in religious traditions, under the guidance of prophets, priests and other religious intermediaries. Religious authorities established scriptures and rituals, using rational principles and insights currently in vogue to formulate dogmas and creeds, which became part of the ongoing tradition. Scripture, creeds, and doctrine further shaped spiritual experience. Over time, free-thinking individuals and their followers questioned the methodology and conclusions of organized religion. They began to embrace new spiritual principles valued by progressive people of their time. In the twenty-first century, such values came to include freedom of conscience, reverence for nature, respect for life, compassion for all, non-violence, equality under the law, appreciation of spiritual diversity, openness to new revelation, and the abolition of discrimination based on race, color, sex, religion, age, class, or nationality.

Such spirituality, reinforced by organized religion, has the potential to lead humanity into spiritual enlightenment. While not all evolution, spiritual or psychological, biological or political, is progressive, authentic spirituality seeks the trajectory of an upward spiral.

It is easy, indeed too easy in our day, to drive a wedge between spirituality and religion, to declare that organized religion is the source of many of the world's ills, and that to solve the world's problems we must eliminate religion. Such is the view of zoologist Richard Dawkins, who views religion as a cancer, as the enemy of humanity and the progenitor of endless violence. He is quick to cite remarks by some of America's most illustrious Founding Fathers, such as Thomas Jefferson's "Christianity is the most perverted system that ever shone on man," the anticlericalism of James Madison, "During almost fifteen centuries has the legal establishment of Christianity been on trial. What have been its fruits? More or less, in all places, pride and indolence in the clergy; ignorance and servility in the laity; in both, superstition, bigotry and persecution," and John Adams's ringing critique, "This would be the best of all possible worlds, if there were no religion in it."[7]

Neale Donald Walsch, in his celebrated *Conversations with God*, asks the question, "Do we need to return to religion? Is that the missing link?" To which his God replies: "Return to spirituality. Forget about religion." When Walsch asks for clarification, "God" responds: "[Religion] is not good for you. Understand that in order for organized religion to succeed, it has to make people believe they *need* it. In order for people to put faith in something else, they must first lose faith in themselves. So the first task of organized religion is to make you lose faith in yourself. The second task is to make you see that *it* has the answers you do not. And the third and most important task is to make you accept its answers without question."[8]

Walsch attempts to clarify this point by addressing the differences between "spirituality" (what we might call "natural or authentic religion") and "religion" (what we might call "authoritarian or fundamentalist religion"), contrasting their views in the following manner:

- religion fills the hearts of humans with *fear of God*, where once individuals loved That Which Is (God) in all its splendor;
- religion ordered humans to *bow down before God*, where once individuals rose up in joyful outreach;
- religion has burdened humans with *worries about God's wrath*, where once individuals sought God to lighten their burden;
- religion told humans to be *ashamed of their bodies* and their most natural functions, where once individuals celebrated those functions as the greatest gifts of life;
- religion taught us that we must have an *intermediary in order to reach God*, where once we thought ourselves to be reaching God by the simple living of our lives in goodness and in truth;
- religion *commanded humans to adore God*, where once humans adored God because it was impossible not to;

The list concludes with a broad condemnation of organized religion in the past: "Everywhere religion has gone it has created disunity—which is the opposite of God. Religion has separated man from God, man from man, man from woman—some religions actually telling man that he is above

---

7. Dawkins, *God Hypothesis*, 43.
8. Walsch, *Conversations with God*, Book 2, 247.

Introduction

woman, even as it claims God is above man—thus setting the stage for the greatest travesties ever foisted upon half the human race."[9]

Despite Walsch's penetrating insights, I find an alternative approach more realistic and much more hopeful. According to world religions scholar Huston Smith, the contrast between spirituality and religion is both unnecessary and unwise. Using the analogy that religion is to spirituality as institutions of learning are to education, Smith maintains that while it is possible to become educated without schools, universities, and books, to do so is like reinventing the wheel in every generation. Just as institutions of learning are the way education gets traction in history, so also religion is the way spirituality gains traction in history.[10] While there are perversions and extremes in religious beliefs and behavior, religion's external forms should be regarded as vessels of spirituality rather than as virulent cancers or useless vestiges, as some suggest.

The Journey of Faith: A Holistic Pattern

I am a teacher by profession. For forty years I have taught at the college and graduate levels. But teaching is not just something I do; teaching is my identity. My passion for learning led me to consider a career in religious studies, a choice that was confirmed by my fondness for the subject matter and because my initial teaching experiences created moments that were lively and true. I learned early on that the best teachers—the most effective—are committed to the *process* of education, a process that revolves around two priorities: (1) commitment to the pupil—as person and as learner—and (2) commitment to the joy of learning, to ever fresh insights and possibilities. An effective teacher in the field of religious studies provides students with tools for inquiry and keeps the conversation going, not arriving at conclusions too quickly or using authority to clinch an argument. I try to follow that advice in this book, and I trust you too will value that approach as you read further.

During the past decade, the mindset of college students has changed dramatically. In almost every discipline, the level of engagement with the subject matter has transformed students from passive to active learners. In addition, the theological preunderstanding of students in my classes seems to have changed as well. While a majority continue to be reared in Christian homes, an increasing number enroll in religion courses not

9. Ibid., 248.
10. Smith, *Why Religion Matters*.

Introduction

simply to build upon an existing foundation but to wrestle with matters of faith. Large numbers of college students today self-designate as agnostics and atheists, and those who arrive at these positions thoughtfully rather than out of boredom or apathy add profoundly to class dynamics. On the whole, skeptical students become exemplary students, for they approach life passionately rather than perfunctorily.

Individuals today find themselves attracted to a religious paradigm that describes one's faith story as a journey through three stages. This journey has become instructive for many of my students in articulating their own faith story.

Precritical understanding (also called *precritical naiveté*) is an early state in which children accept whatever significant authority figures in their lives tell them to be true as indeed true. For some this state is short-lived; for others, it can last a lifetime. In this stage children generally accept conflicting teachings that God is everywhere present and that God is in heaven. Theologians speak of this tension as the relationship between the immanence and transcendence of God. While most children live with the ambiguity, others feel the need to resolve the tension one way or another.

In their early teens, some begin to doubt the existence of God, an experience that can be traumatic for those who believe in hell or who fear eternal punishment. From a psychological perspective, such an experience represents a collision between one's childhood beliefs and those of modernity. Those who undergo this transition are entering the stage of *critical understanding*, and there seems to be no way back.

In late adolescence college students may become exposed to the scholarly study of religion. The answers provided by the great intellectual figures of Western theology may not restore their former beliefs, but they do provide a framework that allows then to take their perplexity seriously. Those who wrestle with the nature of scripture and learn about early Christianity discover that the Bible, including the gospels and the rest of the New Testament, is neither a divine document nor a straightforward historical record. Some are exposed to the well-known scholarly distinction between "the Jesus of history" and "the Christ of faith." The first concept refers to Jesus as he truly was—a Galilean Jew who was executed by the Romans—and the second concept refers to what Jesus became in the faith of the early Christian communities: the Christ of the developing Christian tradition. The gospels, it seems, contained mostly later traditions about Jesus, so it is the "Christ of faith" rather than the "Jesus of history" that one encounters in the gospels and in the later creeds. From this perspective the image of Jesus as divine savior, central to the church's theology, was not something Jesus had taught concerning himself but rather came from the church's later understanding. The longer one studies the Christian tradition, the more transparent its human origins become. The same applies to all of the world's religions; all seem products of culture. Those who accept this become perplexed about God and conclude that there probably is no such reality.

Eventually those who persevere in their faith journey discover that agnosticism and atheism are not final destinations but temporary stops. Their religious perception is transformed by what might be called "an experience of sacred mystery." Something happens to them—a mystical experience, something traumatic, a relationship, a sudden realization, a wilderness experience, an experience of "something more"—and the word "God" becomes meaningful once again, only this time not as a reference to a supernatural being "out there" but to the sacred at the center of existence, the holy mystery that is all around us and within us. God is no longer a mere idea or an article of belief external to oneself but rather an element of experience. Such persons have reached the state of *postcritical understanding* (*postcritical naiveté*), a state where one participates in religious rituals because they are meaningful and not because they are required, where one hears ancient biblical stories as "true" while knowing them as not literally true.

Though the expression "postcritical understanding" or "postcritical naiveté" seems to represent accurately this sophisticated state of innocence, I prefer "mature faith." By faith, I refer to an existential state that is unique to each individual, and by "mature" I refer to a conscious, heartfelt examination of conviction based upon one's cumulative life experience. Mature faith challenges one's conceptual framework and provides a new understanding of the religious task. This book is written for those who desire to learn more about postcritical spirituality or to enjoy more fully its benefits.

Overview

Those who know my theological disposition or have read my earlier books may be surprised by my bluntness in the opening chapters of this volume. That material was written in response to The Outsider Test for Faith, formulated by former evangelical John W. Loftus. This approach encourages individuals of various faiths to assess their truth claims

Introduction

from the perspective of an outsider and with the same level of skepticism they use to evaluate other religious traditions. Applying this methodology to my own religious perspective, I spent a year subjecting my religious beliefs to logical scrutiny, temporarily setting aside my faith presuppositions and replacing them with rational and scientifically verifiable premises. The short-term results of this deconstructive undertaking were disastrous; reason, it seemed, trumps faith every time. As I worked out the details of my project, it became evident that as long as one is constrained by the modern mentality, one cannot achieve "a sufficiently deep understanding of Christianity to find God, as revealed in Christ."[11] Other possibilities emerged, challenging the validity of my conclusions and commencing the reconstructive approach I describe as "postcritical understanding." Those possibilities could not be ignored. The remainder of the book addresses topics vital to the reconstructive task. The results demonstrate that science and religion can work cooperatively in mutually beneficial ways: scientific knowledge can broaden the horizon of religious faith and religious faith can deepen our understanding of the universe.

Part One tells my faith story honestly, starkly, and vividly. Chapter 1 highlights decisive events in my life that helped shape my precritical belief system and introduces the critical phase of my journey. Chapter 2 examines various religious topics impacted by my experiment with The Outsider Test for Faith, including prayer, miracles, prophecy, salvation, and the afterlife. Chapter 3 explores two traditional ways of knowing: *logos* (reason) and *mythos* (myth). Both are essential and neither is superior to the other. Although *logos* is essential to human survival, it has limitations. It cannot provide ultimate meaning or help cope with tragedy or with death. For help people turn to *mythos*. The task of religion is to enable followers to find wisdom, the sort of wisdom that helps them live creatively, peacefully, and even joyously with realities for which there are no easy explanations.

Parts Two and Three represent the reconstructive task. Chapter 4 challenges conventional Christians to replace belief with faith. The difference between these is explained by two competing models for truth: the circle and the ellipse. The circular model is based on either/or thinking, meaning that something is true *or* false, literal *or* fanciful, revealed *or* invented. Dichotomous ways of thinking are reductionistic, suggesting

11. Allen, *Christian Belief*, 19.

Introduction

that such options exhaust the alternatives. Either/or thinking is intolerant of ambiguity and uncertainty and is dissatisfied with anything less than certainty. The elliptical model, by contrast, follows a both/and approach to reality. It is holistic and inclusive; it embraces adventure and ambiguity and finds ways to feed the imagination. Truth, for elliptical thinking, is not one-dimensional but dialectical. Postcritical understanding (mature faith) places equal value upon faith and reason, and holds the two in tension. In this chapter I apply the elliptical model to five theological topics, demonstrating the potential interconnectedness of Jewish and Christian approaches to reality.

Chapter 5 questions the appropriateness of the conception of God as personal. Building on the contributions of depth psychology, process theology, and the insights of numerous twentieth-century religious thinkers, readers are asked to consider a panentheistic perspective (the view that the universe is in God, yet God is more than the universe), focusing on the transpersonal or superpersonal aspect to God found in many religious traditions. In this chapter we examine two models of God found in the biblical and Christian traditions, the "monarchical model" and the "Spirit model." The monarchical model, which portrays God as male, all-powerful, lawgiver, and judge, suggests that God is distant. Those who use this image today tend to be doctrinaire and to associate God with belief, the sort of belief that appears dogmatic and hostile toward science and modernity. The Spirit model, by contrast, appears relational and tolerant, more accepting of uncertainty and ambiguity and less combative. Adherents of this perspective are more amenable to science. Chapter 6 examines the Christian doctrine of creation and provides both historical and current examples to demonstrate how belief in God and in an evolving creation—the universe of Darwin and Einstein—stand squarely in the tradition of faith seeking understanding. In the words of eminent biologist Theodosius Dobzhansky: "It is wrong to hold creation and evolution as mutually exclusive alternatives. I am a creationist and an evolutionist."

A panentheistic understanding of God requires a re-examination of Christian theology in its entirety, a task I leave to others. Part Three addresses three topics, scripture (chapter 7), Jesus and the gospels (chapter 8), and the doctrines of resurrection and eternal life (chapter 9), utilizing early Jewish-Christian methods and perspectives that harmonize with panentheism. Chapter 7 examines biblical authorship, acknowledging the obvious human element in the Bible. It critiques the widely held assumption that the Bible is both divine and human, arguing that the Bible in its

Introduction

entirety is a human product. As such it contains ancient Israel's perceptions and misperceptions, just as it contains the early Christian movement's perceptions and misperceptions. This chapter uncovers an essential feature of the Bible, its narrative framework.

Chapter 8 underscores the fact that the Jesus most Christians worship today (the second person of the Trinity) is far different from the historical Jesus. That Jesus was Jewish, and his mission was focused within Judaism. As a first-century Palestinian Jew, Jesus would have viewed his mission as prophetic, announcing God's coming kingdom. That Jesus never intended to establish a new religion. Those who fail to understand Jesus as a Jewish figure, teaching and acting within first-century Judaism, misunderstand what he was about.

This chapter introduces the Jewish exegetical method known as *haggadic midrash* in order to help us understand how the New Testament writers constructed their literature. Midrash is the act of rereading and expanding a text in the form of a new narrative to update the existential meaning. Gospel writers, for example, less concerned with recording history and more focused on writing edifying literature, recontextualized ancient material for a new situation. The gospels, like the rest of the New Testament, are the products of developing traditions of the early Christian communities in which they were written. Some of the events reported in the gospels really happened and reliably represent Jesus as a figure of history, but much of the tradition is history metaphorized, meaning it is not literally true but represents the revised understanding of the evolving Christian communities following Easter.

The first generations of Christians, the vast majority of whom were Jewish, undoubtedly saw midrash at work in their scriptures. Later generations of Christians, who tended to be gentiles, read these Jewish antecedents in their scriptures with an anti-Jewish bias that distorted the message of these books. By the start of the second century the common ground between Jews and Christians, once vast, became nonexistent. The gentile way of reading the New Testament became increasingly dominant, until the Jewish perspective was lost altogether.

Understanding the Jewishness of Jesus and of the New Testament also has profound implications for core Christian doctrines such as the resurrection and the hope of eternal life. Chapter 9 addresses the centrality of Easter to Christianity. What really happened on Easter, and what does Easter mean for Christians? Is it possible to affirm the reality of the Easter experience without the necessity of literalizing the details of the resurrection moment? Did the loss of a Jewish *haggadic* perspective toward sacred stories result in a distortion of the intended message?

A clue to the answers can be found in the intention of the gospel writers, whose symbolic language signaled they were not writing history or biography. They were trying to interpret a life-changing experience, but all they could use were limited human words. The gospel writers signaled this weakness of vocabulary to their readers by exaggerating their language to the point at which their words became incongruous if understood literally. Once we admit the inadequacy of human language to describe the realm of the divine, we must address the inconsistencies present in the biblical texts of Easter. The discrepancies in these texts indicate that the core message of Easter is spiritual, not physical: Jesus continued to be experienced after his death, but in a radically new way, as a spiritual and divine reality.

As Christianity evolved, the process required metaphorical and conceptual development, a process akin to what modern theologians call "remythologization." During the following century, when the traditions found in the New Testament took shape, Christian communities used a large number of metaphors or images, mostly drawn from the Hebrew Bible, to speak about Jesus and his significance. Over time, these metaphors produced a transformed perception of Jesus that led to the "canonical Jesus" of the New Testament and the "creedal Jesus" of later Christianity.

Part Four addresses the topic of science and religion. Are they compatible? Can they be harmonized? Can one believe in God in an age of science? Chapter 10 examines three contemporary models in which science and religion can be related: (1) opposition (conflict), which views science and religion as fundamentally irreconcilable; (2) separatism (contrast), which avoids conflict by placing science and religion into totally independent and autonomous realms, each with its own domain and its characteristic methods; and (3) engagement (consonance), which affirms interaction between the disciplines.

Within the opposition camp two antagonistic viewpoints venture forth to provide an ultimate explanation of reality: (1) scientific materialism (also known as "scientism" or scientific naturalism), in which scientific evidence provides ultimate truth, and (2) biblical literalism, in which religious faith provides ultimate truth. Both represent opposite ends of the theological spectrum, but they share characteristics in common. Locked in an either/or approach to reality, both claim that science and theology make rival claims about the same domain, namely the history of nature, so that one must choose between them. Both clearly misrepresent science.

Scientific materialists start from science but end up making broad philosophical claims. Biblical literalists, on the other hand, move from theology to make claims about scientific matters. Both fail to respect the differences between the two disciplines.

The separatist approach views science and religion as totally independent and autonomous realms, each with its own domain and its characteristic methods. Proponents of this view claim there are two distinct jurisdictions, each tending to its own business and neither meddling in the affairs of the other. Because there should be no real competition between evolutionary science and religion, the separatist approach appeals to many theological camps within Christianity.

While separatism is a good starting point for analyzing the relation between science and religion, it is ultimately unsatisfactory, for its theological adherents end up with a distorted view of religion. For some Christians, nature is devalued and the gulf between God and the world remains vast. Other Christians end up privatizing and interiorizing religion, limiting God to the realm of selfhood and rendering nature devoid of religious significance. Such an anthropocentric framework offers little protection against the exploitation of nature; furthermore, relegating science and religion to watertight compartments rules out the possibility of constructive dialogue and mutual enrichment.

Despite the presence of distinctive functions and attitudes in religion that have no parallels in science, there are also functions and attitudes in common. Some of these comparisons are spelled out in chapter 10, which endorses consonance. Engagement maintains that science and religion are logically and linguistically distinct, but it acknowledges that in the real world they cannot be easily compartmentalized; science is not as objective, nor religion as subjective, as some assume. Since truth cannot contradict itself, scientific and religious truth must be reconcilable. However, the engagement approach acknowledges that after Darwin we simply cannot have the same thoughts about religious faith as we may have had before. After Darwin the entire universe and the story of life look different. So also do a lot of other things: human existence, morality, culture, and, above all, God. According to the engagement approach, evolution does not require that we abandon faith and theology, but it does demand that these undergo a kind of development of their own.

There is no danger to religious faith or theology in opening itself to such transformation. In fact, such growth helps to keep faith and theology alive and healthy. Engagement does not strive to prove God's existence

Introduction

from science but is content to interpret scientific discoveries within the framework of religious meaning.

Chapter 11 presents a hierarchical model to depict the relations between theology and the sciences. Physics, the study of the simplest building blocks of reality, appears at the bottom. The rest of the sciences, including psychology and the social sciences, are located in order above physics, to represent the fact that they study increasingly complex systems. Adopting this model, the Anglican theologian and biochemist Arthur Peacocke proposes that theology be considered a science and then places it at the top of the entire hierarchy, since theology involves the study of the most encompassing system of all: God in relation to both the natural world and human society. This model reconciles the best insights of the Opposition and Separatism viewpoints. In addition, it also affirms the Engagement model, since it recognizes that theology cannot be isolated from the rest of knowledge.

The relation between theology and the sciences is much like the relation between one science and another. Each science employs its own proper language and subject matter and provides a relatively autonomous description of reality. Yet each science can learn from its neighbors. Thus theology provides a relatively autonomous description of reality, yet has some things to learn from the sciences and some things to teach them as well. While some may object that classing theology among the sciences is a mistake, theology operates much like a science. It has its own proper data—from history, revelation, and the cumulative experience of the church—and its doctrines are comparable to theories in the sciences, rationally justified by their ongoing ability to explain the data.

At this point we revisit the role of scripture in Christianity, examining the concept of the "Two Books," the Book of Nature and the Book of Scripture. This influential notion has a long-standing tradition in Christian theology, having been articulated early in the third century by Tertullian. Theologians who first promoted this concept were concerned to defend the integrity of both the study of nature and the study of scripture. This concern occupied many of the church's greatest thinkers throughout its long history. When the language of scripture appeared to contradict that of science, theologians such as Augustine and Calvin encouraged readers to invoke the principle of accommodation, meaning that when biblical writers spoke of natural phenomena, they were using the common language of their day and applying limited human understanding.

Introduction

Chapter 12 introduces the topic of evolution, the overarching paradigm that governs the modern scientific worldview, tackling the most troubling aspect of evolution for many Christians, namely the notion that humans have evolved from earlier life forms. Chapter 13 considers the nature of human beings in greater detail, including the implications of human evolution for the biblical view that humans are created "in the image of God." This brings us to the matter of dualism, a divisive issue in our culture. Many people, especially Christians, assume humans are made of two parts: a physical body and a nonmaterial mind or soul. Increasingly, scientists, philosophers, and biblical scholars are calling this theory into question. A non-dualistic approach seems more consistent with science than dualism but also more consistent with biblical thought. This "non-reductive physicalist" account also fits nicely with the hierarchical model described in chapter 11. As we go up the hierarchy of levels from physics and chemistry to biology—from nonliving to living, we see that life is a result of the special *organization* of nonliving matter rather than of the addition of any new substance such as a vital force. Similarly, as we go from the non-human to the human level, entities such as a soul or mind need not be added. The chapter examines two themes that are central to creationist theology: the assumption of an original perfection of creation and the assumption of original sin. These doctrines have had a long history in Christian thought, but upon further examination they appear to be based more on shallow biblical literalism than upon general Christian teaching regarding sin and redemption.

Chapter 14 discusses the topic of teleology, noting that while Darwinism challenges traditional understandings of design in the universe, a panentheistic perspective is compatible with faith in the biblical God of self-giving love. Such a view not only allows for randomness and uncertainty in the universe, it actually anticipates an evolving universe. This chapter concludes the argument that one can be both an evolutionist and a Christian.

Part One

Beyond Belief

> God is more interested in
> adventure than in the status quo.
>
> —John F. Haught, professor of theology

> In soul faith there are always at least two figures—the "believer" and the "disbeliever." Questioning thoughts, drifting away temporarily from commitments, constant change in one's understanding of faith—to the intellect these may appear to be weaknesses, but to the soul they are the necessary and creative shadow which actually strengthens faith by filling it out and ridding it of its perfectionism. Both the angel of belief and the devil of doubt play constructive roles in a full-rounded faith.
>
> —Thomas Moore, psychotherapist

1

Autobiographical Sketch

FIFTEEN PASSAGES, TAKEN FROM seven books of the Bible, contain an understanding of reality that has profoundly influenced the Western world. Indeed, prior to the Enlightenment—an epoch of Western civilization informed by scientific discovery and the rigorous application of reason—the prevailing cosmological and anthropological perspectives of the West had been undergirded by religious notions rooted in these passages. The passages I have in mind are: Genesis 1:1; Genesis 1:26–27; Genesis 2:7; Psalm 8:3–8; Psalm 19:1; Psalm 139:13–14; John 1:1–3; Romans 5:12–14, 17–19; Romans 8:28; 1 Corinthians 15:21–26; Colossians 1:15–17; Revelation 21:1–4, 23–27; 22:5.

Taken together, these passages teach that humans are part of a vast providential plan of creation by a singular deity called God who is personal, all-powerful (omnipotent), and all-knowing (omniscient), and who is intimately involved with his creatures, particularly with humans, who are objects of God's attention and who have been designated vice-regents of God's magisterial rule. From passages like these, Christians have deduced that God is just, merciful, and altogether good (omnibenevolent). History, with its origins in the Garden of Eden and its consummation at a time known only to God, is filled with promise. The role of humanity is to perpetuate divinely instituted models for the well-being of society (according to Martin Luther, God providentially established specific "orders" within society, including family, church, and state in order to prevent creation from collapsing into chaos), which, if properly implemented, would accomplish God's cosmic purpose and plan for creation. Those who accept God's plan will be rewarded with eternal bliss, and those who resist or deviate unforgiven from that path will be lost forever.

That's the message I received as a child, and in time I recognized the biblical story, in its entirety, to be my story as well. That story essentially framed my self-understanding, in whole or in part, for much of my adult life.

Beyond Belief

As the only child of Protestant missionary parents, it was altogether natural that at an early age I should adopt my parents' worldview as my own. One of my earliest recollections was the experience of kneeling by my bed and "accepting Christ as my Lord and Savior." I was four years old, and I had just learned that the only way to get to heaven to be with Jesus was to confess my sinful condition and acknowledge Jesus as my Savior, meaning that I needed to believe that Jesus had died on my behalf as God's plan for my eternal salvation. The alternative to heaven was a place called "hell," and I certainly didn't want to end up there. Choosing Jesus was a sensible alternative to eternal damnation, but it also brought with it a particular lifestyle undergirded by specific doctrines and specific ethical priorities.

To thwart those occasional moments when I might question the rationale behind my conversion to Christ, I was reminded to read the Bible and pray daily as well as to participate in daily family devotions. This family time allowed me to ask questions and helped me to "grow in my faith." Over time, I became effective in "sharing my faith with others," which increased my confidence and shored up the foundation of my beliefs.

Around the start of my teenage years I entered a short period of rebellion, losing some of my youthful charm and my desire to please others while questioning aspects of my religious beliefs. Though my parents interpreted my negative behavior as a conflict with evil, I was simply growing up. When my parents left Costa Rica to continue their missionary work in Colombia, a turbulent South American country emerging from a decade-long period of civil strife, I enrolled at The Stony Brook School, a private college preparatory school on Long Island, remaining there until my graduation three and a half years later. At that boarding school, known for its adherence to Christian values, I grew physically, intellectually, and spiritually, all under the watchful care of a distinctive Christian staff. I enjoyed my studies and came to acquire a deep appreciation for history and literature.

My faith deepened during that period, due in part to compulsory daily chapel and to additional opportunities for spiritual growth such as leading a Christian youth group in the community, representing the school at religious conferences, and embarking on a summer cross-country tour with a teacher and several international students. In school I excelled in religious and theological studies; my religious zeal was such that I was one of two seniors to complete the headmaster's challenge to memorize a book of the Bible in order to receive a Bible of my own choice.

Assisted by an academic scholarship, I registered at The King's College, a Christian college now located in New York City but then on a beautiful campus in Briarcliff Manor, thirty miles north of the city.

King's provided a perfect environment in which I could excel spiritually and academically. All students enrolled in required religion courses, and since there was no major or minor offered by the department, I opted for numerous electives. My faith was nurtured at chapel services, Sunday evening services, and accompanying the college president on his speaking and preaching engagements. I also spent two summers traveling the country representing the college as pianist for musical gospel teams. One summer, in addition to musical accompaniment, I preached over sixty times at church services and other church-related events.

Graduating with a major in Modern Foreign Languages, I remained at the college for a year, assisting the language department and serving as resident director of an off-campus dormitory. I also audited a class in Church History taught by world-renowned Yale professor Kenneth Scott Latourette at General Theological Seminary in New York City. A disappointment occurred at the start of the term when my Baptist church in Paterson, New Jersey denied my request for funds to study at the seminary on account of the church's policy to support only students attending conservative denominational seminaries. I concluded that my theological affiliation lay elsewhere.

The following year I enrolled in a graduate program in Latin American Studies at Indiana University. Though I found the topic fascinating, I remained undecided about a career and applied to Princeton Theological Seminary, one of America's leading theological institutions, intending to study ethics and ecumenism. During my first year in the divinity program my attention gravitated to biblical studies, partly because of my strong background in the subject but also through the influence of one of the leading scholars at the institution, Dr. Bruce Metzger, a gracious scholar with a stellar international reputation and a conservative approach to the Bible.

Upon completing a divinity degree I transferred my church membership to the Presbyterian Church and remained at Princeton Seminary, enrolling in the PhD program in biblical studies. Discerning a call to ministry, I sought ordination in my adoptive denomination and accepted the pastorate of a small congregation while I completed the dissertation phase of my program. Though my work at the church was meaningful, I found the administrative side tedious. Aware that my gift definitely lay in academics, I accepted a teaching position at Grove City College, a Presbyterian-related liberal arts college.

An area of theological study that had fascinated me for a long time was the topic of eschatology, which dealt with the end of history and the return of Christ. This topic had also intrigued the earliest Christians and many others throughout church history. My evangelical upbringing emphasized the imminent return of Christ, which led to a literalistic interpretation of eschatological passages in the Bible, particularly apocalyptic passages in the gospels (see Mark 13, Matthew 24, and Luke 21), in the epistles (2 Thessalonians 2), and in the books of Daniel and Revelation.

Princeton Seminary, known for its commitment to a Reformed and amillennial approach to eschatology,[1] encouraged less literal approaches to the topic. Seminarians at Princeton, after all, were training for careers in ministry and society, and not for the impending end of history. Nevertheless, the centrality of eschatology in the Bible and for early Christianity was undisputed by scholars at the seminary. While some students believed in an imminent rapture (the expectation that believers would soon be "caught up in the clouds" to meet Christ at the time of his return, a view based upon a literal interpretation of 1 Thessalonians 4:15–17), I no longer agreed. My changing views on eschatology resulted in fervent debates with my evangelical parents, who clung tenaciously to literal premillennialism.[2] They disagreed with my interpretation of scripture and feared that my understanding of eschatology indicated an alarming compromise with biblical principles. Prolonged disputes on the topic, with neither side relenting, led to the conclusion that it was best to avoid the topic altogether.

A corollary to eschatology is the doctrine of heaven and hell, a topic with important implications for soteriology (salvation). Though I still maintained a traditional understanding of salvation (that individuals are saved through Christ's work on the cross), the doctrine of hell kept resurfacing, and the more I thought about it, the more inclined I felt to abandon it. C. S. Lewis's witty and subtle approach to heaven and hell described in his allegory, *The Great Divorce*, became increasingly attractive at that time. Questioning eschatology led to my questioning other religious topics as well, particularly biblical prophecy.[3]

Despite these concerns, the bedrock of my belief was intact and continued to be based on scripture. While the Bible seemed largely the product of human authorship, I saw no need to question the doctrine of

---

1. Amillennialism utilizes a symbolic interpretation to the early Christian focus on the concept of a millennium, a reference to the restored earthly kingdom that was understood to last for a period of one thousand years between the first coming of Christ and the establishment of a totally new cosmic order at his second coming.

2. Premillenialism refers to the view that the imminent rapture of believers will be followed by a seven-year period of tribulation for those "left behind" during the rule of the antichrist.

3. These topics will be addressed in chapter 2.

divine inspiration. I no longer believed in verbal inspiration—the notion that the actual words of scripture were inspired—but I still maintained that the Bible was a product of special revelation, and that it was sufficient for faith and practice.

When I interviewed successfully to teach in the Religion Department at Grove City College, a college of some 2,300 students on a beautiful 170-acre campus in western Pennsylvania, I was elated. Despite several drawbacks—classes taught on Saturday mornings and a high student-faculty ratio—the students were bright and well-mannered and the faculty members were engaging.

My first years of teaching were challenging, due to new course preparations, a student load of some two hundred per semester, and the completion of my doctoral dissertation. I also advised five student organizations while supplying pastoral services with my wife at a local Presbyterian congregation. In addition, our two children were born during this period.

At the same time, members of the religion department were creating a textbook to supplement the teaching of an all-college requirement on the religious/philosophical dimension of life. I collaborated on several chapters in biblical theology. The team, including colleagues from other departments, met regularly to review and edit the essays for the project. The two-volume work, *Building a Christian World View*, utilized six concepts that comprised a Reformed (Calvinist) approach to Christianity. The intention was to develop a biblical view that encompassed all of life, based on the assumption that the Bible presents a unified view of reality that is coherent and consistent and that accurately describes the human situation.

The six themes of the worldview presented in the text are: theology (the study of God), anthropology (the study of humankind), epistemology (the study of knowledge), cosmology (the study of the universe), society, and ethics. The methodological approach to the worldview required that one start with the category of theology, specifically with biblical teaching concerning God. That viewpoint, in turn, was understood to impact directly all other categories of the worldview, beginning with anthropology and epistemology. The starting point for an understanding of the topic of anthropology was the belief that humans were created by God and were therefore related to God in particular ways. The starting point for a biblically-based epistemology was that all truth begins with revelation. It was assumed that what one believes concerning theology, anthropology, and epistemology directly impacts beliefs in the related fields of cosmology, society, and ethics. The following diagram suggests the flow of influence between the six themes of the worldview:

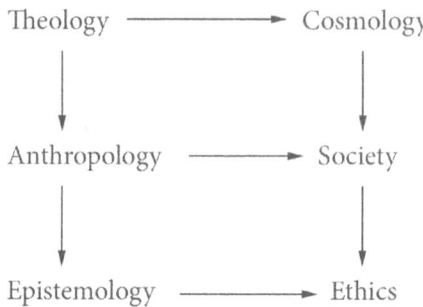

According to this perspective, what one believes about God, man (anthropology), and knowledge (epistemology) correlates directly to beliefs about the nature of the cosmos (it was created by God and was totally good at the point of its creation), society (social institutions such as the family and the state were conceived by God and introduced by divine revelation and did not originate with humans solely as means for their survival and progress), and ethics (ethical codes and norms that serve as the basis for human behavior were predetermined by God and revealed throughout history). In contradistinction to modern views, which approach ethics humanistically and consider values to be relative, a Reformed perspective looks to biblical norms for guidance on most, if not all, ethical concerns. The question, "How, then, shall we live?" is the corollary of, "What, then, do we believe?" Ultimately, all that is true comes from God, who is Truth. Reasoning deductively, this approach builds on the premise that all truths are rooted in divine Truth, for "all truth is God's truth."

In 1980, after five fulfilling years at Grove City College (GCC), I resigned to assume a teaching position at Washington & Jefferson College, a position that encompassed regular teaching duties in addition to administrative responsibilities as Chair of the Religion Department and College Chaplain.

After more than thirty years of teaching at W&J, I value the college stance as independent and non-denominational, for it has provided me with unlimited opportunities for personal and intellectual growth. During this time I have introduced over twenty different courses in world religions, spirituality, and biblical studies, in addition to studies in global Christianity, religion and ecology, and Christian theology. I have spent summers at Chautauqua Institution in upstate New York, where I met world-class theologians and listened to some of America's most innovative thinkers. I have also remained active in my denomination, serving on various committees of Washington Presbytery and preaching in numerous ecumenical settings.

The cumulative momentum of my experience at W&J has led me to reevaluate my worldview. I pondered the consequences of replacing theology—the traditional starting point for faith—with biology and cosmology—the starting points for modern science, utilizing these disciplines as building blocks for understanding the topics of anthropology, society, epistemology, and ethics. The following diagram indicates the redirected flow of influence between the categories of the worldview, giving theology a "bottom-up" rather than a "top-down" role.

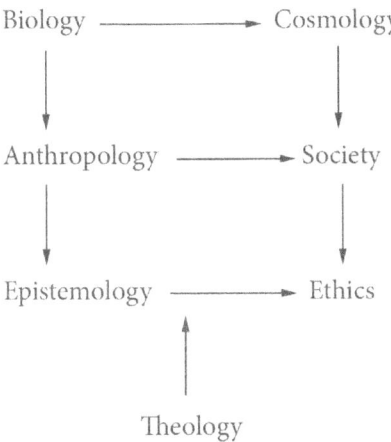

A Tale of Two Paradigms

It is no secret that we are living in a time of major change, resulting in monumental religious conflict, chiefly in North American mainline denominations. While there are many ways of being Christian in our day, two paradigms—two overarching interpretive frameworks—may be helpful to describe the current conflict in Christianity. The first, the Precritical Paradigm, has been a common form of Christianity for the past several hundred years. This approach should not be associated with Christianity as a whole, though it remains a major voice, perhaps the majority voice in global Christianity. Its adherents

a. view the Bible as a divine product, as the unique revelation of God;
b. interpret the Bible literally;
c. equate faith with belief; the Christian life centered in believing now for the sake of salvation;
d. view the afterlife as central; the Christian life being about requirements and rewards, with the main reward a blessed afterlife;
e. view Christianity as the only true religion, and belief in God, the Bible, and Jesus as the way to heaven.

This paradigm should not be equated with "the Christian tradition," as though it were the dominant or only way of being Christian throughout history. In actuality it is the product of modernity, shaped by the birth of modern science and scientific ways of knowing. Since the Enlightenment of the seventeenth century, modernity has questioned both the divine origin and the literal-factual truth of many parts of the Bible, and the Precritical Paradigm is a response to that modern critique.

A second way of seeing Christianity, the Postcritical Paradigm, has been in existence for over a hundred years and has become an increasingly attractive movement within mainline Protestant denominations and in the Catholic Church. Like the earlier paradigm, its central features are a response to the Enlightenment, only in this case it embraces many Enlightenment ideals, including an appreciation of science, historical scholarship, religious pluralism, and cultural diversity. It also arose out of awareness of how Christianity had contributed to racism, sexism, nationalism, exclusivism, and other harmful ideologies. Its adherents

a. view the Bible as a human response to God;
b. interpret the Bible historically and metaphorically;
c. view faith relationally rather than dogmatically—faith being the way of the heart, not the way of the head;
d. view the Christian life as one of relationship and transformation. Being Christian is not about meeting requirements for a future reward in an afterlife, and not very much about believing. Rather, the Christian life is about a relationship with God that transforms life in the present;
e. affirm religious pluralism. This paradigm considers Christianity as one of the world's great enduring religions, as a particular response to the experience of God in our Western cultural stream.

From the perspective of the Postcritical Paradigm, the Precritical Paradigm seems anti-intellectual and rigidly (but selectively) moralistic. Its insistence on biblical literalism seems inadequate, as does its rejection of science whenever it conflicts with literalism. It seems to emphasize individual purity more than compassion and justice. And its exclusivism, its rejection of other religions as inadequate or worse, is objectionable. Can it be that God is known in only one religion—and perhaps only in the "right" form of that religion?[4]

---

4. Borg, *Heart of Christianity*, 16.

2

Embracing the Critical Phase of the Journey

IN THIS CHAPTER I examine nine perceptions acquired during the precritical phase of my religious journey. Having begun with notions based upon or deduced from a literalistic understanding of the Christian scriptures, I reexamine them, applying critical thinking, intuition, and personal experience.

Adopting pedagogical methods and topics compatible with current scholarship, my teaching style challenges students to question the validity of inherited belief systems. The rationale comes from the Outsider Test for Belief, which claims that beliefs based on unquestioned faith generally lead people to justify what they were raised to believe. Such reasoning is ultimately circular.

By way of support I cite an insight gained during my qualifying exams at Princeton Theological Seminary, a battery of exams in the doctoral program that one must complete prior to commencing the dissertation phase of the PhD program. While preparing for an exam on Paul's letters, it became evident that my assumption about the authenticity or inauthenticity of those letters could always be confirmed by research. In other words, if I assumed that a disputed letter of Paul was actually written by Paul, it was not difficult to marshal sufficient argumentation for that assumption. Conversely, if I assumed that the disputed letter of Paul was not Pauline, I could present an equally convincing argument. However, if I started from a position of neutrality, I had to investigate all sides of the debate equally, and this became more challenging. Furthermore, such results were more compelling, since this approach forced me to examine all of the evidence and not simply argumentation that could be dismissed or filtered through my assumptive lens. Allowing the evidence to dictate the results required difficult evaluative work and exposed me to a wide range of methodologies, including conclusions not yet envisioned by scholars.

The same applies to all religious premises. If one begins with unexamined assumptions, one can easily arrive at foregone conclusions and overlook opportunities for learning, growth, or change of perspective.

1. The Insider Bias against Other Religions

While teaching world religions and global spirituality at Washington & Jefferson College, I uncovered numerous parallels between Christianity and other religions, including beliefs, practices, and historical development. This discovery convinced me that questioning beliefs, dogmas, and practices of other traditions but not one's own is inconsistent and biased. After all, had I been born Buddhist or Muslim, I would likely view everything from that perspective, so what makes my theological bias true but theirs false? In a pluralistic age, particularity is an invalid test for truth.

The Outsider Test for Truth makes clear that no one religion can lay claim to ultimate truth, though most have done so with regularity, particularly when challenged by competing perspectives. In the absence of an absolute, objective vantage point whereby all religious truths can be judged, it seems best to acknowledge that none have more than a temporal or subjective value.

2. The Role of Apologetics, Evangelism, and the Doctrine of Predestination

At W&J I initially offered a course in Christian apologetics that offended some colleagues but was popular with conservative Christian students. Such students were eager to share their faith with others on campus, and I supported their efforts, assenting to the claims that their action was based on the missionary nature of Christianity. Eventually the apologetics course disappeared from the curriculum, partly in response to an increased departmental emphasis on world religions but also by my genuine desire to embrace diversity and religious pluralism. The rationale for my decision was clear: I no longer adhered to Christian exclusivism (the view that only those who accept the Christian gospel are saved), and I no longer believed in hell or eternal damnation.

I became intrigued by the perspectives of two modern Christian thinkers: theologian Karl Barth—the systematic theologian who applied the doctrine of predestination to modern concerns in unanticipated ways—and philosopher John Hick, who developed a "pluralist" approach to religious traditions, arguing that they represent different yet equally valid responses to the same ultimate reality.

The traditional view of predestination, as articulated by Augustine, Calvin, and other representatives of orthodoxy, claims that all of humanity is contaminated by sin and unable to break from its grasp. Only grace can set humanity free. Yet grace is not bestowed universally; it is only granted to some individuals. As a result, only some will be saved—those to whom grace is given. Predestination involves the recognition that God withholds the means of salvation from those who are not elected. Later followers of Augustine taught a doctrine of "double predestination," whereby God allocates some to eternal life and the rest to eternal condemnation, solely on the basis of divine will, without any reference to their merits or demerits.

Building on the contributions of Augustine and Calvin, Barth used a unique Christological approach to arrive at a startling conclusion. For Barth, predestination refers not to the election of select humans for preferential treatment but rather to God's election of Jesus Christ to serve as mediator between humanity and deity. Barth's starting point is with God's free and sovereign decision to enter into fellowship with all humanity. By electing Christ for the redemption of humanity, it is Christ who is rejected, not humanity. The cross, representing God's judgment upon sin, is God's "No" to humanity. However, this "No" does not result in the exclusion and rejection of humanity, for God's "No" to sin is borne by Christ, who died for all. In Christ, then, we find God's judgment *and* God's redemption, God's "No" to sin and God's "Yes" to grace. Because Christ is the sole elected individual, his mediatorial role leads to God's final word to humanity, which remains "Yes." Barth's doctrine of predestination, pointing to universal restoration and the salvation of all humanity, eliminates condemnation of humanity. The only one who is predestined to condemnation is Jesus Christ, who from all eternity willed to represent humanity. Barth's perspective, though hopeful, is rejected by many evangelical and fundamentalist Christians, who consider that his methodology and conclusions compromise the traditional Christian doctrines of human nature, sin, and grace.

Whereas Barth maintained a strongly Christological orientation to predestination and consequently to the doctrines of sin and grace (salvation), John Hick argued that Christianity needed to move from a Christ-centered to a God-centered approach. Describing his stance as a "Copernican revolution" in our understanding of world religions, Hick argued that it was necessary for Christians to abandon the dogma that

Embracing the Critical Phase of the Journey

Christ—and therefore Christianity—represents the center of faith and come to the realization that it is God who is at the center, meaning that all religions revolve around the same divine reality.

For Hick, what is of central importance to God's nature is God's *universal* saving will. Assuming God desires that everyone be saved, it would be inconceivable that the divine self-revelation be addressed to only one religion and in such a way that only a fraction of humanity could be saved. Concluding that all religions lead to the same God, Hick argues that Christians have no unique access to God, for God is universally available through all religious traditions.

As intriguing as these views appear, they seem less attractive now. Barth's perspective ultimately provides an apologetic based on an outmoded theology—on the notion that reconciliation with a supernatural deity requires sacrifice, and that the atoning sacrifice of Christ is efficacious. Hick's idea has greater merit, for it assumes that if God exists, then all understandings of God (that is, all religions) are equally valid. In my estimation, the weakness in pluralism (in addition to its relativism) is that many of its exponents assume the validity of supernatural theism, of the existence of a personal and omnipotent deity or deities with whom humans can interact meaningfully and directly. In all fairness, Hick doesn't believe that the personifications of deity worshiped by devotees of the world's religions are real in any final sense. He argues that a distinction must be made between the ultimate inaccessible spiritual reality, which he calls "The Real," and the various contradictory perceptions or experiences of that reality which are concretized and personalized in the radically different beliefs and practices of the religions of the world.

While this idea holds promise, it has numerous intellectual shortcomings. Hick's view has been criticized for assuming the possibility of a "detached" or "objective" view of religion or reality, which contradicts the understanding that all theological reflections arise from within specific traditions. This view is similar to that propounded by Deist writers of the Enlightenment, an idea corrupted over time and seemingly dismissed by scientists, psychologists, and philosophers as simply another vestige of wishful thinking. In his critique of Hick, Alister McGrath argues that pluralists are caught up in a tension that they cannot resolve: the tension between the need to argue for the superiority of their own pluralist views over and against traditional religious views, on the one hand, while maintaining the legitimacy of traditional religious views that exclude the legitimacy of precisely these arguments, on the other. As Gavin D'Costa has pointed out, Hick's approach to religious pluralism actually "represents a tradition-specific approach that bears all the same features as exclusivism—except that it is western liberal modernity's exclusivism."[1]

3. Corporate Worship, Prayer, and Other Disciplines of Devotion

When I was younger, spontaneous prayer was easy. God was a friend, and speech with God seemed natural. But as I grew older and began to question the experience of prayer, analyzing it logically and construing it relationally, I became discouraged.[2] Whenever I complained that prayer seemed like a one-way street, I generally got a clever argument, such as: "God always answers prayer; however, some prayers are answered with a No"; or, "our responsibility in prayer is to be faithful, not to achieve desired results." Over time, while I enjoyed the therapeutic benefits of what Richard J. Foster calls the inward and the outward disciplines,[3] I viewed worship and other corporate disciplines with skepticism. I had been taught that public worship was instituted by God for God's glory, and this concept seemed nonsensical, for my experience of worship was that it was for my benefit. I went to worship for inspiration (beautiful music and a good sermon were essential), communion with God, and fellowship with others; the rest seemed peripheral and redundant.

I have become increasingly convinced that the way we worship augments God's silence and unresponsiveness. For years I prayed and read the Bible devotionally, supplementing these disciplines with meditation and other spiritual activity. I was reaching out to God as I would communicate with another person, but God did not reciprocate. As my spirituality deepened, I discovered that the God I worshipped no longer squared with the supernatural God of traditional Christianity.

As I ponder the notion that God "dwells in the midst of our praise," as many believers sing and affirm through prolonged ritualistic acts, the opposite seems true, that God might actually be worn-out by our repetitive religious practice. This feeling surges when parishioners intone self-deprecating prayers of confession. Such congregational put-downs appear

1. McGrath, *Christian Theology*, 442.
2. For additional (postcritical) discussion of prayer, see segment 2 in chapter 4.
3. In his classic book *Celebration of Discipline*, Foster selects twelve spiritual disciplines that have been central to Christianity, dividing them into three categories: Inward Disciplines (meditation, prayer, fasting, study); Outward Disciplines (simplicity, solitude, submission, service); and Corporate Disciplines (confession, worship, guidance, celebration).

Embracing the Critical Phase of the Journey

trite and ineffectual, engendering little more than a sense of unworthiness on the part of penitential worshippers. Persistent questions arise: Wouldn't prayers of confession, offered by truly penitent individuals, be more beneficial if addressed directly to the offended party? Should corporate petitionary prayer be "forgiven" at all, particularly when offered by rote?

Treasuring the concept of simplicity and spiritual solitude, I question the biblical command to observe the Sabbath. It served a definite purpose in biblical times, as Judaism and then Christianity modeled a distinct way of life in a pagan world, but the thought of God mandating such practice for all time seems unrealistic and impractical, particularly when subsequent Jews and Christians became adept at circumventing its observance. There are many reasons why communities should observe public holidays and periodic days of rest, but making them mandatory or burdening humans with vast systems of religious legislation became nonsensical during the critical phase of my faith journey.

While I value spirituality and believe it should be held in the highest regard on account of its transformative power for people of all religious and cultural traditions, including many who claim no religious affiliation, my understanding of the spiritual life comprises ordinary, everyday life lived in an ever-deepening relationship to God and therefore to one's true self, other people, and the whole of creation. Human life has a personal dimension and a social dimension, which include an inner and an outer journey respectively. Such life includes both a secular character, which is rational, immanent, this-worldly, physical, political, and human, and a sacred character, which is intuitive, transcendent, otherworldly, spiritual, pietistic, and divine. A healthy human spirituality oscillates between a subconscious reliance on God's presence and conscious attention to God's presence. In the first instance, we are involved with other human beings in daily life and work. In the second, we intentionally look to God so that God might transform, restore, and nurture us, sending us back into the world to live more fully.

One way to describe the movement between these two dimensions of life is to imagine a child sitting on a parent's lap in the park. When the child feels loved and secure, the child ventures off to play. Eventually, the child gets tired, has a confrontation, becomes lonely, or suffers a mishap and runs back into the parent's arms to be consoled. Then, after experiencing love and security, the child returns to play. The spiritual life of prayer, meditation, and worship is like this, a movement between prayer as devotional life and prayer as daily life and work.

4. Belief in Miracles

The modern world, based on a universal human rationality independent of faith, has long been skeptical of ways of thinking based on improbable religious truth, including belief in miracles. Unless one compartmentalizes faith and religion divorced from reason and science, it seems likely that the majority of the miracles in the Bible did not happen as stated and were inserted into the tradition to elicit faith in God or in Jesus as well as to undergird credibility for early Christianity. We now know that Jews and Christians were not alone in claiming miracles on behalf of their God. Many other sects, cults, and religions have appealed to resurrections, healings, and exorcisms in their traditions as well.

When one applies The Outsider Test for Faith to miracles, it becomes obvious that while people can easily justify whatever they were raised to believe, they can just as easily dismiss what people in other religions traditions believe. Even today many Christians reject miracle accounts in other religions, such as miracles in the Hindu tradition or, closer to home, those attributed to Joseph Smith, the founder of Mormonism, while not questioning miracles in their own tradition or those found in their scriptures. This inconsistency is not justifiable, unless one postulates that the laws of the universe are bent only for adherents of one's own faith or denomination.

Despite my skepticism with miracles in general, the concept of miracles, however, should not be easily dismissed. If we accept David Hume's argument that miracles are contrary to experience as well as to the laws of nature, then it seems quite probable that we are justified in not believing in miracles.[4] However, if the so-called "laws" of nature cannot be know with certainty, and if there are documented exceptions to at least some of those laws, then Hume's argument loses much of its force. Furthermore, if there is fairly strong evidence in support of the occurrence of at least one miracle, such as the resurrection of Jesus, or documentable cases where credible nonbelievers claim to have witnessed miracles—and I know scientists and philosophers who fit that category—then Hume's argument can be dismissed as unpersuasive.

The sense of mystery in the universe, the need to remain open to unknown possibilities, has been held inviolate by peoples in all cultures

---

4. The most celebrated article ever written on miracles is by David Hume. In section 10 of *An Enquiry Concerning Human Understanding* (1748) he set forth an argument against belief in miracles that provoked a lively response in his day and has continued to be the subject of rigorous dispute to the present day.

and places throughout history. Even the most rigorous scientist cannot declare with absolute confidence that reality can be limited to what is known through the senses. In a materialistic universe governed exclusively by natural laws, belief in miracles could be construed as violations of the laws of nature, but only the most rigorous reductionist today would argue that humans possess ultimate knowledge of nature, something modern physics clearly disproves. Today, when speaking of miracles, intellectual honesty requires that we be very clear in our definition and, even then, that we remain open to an unknown present and an indeterminate future.[5]

5. Biblical Prophecy

I was once fascinated with the topic of biblical prophecy, for it is vital to Christian apologetics. Popularly understood, the task of biblical prophets was to "prophesy," and when they prophesied they were predicting future events. Though modern scholarship downplays this understanding of the role of prophets, this perspective was quite common in first-century Judaism and Christianity, and it has prevailed until modern times.

Biblical scholars now understand the prophetic role as having involved three distinct yet related tasks, each with a different temporal focus: (a) they were predictors of the future (*foretelling*); (b) they were reformers who kept alive the Mosaic past through continuous appeal to the theocratic ideals expressed in the covenants (*retelling*); and (c) they were social critics who spoke out boldly and without compromise against current disobedience and disbelief within the social, religious, and political establishment (*forthtelling*). Of the three tasks, the most significant was forthtelling and the least significant was foretelling. Biblical prophets rarely, if ever, made open predictions about the future, and when they did so, the predictions were linked to their role as social critics, which focused on the consequences for unrepentance. The prophet's futuristic role was associated primarily with the certainty of the coming of the Lord, a coming to make things right through judgment and reward.

---

5. By "miracle" I have in mind a marvel, popularly understood as an event or set of events inexplicable by the laws of nature and thereby held to be supernatural in origin. When I question miracles what I question is the notion of marvels performed by an omnipotent deity solely to accomplish divine will. I accept more nuanced understandings of miracle, such as the definition suggested by my colleague Dan Stinson: "vulnerability to the presence of God." For additional (postcritical) discussion of miracles, see segment 3 in chapter 4.

Beyond Belief

To discredit the notion that biblical prophets predicted history in advance, I cite examples from both testaments of scripture, beginning with the Old Testament book of Daniel. This book, read by many Christians as a prophetic blueprint of the future (the end of history), has been attributed to Daniel, who is said to have written the book from Babylon in the sixth century BC (about 530 BC). That is surely wrong. The book is actually one of the few Old Testament books that can be given a reliable date. It is now known to have been given its final form during the second century BC, by an unknown author who was a member of a resistance movement called the Hasidim, a group of nonconformists who resisted the Seleucid policy of forced Hellenization of Jews from 167 to 164 BC. The second half of the book, which contains detailed prophecies concerning the intervening period, particularly the second century, is an example of what scholars call postdiction, meaning that it was written after the fact, in the time of its fulfillment.

The two halves of the book seem to have originated separately. Chapters 1–6, which refer to events from 595 to 535, probably circulated orally during Israel's Restoration Period (fifth through second centuries) and then were attached to the "prophetic" second half (chapters 7–12) around 164 BC, the last year of the Maccabean Revolt. This latter half of the book, known as "the Manifesto of the Hasidim" because it sets forth the theology of the Maccabean revolution, would have been written at that time.

The problems with the traditional dating are legion: for starters, when the author talks about the sixth century (if that is indeed his own time period), he is vague and inaccurate, but when he talks about the second century BC, especially about the events of 167 to 164, he is quite detailed and exact. The book, if written circa 164, does contain one prophetic detail, a reference in Daniel 11:45 to the death of Antiochus Epiphanes, then-current Seleucid king. Although the author knows the career of Antiochus intimately, he gets this one detail wrong. The reason is simple: the author of Daniel is not a prophet, and the one time he attempts to prophecy, he fails, because the future cannot be predicted accurately. And that is true of biblical and nonbiblical authors alike.

I wish to make another point about prophecy in Daniel, pertaining to two mystifying glosses found at the conclusion of the book (chapter 12:11–12), two verses added by the author or by a later editor. These verses, which lengthen the time before the anticipated culmination (the defeat of the Seleucids, not the end of the world) to 1290 days and then to 1335 days, were inserted most likely as an anxious adjustment when the end did not materialize as expected.

Embracing the Critical Phase of the Journey

New Testament examples abound, so I limit myself to Matthew's use and understanding of prophecy, which by modern standards is quite skewed. Take the bizarre version of Zechariah 9:9 found in Matthew 21:7, where the Evangelist misunderstands the poetic parallelism in the original and has Jesus riding on two animals at the same time (although some modern translations attempt to clarify the confusion by eliminating the reference, it is clearly present in the original Greek of the passage). The parallel passages in Mark and Luke provide a much more sensible explanation. Matthew's gospel often interprets prophetically Old Testament passages not prophetic in their original context. This was done to demonstrate that events in the life of Jesus, particularly his birth, were part of a divinely pre-arranged pattern. The best-known example, the Emmanuel passage from Isaiah 7:14 (cited in Matthew 1:23), bore no reference in the original Hebrew text to the distant future. The context makes clear that it was given as a promise to King Ahaz, who ruled from approximately 735 to 715 BC. As a contemporary of the prophet Isaiah, the prophecy was a sign to the king that his wife was already, or soon would be pregnant. The birth of that child, born in the near future, was a promise to Ahaz that God would provide relief from impending political threat. Only later, through a Jewish interpretive technique known as midrash, which recasts older stories into newer ones and thereby reads "deeper" meanings into old texts, were prophecies of this nature updated and applied to future events such as the coming of the messiah (Matthew 1:22–23).[6]

There are numerous additional midrashic examples in the New Testament writings that biblical literalists misread, misunderstand, and misapply. One such example appears in Matthew 2:23, where the relocation of the infant Jesus from Egypt to Nazareth is said to be a fulfillment of a saying found "in the prophets" to the effect that someone would be called a Nazarene. The vagueness of the reference (no particular biblical text seems to be in mind) makes clear that this is a piece of redaction made up by the author to prove his point and not the fulfillment of any specific prophetic message. A few verses earlier we read about the return from Egypt to Judea of Joseph, Mary, and Jesus. The author of Matthew cites this event as the

---

6. In the extensive history of Jewish life and literature, there developed a need for commentary and reinterpretation of traditional texts in light of the ever-changing present situations. Midrash is the hermeneutical act of rereading and expanding a text in the form of a new narrative to update the existential meaning. Such an approach is not concerned with historic accuracy but with meaning and understanding. This topic is addressed more fully in chapter 8, in the segment titled "The Jewishness of the New Testament."

fulfillment of a passage from Hosea 11:1, but that passage clearly referred to the original Exodus and not to the future at all. As many scholars note, Matthew's account contains numerous parallels to the story of Moses in Exodus. The exodus story was used by Matthew as the base material for the story of the birth of Jesus, including the flight from Egypt and the slaughter of the male children by the Pharaoh and by Herod. While the midrashic approach might astound conservative readers of the Bible, the author of Matthew would not have considered this method questionable, since he was following a common Jewish exegetical approach.

A related approach to biblical prophecy, known as *pesher* (meaning "deciphering" or "interpretation"), was commonly used in the biblical commentaries found among the ancient writings known as the Dead Sea Scrolls, discovered around 1950 but written by an apocalyptic sect of Jews in the decades before and around the birth of Christianity. This sect wrote biblical commentaries, such as the renowned commentary on the book of Habbakuk, in the belief that its members were living in the final, climactic days of history, and with the understanding that the ancient prophetic oracles were being fulfilled in the events of their time. The sectaries were convinced that they belonged to a community that alone interpreted the scriptures correctly, and that biblical prophecy was intended primarily for them. The earliest Christians certainly held similar attitudes. As Paul makes clear in 2 Corinthians 1:20, Christ is the affirmative answer to all God's promises, meaning that all of the hopes and promises of God were fulfilled in him, and, we might add, by his followers, known both as "the body of Christ" and as Christians, meaning "little Christs."

Rather than forcing the prophetic passages of scripture into an either/or straightjacket, meaning that either they were predictive—and consequently were fulfilled at some later time, whether during the Intertestamental Period, the New Testament period, or else literally at some future time—or else that they had only one level of meaning, and that for the original audience, it is better to assume that Jews and Christians searched the scriptures looking for passages that helped them understand the experiences of their time or the meaning of Jesus and the events of his life. Such an approach required clever biblical exegesis, whether allegorical, typological, or midrashic. Like all these approaches, prophetic application was clearly postdictive, that is, after the fact.

6. Heaven, Hell, and the Doctrine of the Afterlife

In our time, belief in a God who is all-good, all-benevolent, and all-just is widely viewed as incompatible with the traditional doctrine of hell. Indeed, such a belief seems impossible. The contradiction of holding such views simultaneously is so great that many Christians today are moderating their understanding of hell, viewing the concept as a metaphor for the absence of God's presence rather than as a place of eternal punishment.

Some skeptics, following the Christian logic that non-believers will spend eternity in hell if they reject the message of the gospel, have proposed that it would be better if Christians would simply stop evangelizing the world, for then non-Christians would not find reasons to reject the message and thereby have a better chance of going to heaven. Others, underscoring the perverse logic of heaven and hell, have argued that the universal killing of children before they reached the hypothetical "age of accountability"—when the church considers them morally responsible—might be construed as merciful, for such would actually enhance their chances of eternal salvation.

The idea of hell, like belief in heaven, is a step-child of the doctrine of the afterlife. If one can demonstrate that belief in a physical afterlife is flawed or even questionable, and if one can demonstrate that behind all thought, desire, and life there is only one prime force—a God who is love—then belief in the doctrine of hell is weakened and possibly eliminated.

The presence of the doctrine of hell in the Bible, like belief in the afterlife in general, is quite late. Before the sixth century BC the Hebrews, along with the Phoenicians, Babylonians, Greeks, and Romans, did not emphasize life after death, for they had no clear belief in the existence of a soul as separate from the body. The dead, righteous and wicked together, survived as "shades" in an underworld called Sheol, similar to Hades in the Homeric poems, but they were limited to a dull, shadowy existence without clear consciousness. There was nothing desirable here; it was simply one step removed from annihilation. As anthropologists and social historians point out, the reason behind this emphasis was a concept known as "corporate personality," meaning that in the ancient world, the tribe was the basic social unit.

The Hebrews lived and thought tribally. When a single individual sinned, as in the classic case of Achan in the biblical account of the battle of Jericho (Joshua 7:11–26), the entire tribe was punished. According to the book of Exodus, the people of Egypt were afflicted with dreadful plagues on account of the hardness of heart of the Pharaoh. This belief made sense in an era when the overwhelming value and chief virtue was the survival of the tribe, not the survival of the individual. In the sixth century, around the time the Hebrews came under the influence of the Persians, biblical literature gives evidence of the rise of a concept of individualism. A current proverb: "The parents have eaten sour grapes, and the children's teeth are set on edge," quoted by Jeremiah and Ezekiel, was questioned by these prophets and by their generation.

Ezekiel is quite possibly the first figure in Jewish religious history to assign reward and punishment based on a sense of individual responsibility when he challenged the moral principle underlying that proverb with these words: "As I live, says the Lord God, this proverb shall no more be used by you in Israel. Know that all lives are mine; the life of the parent as well as the life of the child is mine: it is only the person who sins that shall die" (Ezekiel 18:3-4). Ezekiel then goes on to spell out his understanding of righteous and unrighteous behavior. Individuals who do righteous deeds "shall surely live," and those who do evil deeds "shall surely die." To make his point absolutely clear, Ezekiel repeats himself: "A child shall not suffer for the iniquity of a parent, nor a parent suffer for the iniquity of a child; the righteousness of the righteous shall be his own, and the wickedness of the wicked shall be his own" (Ezekiel 18:20).

To think individualistically, a quantum leap in consciousness was required of ancient communities, and later biblical history informs us that throughout the Intertestamental and New Testament periods, Jews and Jewish Christians continued to think corporately. One need recall the story of the blind man brought to Jesus by his disciples with the question: "Rabbi, who sinned, this man or his parents, that he was born blind?" (John 9:2). One possible answer, certainly on their minds, was that the individual's blindness had been caused by parental sin (the origin of the view is often attributed to the commandment in Exodus 20: 5, which declares that God is a jealous God, "punishing children for the iniquity of parents, to the third and the fourth generation of those who reject me").

The first person believed to have had ideas about the soul perhaps close to modern notions was Zoroaster, a Persian who may have lived about 600 BC. As the founder of Zoroastrianism, he taught that humans have a body and a soul, and that the soul is associated with the faculties of reason, consciousness, conscience, and free will. Free will, according to Zoroastrianism, enables people to choose good or evil actions, for which they are morally responsible. On the basis of their actions, God is justified in rewarding or punishing individuals by sending them to heaven or hell. Following the Babylonian Exile, the Jews had very close contact with the

Embracing the Critical Phase of the Journey

Persians, at which time Jews may have begun adopting beliefs similar to those of the Zoroastrians, including a final judgment and the resurrection of the dead.

The first Jewish text to suggest the possibility of an afterlife as a venue for righting earthly wrongs is the *Book of the Watchers*, as scholars call the work preserved as 1 Enoch 1–36. This work, which reached its final form by the end of the third century BC, was extremely influential in the Intertestamental Period. In the last portion of this volume, the patriarch Enoch (mentioned in Genesis 5:21–24), is taken on a tour of the earth in the company of the archangels. After seeing the fiery abyss in which the watchers (the Nephilim of Genesis 6:4—angels who descended to earth to marry women) are imprisoned, Enoch comes to a mountain with four chambers. The passage suggests that the chambers house the souls of the dead, with the souls of the wicked relegated to the dark chambers while the souls of the righteous enjoy temporary blessing as they await their final disposition on the Day of Judgments. In at least one of the dark chambers the souls of the wicked are already undergoing punishment.

It is difficult to ascertain how quickly the new picture of the afterlife became widespread among Jews, but by 165 BC, during the Maccabean Period of Jewish history, the idea of individual life after death based on merit is found in the apocalyptic book of Daniel. Apocalyptic thought was a form of prophecy that flourished in the Jewish literature of the postexilic period, beginning particularly with the Maccabean period. The chief examples in the Bible are the book of Daniel in the Old Testament and the book of Revelation, the closing book in the New Testament. This type of writing focuses on the last things and anticipates the imminent end of the world. It is caused by a religious outlook that envisions a final conflict between God and the powers of evil, whereby enemies are defeated and punished while insiders, generally persecuted minorities, are rewarded in a new world order established by God. Apocalyptic literature, written by victims, expresses their hopes through visions with complex and sometimes gruesome symbolism. This outlook led to extreme characterizations of the afterlife as consisting of two options, heaven and hell. Heaven, of course, is for insiders, while hell is for the rest.

The book of Daniel emphasizes God's providential role in history. In chapter 12, those who resist the enforced Seleucid program of Hellenization are called "the wise." It is they who are promised a glorious and eternal future: "Many of those who sleep in the dust of the earth shall awake, some to everlasting life, and some to shame and everlasting contempt"

(Daniel 12:2). Here, according to some scholars, we have the first explicit biblical reference to resurrection. Further confirmation of second- and first-century Jewish belief in a corporeal resurrection comes from the apocryphal book of 2 Maccabees, written in Greek in the decades following the Maccabean revolt (167–163 BC). The story of the extreme torture and martyrdom of seven brothers in chapter 7 presupposes a resurrection of the body and even a reassembling of dismembered limbs, while the passage in 12:43–44 assumes on the basis of resurrection that prayers for the dead are efficacious (see also 1 Corinthians 15:29). The Maccabean material clearly grew out of the need for justice. If young Jewish people died as martyrs rather than compromise their faith, then surely God must reward them.

Earlier biblical references to the afterlife, including the notoriously difficult passage in Job 19:26–27 and the undateable Isaiah 26:19, are unclear in the original Hebrew version and cannot support the later doctrinal meaning imposed on them by Christian translators. Two passages found in the book of Ecclesiastes also should be mentioned. The remark about the possibility of an afterlife inserted in Ecclesiastes 3:21 should not be interpreted out of context, since it is prefaced by the clearer meaning of the preceding verse: "All go to one place; all are from the dust, and all turn to dust again." Another passage, Ecclesiastes 12:7, suggests that the human breath or "spirit" returns to God, but this verse is simply affirming the viewpoint of Genesis 2:7, in which human life and death are said to be dependent upon the breath of God, which returns at death to God, from whence it came.

By the start of the Christian era, Jews were divided on eschatological beliefs, with the Sadducees holding the older belief that there is no afterlife and consequently no resurrection and the Pharisees accepting the newer belief that there is an afterlife as well as a resurrection. Belief in rewards and punishments became significant in rabbinic Judaism, which emerged in the aftermath of the destruction of the temple in AD 70. The apostle Paul, called "the second founder of Christianity" for his theological influence on earliest Christianity, was a Pharisee before his conversion. Through him the key doctrinal beliefs of the Pharisees became central to Christianity, including their doctrine of the afterlife.

It is important to keep in mind that the New Testament remains ambiguous about life after death. While the idea of Jesus' resurrection is central to Christianity, its meaning is debated within the New Testament. As Paul writes in 1 Corinthians 15:50, "flesh and blood cannot inherit the kingdom of God, nor does the perishable inherit the imperishable." And

Paul did not address the notion of hell. As scholars now note, most of the images of fire and torment in the afterlife come from the gospel of Matthew and the book of Revelation. As notions of heaven and hell evolved over time in the Christian tradition, related concepts and adjustments were added, including such notions as purgatory, limbo, and child limbo. Since all sins were not considered equal, time sentences and other forms of plea-bargaining entered the equation.

In his *Divine Comedy*, Dante Alighieri gives poetic expression to medieval Christian beliefs concerning the afterlife. Describing a journey through Inferno (hell), Purgatorio (purgatory), and Paradiso (heaven), the poem makes substantial use of the leading themes of Christian theology and spirituality, culminating with heaven, the ultimate goal of the Christian life. Dante portrayed the geography of hell as consisting of nine successive levels, each circle exponentially greater in torture and pain. The first circle, populated with virtuous non-Christians such as Aristotle, Seneca, and Virgil, was a place called "limbo," seen as a kind of "ante-hell," where no pain is experienced. Dante's work, written during an age when society and human life were precarious and under constant threat, helped establish medieval perceptions of the afterlife.

During the Enlightenment, many if not all Christian doctrines came under intense scrutiny. Belief in the afterlife was viewed as superstition and wish-fulfillment, a projection of human longing for rewards and retribution. Particular criticism was directed against the idea of eternal punishment since it seemed to serve no useful purpose. The twentieth century, however, saw a rediscovery of eschatology. Though the doctrine's revival can be attributed to a number of factors, it was primarily due to a general collapse in confidence concerning human goodness and human civilization. The First World War, especially traumatic, was followed by the Great Depression and the terrors of Nazism, leading to the Holocaust and the threat of nuclear war. These events and related concerns raised doubts among Christians concerning the credibility of the liberal humanist vision and led to renewed stress on their eschatological beliefs, characterized by apocalyptic solutions focused on the rapture of believers to heaven and the punishment of unbelievers in hell.

Despite the residue of apocalypticism in twenty-first-century America, exacerbated in part by the global war against terrorism and other ongoing threats to our well-being, it is hard to imagine that any reflective person today believes in a literal doctrine of hell. It should be obvious by now that all these images of the afterlife, including heaven and hell, are born of fertile human minds.

7. The Doctrine of Salvation

Concerning the concept of salvation, Christian scholars are convinced that modern evangelical emphasis on "being saved," that is, viewing salvation primarily as an assurance of entrance to heaven, is at best a rather recent emphasis in Christian tradition, going back no earlier than the nineteenth century. In the Bible the concept of salvation was essentially this-worldly, a means to assure believers of security from external threats and dangers and their place in the coming kingdom of God on earth. Only rarely might it be viewed as a vehicle to transport deceased or end-time believers to a heavenly kingdom.

The doctrine of salvation is complex, and different aspects of the Christian understanding of sin and salvation have had particular attraction during different periods of church history or for specific situations. Recent studies of the biblical notion of salvation have placed considerable emphasis upon the importance of contextualization, meaning that, because the Christian gospel always addresses specific situations, the doctrine of salvation should be contextualized in those circumstances. For example, to the oppressed—whether spiritually, economically, or politically—the gospel message is that of liberation; to those burdened by personal guilt, the message is one of forgiveness; to the despondent, the message is one of hope.

Christianity holds that the created order, particularly humanity, has fallen into disorder. Things are not what they were meant to be, and something needs to be done about this. The same God who made the created order must act to reorder it, and this God has accomplished through the life, death, and resurrection of Jesus Christ. In his widely used text on *Christian Theology*, Alistair McGrath provides answers given by Christians throughout their history to the question, "*from* what are we saved?" In each case, the doctrine of sin tries to give an answer. Each model, in turn, also points to the doctrine of salvation, with its hopeful answers.[7]

From what, then, are we saved? McGrath provides six answers: Christians are saved from (1) their human condition, (2) their guilt, (3) their lack of holiness, (4) their inauthentic human existence (characterized by faith in the transient material world), (5) oppression, and (6) from forces that enslave humanity—such as satanic forces, evil spirits, fear of death, or the power of sin. In summary, the Christian doctrine of salvation deals with the restoration of all things, including humanity, to its proper relationship to God.

---

7. McGrath, *Christian Theology*, 339–42.

Salvation, consequently, represents new possibilities, a new state of being. McGrath provides models of salvation that correspond to the six models of sin. Together, they answer the question, "*for* what are we saved?" Christians are saved for (1) relationship with God, (2) righteousness in the sight of God, (3) personal holiness, (4) authentic human existence, (5) social and political liberation, and (6) spiritual freedom.

The understanding of salvation presented above exhibits a radical this-worldly orientation. The reason is clear: traditional Christians followed their Jewish counterparts in placing their faith into a historical context. The basic conviction of the Greeks was that truth was changeless and hence not tied to events. The earliest Christian creeds, such as the Apostles Creed, were composed to counter such views, which tended to overspiritualize Jesus and detach Christianity from history.

For Christians, the doctrine of salvation is closely related to the crucifixion of Jesus. This connection is already evident in the gospels, which make the accounts of Jesus' passion central and paramount to the Christian story. Rich in meaning, the death of Jesus became the subject of theological reflection throughout Christian history.

For centuries, Christians have viewed the death of Jesus as salvific, as having saving significance and making our salvation possible. According to many Christians, the death of Jesus was the purpose of his life on earth and was central as well to God's purpose for history. In the familiar language of the gospel of John: "For God so loved the world that he gave his only Son, so that everyone who believes in him may not perish but may have eternal life" (3:16). Likewise the Nicene Creed speaks of the saving significance of Jesus' death as the very reason he came: "For us and for our salvation he came down from heaven, (and) for our sake he was crucified under Pontius Pilate." The gospels portray the death of Jesus as integral to his vocation, as necessary, and as the fulfillment of prophecy. The earliest gospel, Mark, contains a threefold prediction of the passion, indicating that Jesus both taught his disciples of his imminent death and of the ensuing resurrection: "Then he began to teach them that the Son of Man must undergo great suffering, and be rejected by the elders, the chief priests, and the scribes, and be killed, and after three days rise again" (8:31; see also 9:31 and 10:32–33).

For those who read these passages as literal quotations of Jesus, the interpretation seems obvious: Jesus knew in advance the details of his death and saw them as central to his messianic vocation and purpose in life. Mainstream biblical scholarship views such prediction as post-Easter creations, for in the decades following Good Friday and Easter, the early Christian movement preserved the memory of those events by adding to their meaning. Several interpretations of the meaning of the crucifixion are found in the New Testament itself, comprising what is called "atonement theology." In the judgment of many scholars, atonement theology does not go back to Jesus himself. His crucifixion was the consequence of his actions and teaching, but not their purpose. Comparing his death with those of Mahatma Gandhi and Martin Luther King Jr., one can appreciate more clearly that these deaths were the consequence of their actions and teachings, but certainly not their intention or purpose. Looking back on the crucifixion of Jesus, the early Christian movement sought a providential purpose in this horrific event. At least five interpretations of the cross are found in the New Testament itself:[8]

1. A *political meaning*: Jesus was a threat to the Roman authorities, who executed him. The authorities said "no" to Jesus, but God has said "yes" (Acts 2:36);

2. A *cosmic meaning*: temporal rulers, whether Roman rulers or Jewish aristocrats in Judea, are viewed as subject to cosmic "principalities and powers," evil systems of domination built into human institutions. According to language found primarily in letters attributed to Paul (Colossians 2:15), Jesus' death defeats such cosmic powers;

3. A *psychological meaning*: the death and resurrection of Jesus are seen as the embodiment of the path of spiritual transformation that lies at the center of the Christian life, the path of dying to an old way of being and being raised into a new way of being (Galatians 2:19–20);

4. A *spiritual meaning*: the death of Jesus reveals the depth of God's love for us (John 3:16; Romans 5:8);

5. A *sacrificial meaning*: this view emphasizes that "Christ died for our sins" (1 Corinthians 15:3). This familiar theological understanding of the cross was formulated in the Middle Ages by Anselm of Canterbury (1033–1109), who defined the doctrine of atonement that became normative in the West: God became man in order to expiate the sin of Adam.

Biblical scholar Marcus Borg argues that in its first-century setting, the statement that "Jesus is the sacrifice for sin" would not have meant that Jesus' death was part of God's plan for salvation. Rather, it would have

---

8. Borg, *Heart of Christianity*, 91–95.

been understood as a challenge to the sacrificial system centered in the temple in Jerusalem. According to temple theology, "certain kinds of sins and impurities could be dealt with only through sacrifice in the temple. Temple theology thus claimed an institutional monopoly on the forgiveness of sins; and because the forgiveness of sins was a prerequisite for entry into the presence of God, temple theology also claimed an institutional monopoly on access to God."[9] Jewish Christians, using the metaphor of sacrifice, were affirming that forgiveness is not rooted in institutional monopoly but in gracious freedom. It is ironic to realize that the Christian religion began to claim for itself a monopoly on grace and access to God that is undermined by this contextual understanding of the meaning of the cross.

8. The Changing Nature of Christianity

While teaching courses on "The Development of Western Christianity" and "Global Christianity," I became aware that Christian dogma has evolved extensively over time, in part because theologians had honed their craft through interaction with current ideologies, cultural progress, and the prevailing ethos. My understanding of the nature of Christianity has been modified further by recent studies in the field of missiology, which indicate that Christianity has changed dramatically over time, reinventing itself at least six times as the missionary movement advanced to different cultures and continents.[10]

The earliest alterations to the Jesus movement are documented in the book of Acts, where the author discerns six stages of movement and growth as primitive Christianity expanded geographically from Jerusalem to Rome, shifting from a primarily Jewish phenomenon to a mostly Gentile one (1:4—6:7; 6:8—9:31; 9:32—12:24; 12:25—16:5; 16:6—19:20; 19:21—28:31).

With this understanding in mind, modern Christians must acknowledge that their beliefs and practices are vastly different from those of the first Christians, who did not even have the New Testament scripture in final form until it received canonical status in AD 367, when the current list of twenty-seven books of the New Testament appeared together for

---

9. Ibid., 94.

10. See the award-winning essays by Walls in *Missionary Movement*, particularly chapter 2, "Culture and Coherence in Christian History," 16–25.

Beyond Belief

the first time in an Easter letter sent to Christians by Bishop Athanasius of Alexandria.

No one hermeneutical or linguistic bridge can be built that will enable modern Christians to read the earliest Christian writings (the New Testament) and understand the meaning of Jesus ("the Jesus event") as the first generation of believers did. And even if that could happen, it is sobering to realize that there were far more interpretations of Jesus in the first three centuries of the existence of Christianity than exist in our world today. It took numerous church councils and a series of edicts and pronouncements by authoritative figures to form even a semblance of ecclesiastical and dogmatic unity, all of which took place before the explosion of practices and beliefs that resulted from the Protestant Reformation.

9. The Ephemeral Nature of Christian Unity

The Christian religion is schismatic. In Europe, following the Protestant Reformation, most regions followed a territorial church model, establishing official state churches and relying on state power to thwart further schismatic tendencies. In North America, due to the disestablishment clause written into the First Amendment, there emerged a proliferation of denominations and sects. One of these is the Presbyterian Church (U.S.A.), known as the PCUSA, the largest Reformed organization in North America and the denomination to which I belong. This entity represents several mergers, the latest being in 1983, when the United Presbyterian Church in the United States (UPCUSA) joined the Presbyterian Church in the United States (PCUS), a southern church formed at the end of the Civil War.

Since the 1740s there have been at least four important divisions in the Reformed churches, centering on such matters as political issues during the Revolutionary War, responses to various revival movements, and the issue of race. In the twentieth century and continuing to the present, Reformed churches and other Protestant denominations have been divided on questions of gender and sexuality. While European churches tend to be more liberal than American ones, in the United States, Reformed churches tend to have a conservative wing that wants to limit the role of women and condemn homosexuality, and a liberal wing that wants to push for total equality.

The PCUSA, which, like America's political system, follows a representative form of government, is no different. Tension about biblical authority over moral and social issues such as the ordination of gay clergy and the blessing of gay unions is resulting in further schism. The easy way out, for those holding minority positions in the denomination, is to form a dissident splinter group, often led by schismatic clergy who have dishonored the vow taken by clergy in the Presbyterian Church (U.S.A.) promising "to further the peace, unity, and purity of the church." Is it possible, in that phrase, that one's understanding of "purity" can trump "peace and unity"? It seems as if everyone carries a trump card these days, which makes one wonder why they join organizations at all.

Presbyterians are known for their polity, determined by the *Book of Order*. A guiding statement in the section on "Ordered Ministries of the Church" (G-2.0105) addresses the issue of freedom of conscience. It dates back to pre-revolutionary days, to the plan of reunion of the synods of New York and Philadelphia. The statement reads: "That when any matter is determined by a major vote, every member shall either actively concur with or passively submit to such determination; or if his conscience permit him to do neither, he shall, after sufficient liberty modestly to reason and remonstrate, peaceably withdraw from our communion without attempting to make any schism."[11]

That advice seems wise, for it has served well the cause of democracy in our country, allowing for peaceable votes and smooth transition in government at all levels. So I wonder, why would ordinarily peaceable, law-abiding citizens set aside this advice in the case of ecclesiastical affairs, particularly when the result is further fragmentation of the denomination? Such dissidents normally respond by pointing to the higher standards of scripture, which are said to guide their conscience and to serve as their religious constitution. But in this case scripture, as we shall see, is not really functioning as a higher authority, for it is transcended—trumped, if you will—by personal interpretations that in many cases are disingenuous. In such cases the individuals themselves have become authorities above scripture, and when this is done by a minority, it is done in defiance of the majority and in a spirit that undermines "the peace, unity, and purity of the church" they vowed to maintain.

And the future of schismatics is not pretty. Sectarianism results when someone's notion of individual purity or prophecy or doctrine or polity trumps majority rule. And sectarianism violates one of the basic principles of scripture, the unity of believers. The author of the letter to the Ephesians

---

11. *The Constitution of the Presbyterian Church (U.S.A)*, Part II: Book of Order 2011–2013, 26 n. 1.

exhorts believers "to lead a life worthy of the calling to which you have been called, with all humility and gentleness, with patience, bearing with one another in love, making every effort to maintain the unity of the Spirit in the bond of peace. There is one body and one Spirit . . . one God and Father of all, who is above all and through all and in all" (4:1–3, 6). What about "unity" can't many Presbyterians (and most other Christians) comprehend?

3

Two Ways of Knowing

The Basis of Religion: Faith, not Belief

If someone asked you to identify the essence of Christianity, where would you start? Conventional Christians, focusing on dogma, begin with belief in Jesus, the atonement, and the authority of scripture and the church. This approach, however, is antithetical to spirituality. It is a by-product of the Precritical Paradigm's vision of the Bible and the Christian tradition. Prior to the modern period, faith was not understood in this way. Faith was not about beliefs in one's head but about loyalty, allegiance, and trust in one's heart. Faith, of course, has always been central to Christianity, but an emphasis on faith as believing difficult things to be true is a relatively recent phenomenon in Christianity, the product of the last few hundred years.

Because religion by nature is primarily experiential, constructing religion on the foundation of belief leads to endless conflict, frustration, and unanswered questions. Children, of course, willingly accept belief, but as they go through adolescence and enter adulthood, many struggle with doubt and disbelief.

Faith, however, makes a better foundation and prepares one more adequately for life. Some readers may wonder about my distinction, because all through life they have equated faith with belief. But faith should not be equated with beliefs. It may reach conclusions about beliefs, but its foundation is experiential and relational rather than doctrinal. Based on experience, faith makes conscious choices that square with that experience.

As I mentioned previously, my childhood experience was essentially belief-based, and even though it was expressed in relational terms—such as "accepting Christ," acknowledging the Holy Spirit's guidance of my life, and speaking personally with God through prayer—it remained theoretical, based on a belief system that was in my head. Eventually my journey led me beyond belief to an understanding of the Christian life as a relationship of trust with a God to whom I am yoked and who participates in my journey of transformation. It is this understanding of the Christian life that I will develop in the remainder of the book.

Logos and Mythos: Two Ways of Knowing

Psychologists today recognize up to nine different forms of intelligence, building on a theory of multiple intelligence proposed by Howard Gardner in 1983. The original list included seven cognitive abilities: spatial, linguistic, logical-mathematical, bodily-kinesthetic, musical, interpersonal, and intrapersonal. In 1999 he added another category, which he called "naturalist intelligence," and later suggested yet another, "existential and moral intelligence." This last category is viewed as a spiritual or religious capacity, for it involves the ability to contemplate phenomena or to pursue questions that go beyond sense data.

Just as there are many forms of intelligence, so there are various ways of thinking, speaking, and acquiring knowledge. The ancient Greeks affirmed two modes of thought, calling them *logos* and *mythos*.[1] Both were essential and neither was considered superior to the other. While they were complementary, each having its own sphere of competence, it was considered unwise to mix the two. Both were pragmatic. *Logos* ("reason") helped people organize their societies, control the environment, and invent new technology. Although *logos* was essential to the survival of the species, it had limitations. It could not provide ultimate meaning or help cope with tragedy or with death. For help people turned to *mythos* ("myth").

Today, because we live in a society of scientific *logos*, myth has fallen into disrepute. But in the past, myth, like *logos*, helped people to live effectively in a confusing and uncertain world. Ancient myths have been called a primitive form of psychology, for these stories were therapeutic, designed to help people negotiate the obscure regions of the psyche, areas that influence our thoughts and behavior but are difficult to access. Myths were never intended to be taken literally, as though they were accurate accounts of historical events. A myth was "something that had in some sense happened once but that also happens all the time."[2] In other words, myths spoke to existential conditions.

1. The material in this segment is adapted from Armstrong, *Case for God*, x–xvi.
2. Ibid., xi.

Two Ways of Knowing

A myth would not be effective if someone simply believed in it, for myths were not designed to provide factual information. A myth was essentially a program of action. Although it could put individuals in the correct spiritual or psychological posture, it was up to them to take the next step and make the truth of the myth a reality in their own life. Myths showed people how to live more fully, how to cope with their mortality, and how to embrace life's suffering creatively. If one failed to act upon myth or to apply it to specific situations, it would remain abstract and incredible.

From an early date, myths were enacted in stylized ceremonies (rituals) that worked aesthetically upon participants and, like any work of art, introduced them to a deeper dimension of existence. Myth and ritual were thus inseparable. Without ritual, myths made no sense.

Religion, which builds upon myth (scripture) and ritual (ceremony), was never intended to provide answers that lie within the competence of human reason. That was the role of *logos*. The task of religion was to enable followers to find wisdom, the sort of wisdom that helps them live creatively, peacefully, and even joyously with realities for which there are no easy explanations.

Of course, religion does not work automatically. It is a practical discipline that teaches humans to discover new capacities of mind and heart. Religion, which connects myth with ritual, is not, like *logos*, something that people believe or think, but something people do. Its truth is acquired by practical action, by translating the teachings of religion into ritual or ethical action.

Like any skill, religion requires perseverance, hard work, and discipline. Some people will be better at it than others, some will be inept, and others will miss the point altogether. But those who do not apply themselves will get nowhere at all. Early Daoists, practitioners of one of China's indigenous religious traditions, considered religion as a knack acquired by constant practice. People who acquired this knack discovered a transcendent dimension of life that was not simply an external reality "out there" but was identical with the deepest level of their being. This reality, called by many names and understood in different ways by different religious traditions, has been understood as a fact of human life, though it was impossible to explain solely in terms of *logos*.

The Value of Unknowing

Theology is a wordy discipline. People have written volumes and talked incessantly about God. But some of the world's greatest theologians—Jewish, Christian, Muslim, as well as Hindu, Buddhist, and Daoist—have made it clear that while it is important to put our ideas about the divine into words, "these doctrines are man-made and are therefore bound to be inadequate. They devised spiritual exercises that deliberately subverted normal patterns of thought and speech to help the faithful understand that the words we use to describe mundane things were simply not suitable for God."[3] God was not good, divine, powerful, or intelligent in ways we humans could understand. We could not even say that God "existed," because our concept of existence was inadequate. Some of the mystics preferred to say that God was "Nothing" because God was not another being, object, or thing. One certainly should not read scriptures literally, as if they referred to divine facts. These theologians would have considered some of our modern ideas about God idolatrous.

This approach was not limited to just a few radical theologians. Symbolism came naturally to people in the premodern world and was utilized more widely than today. Nowadays many own a copy of the Bible and have the literacy to read it, but in the past most people had an entirely different relationship with their scriptures. They listened to them and recited them, always in a heightened liturgical context. Preachers instructed laypeople not to understand these texts in a purely literal way and suggested figurative interpretations. In medieval Europe, Christians were taught to view the Mass as a symbolic reenactment of Jesus' life, death, and resurrection. The fact that they could not follow the Latin added to its mystique. Much of the Mass was recited by the priest in an undertone, and the solemn silence and liturgical drama, with its music and stylized gestures, put the congregation into a mental "space" that was separate from ordinary life. In the "mystery plays," performed annually on the feast of Corpus Christi, medieval believers felt free to change the biblical stories, add new characters, and transpose them into a modern setting. "These stories were not historical in our sense, because they were *more* than history."[4]

Although our scientifically oriented society seeks to master reality, explain it, and bring it under the control of reason, "a delight in unknowing has also been part of the human experience. Even today, poets,

---

3. Ibid.
4. Ibid., x–xi.

philosophers, mathematicians, and scientists find that the contemplation of the insoluble is a source of joy, astonishment, and contentment."[5] A peculiar characteristic of the human mind is its ability to have ideas and experiences that seem to slip naturally into an apprehension of transcendence. Music, for example, has always been inseparable from religious expression, since, like religion at its best, music marks the "limits of reason." Music, a most corporeal art, is also highly cerebral. Yet this intensely rational activity segues readily into transcendence. Since it is rarely about anything, music goes to the frontiers of language and pushes beyond, to the realm of unknowing. Music confronts us with a mode of knowledge that defies logical analysis and empirical proof. It brims with meanings that will not translate into logical structures or verbal expression. In this way all art aspires to the condition of music; so too, at its best, does theology. Although a modern skeptic will find it impossible to accept George Steiner's conclusion that "what lies beyond man's word is eloquent of God,"[6] perhaps that skepticism is because we have too limited an idea of God or because we have lost the knack of religion.

During the sixteenth and seventeenth centuries Western people began to develop an entirely new kind of civilization, governed by scientific rationality and based economically on technology and capital investment. *Logos* achieved such spectacular results that myth was discredited and the scientific method was thought to be the only reliable means of attaining truth. "As theologians began to adopt the criteria of science, the *mythoi* of Christianity were interpreted as empirically, rationally, and historically verifiable and forced into a style of thinking that was alien to them . . . We began to understand concepts such as faith, revelation, myth, mystery, and dogma in a way that would have been very surprising to our ancestors. In particular, the meaning of the word 'belief' changed, so that a credulous acceptance of creedal doctrines became the prerequisite of faith, so much so that today we often speak of religious people as 'believers,' as though accepting orthodox dogma 'on faith' were their most important activity."[7]

This rationalized interpretation of religion has produced two distinctively modern, related phenomena: fundamentalism and atheism. Fundamentalism, a defensive piety that erupted in almost every major faith during the twentieth century, interpreted scripture with a literalism that is unparalleled in the history of religion. In the United States, Protestant

---

5. Ibid., xiv.
6. Steiner, *Language and Silence*, 59.
7. Armstrong, *Case for God*, xv.

fundamentalists evolved an ideology known as "creation science," which regards the *mythoi* of the Bible as scientifically accurate. In their zeal to promote biblical literalism, fundamentalists campaigned against the teaching of evolution in the public schools, assuming evolution contradicts the creation story in the first chapter of Genesis.

Historically, atheism has rarely been a blanket denial of the sacred but has nearly always rejected a particular conception of the divine. At early stages of their history, Christians and Muslims were both called "atheists" by their pagan contemporaries, not because they denied the reality of God but "because their conception of divinity was so different that it seemed blasphemous. Atheism is therefore parasitically dependent on the form of theism it seeks to eliminate and becomes its reverse mirror image."[8] This can be illustrated in two ways: classical Western atheism and a recent movement known as "new atheism."

Classical Western atheism, developed during the nineteenth and early twentieth centuries by Feuerbach, Marx, Nietzsche, and Freud, was essentially a response to the theological perception of God that had developed in Europe and the United States during the modern period. More recently, "new atheism" has taken the atheist polemic in a new direction. Spearheaded by the efforts of extremists such as Richard Dawkins, Christopher Hitchens, and Sam Harris, its exponents focus on the notion of God developed by the fundamentalists, insisting that fundamentalism constitutes the essence and core of all religion. This has weakened their critique, since fundamentalism is in fact an unorthodox form of faith that frequently misrepresents the tradition it is trying to defend. While Dawkins, Hitchens, and Harris are correct in some of their criticism of organized religion—religious people have indeed committed atrocities and crimes—they refuse to dialogue with theologians who are more representative of mainstream tradition. As a result, their analysis is shallow because it is based on poor theology.

The new atheists, it appears, are not radical enough. Jewish, Christian, and Muslim theologians have insisted for centuries that God does not exist and that there is "nothing" out there. In making these assertions, their aim was not to deny the reality of God but to safeguard it. Modern monotheists seem to have lost sight of this important tradition, known as "apophatic," which could solve many of our current religious problems.

---

8. Ibid., xvi.

Credo: How Faith Became Belief

We know very little about the historical Jesus, since most of our information comes from the texts of the New Testament, which, as *mythoi*, were not primarily concerned with factual accuracy.[9] The first Christians had no intention of founding a new religion but observed the Torah, worshipped in the temple, and kept the dietary laws. They continued to think about God in the traditional Jewish way and, like the rabbis, experienced the Holy Spirit—the immanent presence of God—as an empowering force. They took the highly unusual step of admitting non-Jews into their community, building on predictions by the Jewish prophets that in the Last Days the foreign nations would share Israel's success and become monotheists. As gentile converts joined the Christian movement, many of them already sympathetic to Judaism, this confirmed them in their belief that the old order was passing away. One of the most forceful champions of this view was Paul, whose letters demonstrate that the Christians had already started to engage in a radically inventive exegesis of the Torah and the Prophets to demonstrate that Jesus was the culmination of Jewish history. After the fall of Jerusalem in AD 70, Christians saw the destruction of the temple as a sign that the old Israel was dead. Now in the new Israel, the mixed congregations of Jews and gentiles, Christians could experience the divine presence in the person of Jesus, the Christ.

The twenty-seven books of the New Testament, completed by the second century, represented a valiant effort to rebuild the fallen tradition of Israel. Like the rabbis, the Christians used midrashic techniques to enable the new Israel to move forward. Like Paul, the authors of the four gospels searched the Jewish scriptures to find any mention of a messiah who had been "anointed" in the past by God for a special mission and was now seen to be a prediction of Jesus. This was not simply a clever exercise in public relations. Jews had long realized that all religious discourse was essentially interpretive. Calling scripture *miqra*, a "summons to action," the rabbis believed that no exegesis was complete until the interpreter had found a practical new ruling that would serve the immediate needs of his community. Because Jewish exegetes had always looked for new meaning in the ancient texts during a crisis, the basic methodology of Christian *pesher* ("deciphering") exegesis, practiced by the Qumran sectarians in the Dead Sea Scrolls, was not unlike rabbinical midrash.[10] Above all, it was a

---

9. The material in this segment is adapted from Armstrong, *Case for God*, 81–89 and 93–99.

10. As previously noted, the Essenes, believed to be the Jewish sect that authored

spiritual exercise. Like all great religious teaching, Christian doctrine must also be understood a *miqra*, for it makes sense and is most meaningful only when translated into a ritual, meditative, or ethical program.

This understanding would also be true of the third of the monotheistic traditions, which emerged in the early years of the seventh century in Arabia. Muhammad, a merchant of the thriving commercial city of Mecca, began to have revelations that he believed came from the God of the Jews and Christians. These messages were eventually brought together in the scripture known as the Qur'an, the "Recitation." The religion of the Qur'an would eventually be known as Islam, a word that means "surrender" to God, and was based on the same basic principles as the two other monotheistic traditions. The Qur'an has no interest in "belief" in the modern sense; indeed, this concept is quite alien to Islam. Theological speculation that results in the formulation of theoretical doctrines is dismissed as self-indulgent guesswork about matters that remain speculative but serve only to make people quarrelsome and naively sectarian. Like any religion, Islam is a way of life. The fundamental message of the Qur'an is not a doctrine but an ethical summons to compassionate behavior. The five "pillars" of Islam—faith, prayer, fasting, almsgiving, and pilgrimage—are a *miqra*, a summons to dedicated activity; in the Qur'an, "faith" is something people *do*.

The author of Luke's gospel demonstrates the way Christian *pesher* exegesis may have worked in his story of a numinous encounter on the road to Emmaus (Luke 24:13–35). Three days after Jesus' crucifixion, two of his disciples had been walking from Jerusalem to the nearby village of Emmaus and had fallen in with a stranger who asked them why they were so despondent. They explained what had happened to Jesus, the man they thought to be the messiah. The stranger gently rebuked them: Did they not realize that the scriptures had foretold that the Christ would suffer before attaining his glory? Starting with Moses, he began to expound "the full message" of the prophets, and later the disciples recalled how their hearts had "burned" within them when he had "opened" the scriptures to them in this way. After arriving at their destination, they begged the stranger to dine with them, and it was only when he blessed the bread that they realized it was Jesus himself.

---

and preserved the ancient writings known as the Dead Sea Scrolls, wrote biblical commentaries in the belief that its members were living in the final, climactic days of history, and with the understanding that the ancient prophetic oracles were being fulfilled in the events of their time. The sectaries were convinced that they belonged to a community that alone interpreted the scriptures correctly, and that biblical prophecy was intended primarily for them. The earliest Christians held similar attitudes.

Two Ways of Knowing

Like the rabbis, the Christians gathered "in twos and threes" to decipher the old texts. As they conversed together, the scriptures would "open" and bring them fresh insight. As Paul had made clear, Christians would no longer know Jesus "in the flesh" but would find him in one another, in scripture, and in the ritual meals they ate together.

The stories of Jesus found in the gospels—accounts of the virgin birth, of his baptism and temptation, of the transfiguration—are understood by scholars to be exercises in creative midrash, for their object is to show that Jesus' coming was foretold in the Hebrew scriptures. But one thing remains puzzling: Did not Jesus insist that his followers acknowledge his divine status—almost as a condition of discipleship? In the gospels we continually hear him berating his disciples for their lack of faith and praising the faith of gentiles, who seem to understand him better than his fellow Jews. Those who beg him for healing are required to have faith before he can work a miracle, and one is commended for calling out: "I believe; help my unbelief" (Mark 9:24–25). We do not find this preoccupation with belief in the other major religious traditions. Why did Jesus place such emphasis on it?

The answer is that he did not. The word translated as "faith" in the New Testament is the Greek *pistis* (verbal form *pisteuo*), which means "trust; loyalty; engagement; commitment." Jesus was not asking people to "believe" in his divinity, because he was making no such claim. He was asking for commitment. He wanted disciples who would engage with his mission, abandoning their pride, laying aside their self-importance and sense of entitlement, trusting fully in the God who was their father. In this freedom they were to give what they had to the poor, feed the hungry, and spread the good news of God's kingdom everywhere, living compassionate lives. Such *pistis* could move mountains and unleash human potential (Mark 11:22–23).

When the New Testament was translated from Greek into Latin by Saint Jerome early in the fifth century, *pistis* became *fides* ("loyalty"). *Fides* had no verbal form, so for *pisteuo* Jerome used the Latin verb *credo*, a word that derived from *cor do*, "I give my heart." When the Bible was translated into English, *credo* and *pisteuo* became "I believe" in the King James Version (1611). But the word "belief" has since changed its meaning. This English word, coming from the Middle English *bileven*, meant "to prize; to value; to hold dear." It was related to the German *belieben* ("to love"), *liebe* ("beloved"), and the Latin *libido*. So belief originally meant "loyalty to a person to whom one is bound in promise or duty."

Beyond Belief

During the late seventeenth century, however, as the concept of knowledge became more theoretical, the word "belief" started to be used to describe an intellectual assent to a hypothetical proposition. Scientists and philosophers were the first to use it in this sense, but in religious contexts the Latin *credere* and the English "belief" both retained their original connotations well into the nineteenth century.[11]

As Christianity spread in the Hellenistic world, the more educated converts brought with them the insights and expectations of their own Greek education. From an early date, they regarded Christianity as a *philosophia* that had much in common with the Greek schools. The Greek-educated church fathers, like the first-century Christian exegetes, also sought references to Christ in every sentence of the Hebrew Bible. Finding the Hebrew texts difficult to understand and the ancient biblical ethos alien, they read those scriptures allegorically, in which all the events and characters of what they called the Old Testament became precursors of Christ in the New.

One of the most brilliant and influential of these early exegetes was Origen (185–254), who had studied *allegoria* with Greek and Jewish scholars in Alexandria and midrash with rabbis in Palestine. For Origen, scripture was like a human person, consisting of a body, a psyche, and a spirit; these corresponded to the three senses in which scripture could be understood: the literal sense, the moral sense, and the spiritual sense. The student that pressed on to the end of his biblical studies was introduced to this spiritual (allegorical) sense, when he encountered the Word that lay hidden in the literal text (earthly body) of the sacred page. But this encounter would not be possible without the spiritual exercises that put the student into a different frame of mind. At first Origen's exegesis seems far-fetched to a modern reader, because he reads into the text things that are simply not there. But Origen was not asking the reader to "believe" his conclusions. Like any philosophical theory, his insights made no sense unless the disciple undertook the same spiritual exercises as did his master. Origen's commentaries were a *miqra*. Readers had to take the next step for themselves, meditation on the text with the same intensity as did Origen. Without long hours of contemplation (*theoria*), Origen's exegesis was both incomprehensible and incredible.[12]

For the fathers of the church, scripture was a "mystery," not because it contained incomprehensible doctrines, but because it pointed toward a

11. Armstrong, *Case for God*, 87.
12. Ibid., 96–97.

Two Ways of Knowing

hidden level of reality. Scripture was not just a text but an "activity," which you did not merely read—you had to *do* it; and you did so by participating in the Christian "mysteries," also known as sacraments. Like the philosophical schools of old, one participated in the "mysteries" of *philosophia* not to understand them by natural reason but because they were initiations, during which the congregants were taught to look beneath the symbolic gestures to find the sacred meaning within and thus experience a "change of mind," a conversion.

In the lectures of Cyril, bishop of Jerusalem (c. 315–86), we have one of the earliest accounts of the way candidates were introduced to the rituals and doctrines of the church. In Cyril's church, the ceremony of baptism took place early in the morning of Easter Sunday. During the six weeks of Lent, converts underwent an intensive period of preparation, when they had to fast, attend vigils, pray, and receive instruction about the basic facts of the gospel. They were not required to believe anything in advance. They were to be instructed in the deeper truths of Christianity only after the initiation of baptism, because these dogmas would make sense only after the transformative experience of the ritual. As in any philosophical school, theory was secondary to the rites and spiritual exercises that had produced it. Like any *mythoi*, the doctrines of Christianity were only imparted in a ritualized setting to people who were properly prepared and eager to be transformed by them. Like the insights of any initiation, the doctrines revealed at the end of the ritualized process would seem trivial or even absurd to outsiders. It was only after they had been through the transformative process that new Christians were asked to recite the creed, a proclamation not of "belief" but of commitment to the God that had become a reality in their lives as a result of this rite of passage.

On Easter Sunday, at the start of the ceremony, baptismal candidates faced westward outside the church, in the direction of sunset and death. As a first step in their reenactment of the Exodus, they renounced Satan. They were then "turned around" toward the east. Processing into the church, they discarded their clothes, symbolically shedding their old selves, so that they stood naked, like Adam and Eve before the fall. Each initiate was then plunged three times into the waters of the baptismal pool. Each time they were pulled underwater, the bishop asked: Do you have *pistis* in the Father—in the Son—in the Holy Spirit? Each time the initiate cried, "*Pisteuo!*": "I give him my heart, my loyalty, and my commitment!" In the Latin-speaking West, neophytes would cry "*Credo!*" when they were immersed in the water. This was not an intellectual assent to obligatory doctrines, for much dogma would not be imparted to them until the following week. The initiates were not simply stating their belief in a set of empirically unproven propositions but indicating something akin to "I will" in the marriage service. Belief in our modern sense was not a factor. Faith was purely a matter of commitment and practical living.[13]

The Apophatic Tradition: The Way of Unknowing

In the fourth century, when Constantine declared Christianity *religio licita*—one of the permitted religions of the Roman Empire—Christians had to adapt to their changed circumstances. They had to find a way to instruct the flood of new converts presented for baptism. They realized that their faith could be puzzling. Now that Christianity was predominantly gentile, the Hebrew terminology of the first Jewish Christians needed to be translated into a Greco-Roman idiom. Christianity claimed to be a monotheistic religion, but what was the status of Jesus? Was he a second God? What did Christians mean when they called him "Son of God"? And who was the Holy Spirit? The problem was exacerbated by a marked change in the intellectual and spiritual climate of late antiquity.[14]

Previously, Greeks saw no impassable gulf between God and humanity. But the problems of the day resulted in a profound loss of confidence in both the physical world and human nature. By the early fourth century people felt that the cosmos was separated from God by a vast, almost unbridgeable chasm. The universe was now experienced as fragile, and a terrifying void lay ready to engulf all living things. The idea that God had deliberately created all things posed huge problems. Monotheism implied that there was only one omnipotent power; did this mean that God was somehow responsible for evil? The idea of the incarnation was problematic as well. How could a good God become incarnate in material flesh?[15]

In 320 a heated debate about these issues erupted in Alexandria. Arius, a young presbyter of Alexandria, was anxious to safeguard the transcendence of God. God was unique, and he could not see how the immensity and omnipotence of God could possibly dwell in the man Jesus. Athanasius, the brilliant assistant to Alexander, bishop of Alexandria, wanted to safeguard the liturgical practice of the church, which regularly referred to Jesus as divine. If, he argued, the Arians really believed Christ

---

13. Ibid., 97–99.
14. The material in this segment is adapted from Armstrong, *Case for God*, 103–29.
15. Ibid., 103–4.

to be a mere creature, were they not guilty of idolatry when they worshipped him? The emperor Constantine, who had no understanding of the issues, decided to intervene and summoned all the bishops to Nicaea, a resort town in Asia Minor, where they were to resolve the matter. Athanasius managed to impose his views on the delegates, and the council issued a statement that Christ had not been created but had been begotten from the essence of the Father. Although all delegates except Arius and two of his colleagues signed the statement, this attempt to impose a uniform belief was counterproductive. Nicaea led to another fifty years of division, deliberation, and even violence, as creedal orthodoxy became politicized.

Eastern and Western Christians came to understand the incarnation very differently. Anselm of Canterbury (1033-1109) defined the doctrine of atonement that became normative in the West: God became man in order to expiate the sin of Adam. Orthodox Christians never accepted this. The Orthodox view of Jesus was defined by Maximus the Confessor (c. 580-662), who believed that Christ (the *Logos*) would have become flesh even if Adam had not sinned. Jesus was the first human being to be wholly "deified," entirely possessed and permeated by the divine, and all humans could be like him, even in this life.

Maximus fully accepted Athanasius's appreciation of the absolute transcendence of God. The revelation of the incarnate Logos made it clear that God must be absolutely unknowable. Even when we contemplate Christ the man, God remains elusive. Revelation did not provide clear information about God but told us that God was incomprehensible. Paradoxical as it might sound, the purpose of revelation was to tell us that we knew nothing about God: "For having become man . . . [God] himself remains completely incomprehensible . . . What could do more to demonstrate the proof of the divine transcendence of being than this? Revelation shows that it is hidden, reason that it is unspeakable, and intellect that it is transcendently unknowable."[16] For Maximus, such matters could not be settled by doctrinal formulations, because human language is not adequate to express the reality that we call "God." Even common words such as "life" and "light" mean something entirely different when we use them of God, so silence is the only medium by which it is possible to apprehend the divine.

But this did not mean that people had merely to "believe" these profound truths; on the contrary, they had to work very hard to achieve the mental stillness that made the experience of unknowing real in their lives. Maximus's theology was based on a spirituality that had developed shortly

---

16. Maximus, *Ambigua* 5, cited by Armstrong, ibid., 110.

Beyond Belief

after Nicaea. At a time when many Christians were engaged in wordy disputes and technical Christological definitions, others opted for a spirituality of silence. The monks spearheaded this movement, flocking into the deserts of Egypt and Syria to live in solitude, meditating on scriptural texts and practicing spiritual exercises. By the mid-fourth century, some of these desert monks had pioneered an apophatic or "wordless" spirituality that brought them peace and inner tranquility.

Evagrius of Pontus (c. 348–99), who became one of the leading masters of this tradition, taught his monks yogic techniques of concentration that stilled the mind, so that instead of limiting the divine by confining it within rationalistic, human categories, they could cultivate an attentive, listening silence. Prayer was not conversation with God or busy meditation on the divine nature; it meant "shedding of thoughts." Because God lay beyond all words and concepts, the mind must be empty.[17]

The Christians of Western Europe arrived at a similar understanding of the unknowability of God by a more psychological route, charted by Augustine. In one of the most famous passages of the *Confessions* he made it clear that the study of the natural world could not give us information about God: "Behold, you were within and I was outside myself," he wrote. Scripture tells us that we were made in God's image, so it was by looking within that Augustine found a type, an icon, of God. There, in the mind, he discovered a triad of memory (*memoria*), understanding (*intellectus*), and will (*voluntas*) that gives us insight into the triune life of God.

Augustine was fascinated by memory. Far more than the faculty of recollection, memory comprised the whole mind, conscious and unconscious, and was the source of our mental life in the same way as the Father was the ground of being. When he contemplated *memoria* Augustine was filled with awe, for memory gave us glimpses of infinity. But in order to encounter the divine, *memoria* had to press beyond itself to the *intellectus*, the place where the soul could encounter God in deepest intimacy. When Augustine spoke of "intellect," he was not simply speaking of the faculty of logic, calculation, and argument. In the ancient world people saw "reason" as a locality, bounded on the one hand by our powers of rationality and on the other by *intellectus*, a kind of pure intelligence that was higher than reason, without which we would not be able to reason at all. Left to itself, the human mind was incapable of making valid judgment about reality, because it was itself mired in impermanence and change. But when Augustine looked into the depths of his mind, he saw a realm in the

---

17. Ibid., 111.

psyche where the mind was able to reach beyond itself. Using the analogy of love, Augustine looked into the depths of his mind and saw that it was modeled on the Trinity, the archetype of all being. In the mind, memory generates the intellect, as the Father begets the Word that expresses the Father's essential nature. The intellect seeks out and loves the self it finds in the depths of the memory that generated it, just as memory seeks out and loves the self-knowledge encapsulated in the intellect. This activity in our own minds is a pale reflection of the Father, who loves the world through the Son; of the Son, who is the beloved of the Father; and of the Spirit, the bond of love between Father and Son. As in God, the three different human faculties—memory, understanding, and love—constitute "one life, one mind, and one essence."

In Augustine's Trinity, knowledge of God was inseparable from love of God. But Augustine did not expect his readers simply to take his word for all this; they too must undertake the introspection and meditation that had led him to adopt this theology; otherwise, like any *mythos*, it would remain incredible.[18]

Augustine was a complex man, and neither he nor his theology was flawless. But he left his followers a legacy by giving them two principles to follow as they plunged into the unknown future: (1) the principle of accommodation and (2) the principle of the integrity of science. No die-hard biblical literalist, Augustine took science very seriously, and his "principle of accommodation" would dominate biblical interpretation in the West until well into the early modern period. Because God had adapted revelation to the cultural norms of the people who had first received it, biblical passages were couched in the cosmology of antiquity and could not be interpreted literally. God had simply accommodated the truths of revelation to the science of the day so that the original audience could understand them. Whenever the literal meaning of scripture clashed with reliable scientific information, Augustine insisted, the interpreter must respect the integrity of science or bring scripture into disrepute. People who engaged in hostile debate of religious truth were simply in love with their own opinions and had forgotten the cardinal teaching of the Bible, which was the love of God and neighbor. The exegete must not leave a text until he established "the reign of charity," and if a literal understanding of any biblical passage seemed to teach hatred, the text must be interpreted allegorically and forced to preach love.[19]

18. Ibid., 120–21.
19. Ibid., 122–23.

Augustine had absorbed the underlying spirit of Greek apophatic theology, but the West did not develop a full-fledged apophatic spirituality until the ninth century, when the writings of an unknown Greek author were translated into Latin and achieved near-canonical status in Europe. He used the pseudonym Denys the Areopagite (scholars refer to him as Pseudo-Dionysius), referring to Paul's first Athenian convert (Acts 17:34), but he was almost certainly writing toward the end of the fifth and the beginning of the sixth century. During the medieval period, Denys had a profound influence on nearly every major Western theologian.

Denys saw no conflict between Neoplatonism, the leading intellectual *philosophia* of its day, and Christianity. Plotinus (c. 205–70), the leading Neoplatonic thinker, believed that the universe emanated from God eternally, like rays from the sun, so that the material world was a kind of overflowing of God's very being, an outward movement balanced by the yearning of all beings to return to the primal Unity. In like manner, Denys imagined creation not as something that had happened in the distant past but as a continuous, timeless process in which, paradoxically, God was eternally "enticed away from his transcendent dwelling-place and comes to abide within all things," and yet had the "capacity to remain, nevertheless, within himself."[20]

But of course this was impossible to understand rationally, because our minds cannot think outside a universe where beings are unable to do irreconcilable things at once. Although religious people are always talking about God, and it is important that they do so, they also need to know when to fall silent. Denys's theological method was a deliberate attempt to bring his Christian pupils to that point by making them conscious of the limits of language. In his treatise *The Divine Names*, Denys notes that while in the Bible God is given fifty-two names, yet God remains Nameless. Although it is true that God is One, this term properly applies only to beings defined by numerical quantities and therefore does not apply to God literally. To affirm God as Trinity does not mean that the three persons (*personae*) add up to any kind of triad that is familiar to us. God must be Intelligible—and yet God is Unknowable. God is Good, but certainly not "good" like a "good" human being. Gradually, we become aware that even the most exalted things we say about God are bound to be misleading. We cannot even say that God "exists," since our experience of existence is based solely on individual, finite beings whose mode of being bears no relation to being itself: "Therefore . . . God is known by knowledge and

---

20. Pseudo-Dionysius, *The Divine Names* 712A–B, cited by Armstrong, ibid., 123.

by unknowing; of him there is understanding, reason, knowledge, touch, perception, opinion, imagination, name and many other things, but he is not understood, nothing can be said of him, he cannot be named. He is not one of the things that are, nor is he known in any of the things that are; he is all things in everything and nothing in anything."[21]

Such language was not simply a logical conundrum that left people baffled. Rather it served as a spiritual exercise that, if properly performed, would bring participants to a higher level of insight. Denys's spiritual exercise took the form of a dialectical process, consisting of three phases: (1) First we must affirm what God is: God is One; God is good; God exists. But when we listen carefully we fall silent, felled by the weight of absurdity in such God talk. (2) In the second phase, we deny each one of these attributes, while recognizing that even this "way of denial" (*via negativa*) is as inaccurate as the "way of affirmation." Because we do not know what God is, we cannot know what God is not, so we come to the third phase, where (3) we deny the denials. In this phase God is *not* placeless, *not* mindless, *not* lifeless, *not* nameless, or *not* nonexistent. In the course of this exercise we learn that God transcends the capability of human speech, existing "beyond every assertion" and "beyond every denial."[22]

It is as inaccurate to say that God is "darkness" as to say that God is "light"; to say that God "exists" as to say that God does "not exist." Such an exercise points to the limits of logic and leads us to *apophasis*, the breakdown of speech, which fragments before the absolute unknowability of what we call God. Denys's dialectical method leads not to intellectual ignorance but rather to intellectual rapture, which takes us beyond everyday perceptions and introduces us to another mode of seeing and knowing. Like Moses at the top of the mountain, we embrace the darkness and experience no clarity, knowing that we are somehow in the place where God is.

We need to recall that Denys applied his method to the ceremonies of the liturgy, meaning communal rather than solitary rapture. His theology was based on the liturgy of Alexandria, which regarded the Eucharist not merely as a reenactment of Jesus' last supper but also as an allegory of the soul's ascent to God. His method was not for an elite group of contemplatives but seems to have been part of the public instruction of all the baptized faithful. Theology was not a solitary mind game, but like scripture, doctrine, and religion in general, was a *miqra*, a call to action and a way of understanding and living life.

21. Pseudo-Dionysius, 1048A.
22. Armstrong, *Case for God*, 126.

Beyond Belief

In the East, Denys was regarded as a disciple of Maximus, but in the West he enjoyed enormous prestige and became a leading authority. By the medieval period, the apophatic habit had become ingrained in Western Christian consciousness, and it is this practical path to God, this way of the heart, that religion should take if it is to have a central and hopeful role to play in the twenty-first century.

Postmodernism as a Way of Unknowing

Philosophy, theology, and mythology always respond to the science of the day, and a philosophical movement has developed since the 1980s that embraces the indeterminacy of Newtonian physics. It is called postmodernism, a way of thinking that builds on the assumption that what we call reality is constructed by the mind and that human understanding is interpretation rather than acquisition of accurate, objective information. From this it follows that our knowledge is relative, subjective, and fallible rather than certain and absolute, and that truth is inherently ambiguous.[23]

Postmodernism is iconoclastic. Inherited ideas are the products of a particular historical and cultural milieu, including the modern emphasis on science, reason, and *logos* as paths to peace, certainty, and a better future, and therefore are to be deconstructed. Since this analysis is not based on any absolute principle, there is no assurance that we can ever arrive at a wholly accurate version of truth. Fundamental to postmodern thought is the conviction that sense data cannot force us to adopt a particular worldview, so we have a choice in what we affirm—as well as an immense responsibility.

While postmodernism is suspicious of Big Stories—whether theological, scientific, economic, ideological, or political—it is also averse to an atheism that makes absolute, totalistic claims. As Jacques Derrida (1930–2004) cautioned, we must be alert to "theological prejudices" not only in religious contexts, where they are overt, but in all metaphysics—even those that profess to be atheist. Derrida, a secularized Jew, had a messianic hope for a better world and inclined to the view that, since no absolute certainty is within our grasp, we should for the sake of peace hesitate to make declarative statements of either belief or unbelief. While some religious believers are repelled by such unabashed relativism, there are aspects of Derrida's thought that recall earlier theological attitudes. His theory of deconstruction, which denies the possibility of finding a

23. The material in this segment is adapted from Armstrong, *Case for God*, 311–17.

single, secure meaning in any text, is rabbinical. He has also been called a "negative" theologian, for he was greatly interested in Meister Eckhart, the medieval apophatic mystic.

Another Italian postmodern thinker, philosopher Gianni Vattimo, argues that from the beginning religion was an essentially interpretive discourse: it had traditionally proceeded by endlessly deconstructing its own sacred texts, so that from the start it had the potential to liberate itself from metaphysical orthodoxy. "Vattimo is anxious to promote what is called 'weak thought' to counter the aggressively triumphalist certainty that characterizes a good deal of modern religion and atheism. Metaphysics is dangerous because it makes absolute claims for either God or reason.[24]

In opposition to the Enlightenment view, which envisioned freedom as lying in the perfect knowledge of and conformity to the structure of reality, Vattimo substitutes an appreciation of multiple discourses and the contingency and finitude of all religious, ethical, and political values—including our own. He wants to bring down "walls," including the walls that separate theists and atheists; the ideal society should be based on charity rather than truth.

Religion, as described by postmodern philosophers, may sound alien to much "modern" religion, but it evokes many of the insights of the past. Vattimo's claim that religion is essentially interpretive recalls the maxim of the rabbis: "What is Torah? It is the interpretation of Torah." When he affirms the primacy of charity and the communal nature of religious truth, we recall the rabbis' insistence that "when two or three study Torah together, the Shekhinah [the immanence of God] is in their midst," the story of Emmaus, and the communal experience of liturgy.[25]

Like Vattimo, the American philosopher John D. Caputo stresses the importance of the apophatic, arguing that atheists and theists alike should abandon the modern appetite for certainty. Such perceptions, once central to religion, tended to be submerged during modernity, and the fact that they have surfaced again in a different form suggests that this type of unknowing is inherent in our humanity. The distinctively modern yearning for absolute and empirically proven truth is most likely an aberration. Noting that atheism is always a rejection of a particular conception of the divine, Caputo concludes: "If modern atheism is the rejection of a modern God, then the delimitation of modernity opens up another possibility, less

24. Ibid., 314.
25. Ibid., 316.

the resuscitation of premodern theism than the chance of something beyond both the theism and the atheism of modernity."[26]

This raises a tantalizing possibility. If, as Caputo argues, we are entering a "postmodern" phase, is it possible that modern atheism will, like modern theism, become a thing of the past? Will the growing appreciation of the limitations of human knowledge—which is as much a part of the contemporary intellectual scene as atheistic certainty—give rise to a new kind of apophatic understanding of theology?

There are multiple types of fundamentalism in our world today, some religious, others political, and others scientific. Typical of the fundamentalist mindset is the belief that there is only one way of interpreting reality. For the new atheists, scientism alone can lead us to truth. But science depends upon faith, intuition, and aesthetic vision as well as on reason. As theologian Paul Tillich pointed out, men and women continually feel drawn to explore levels of truth that go beyond normal experience. This imperative, called an "ultimate concern" by Tillich, inspired the scientific as well as the religious quest and continues to shape life and give it meaning. The ultimate concern of new atheists such as Dawkins and Harris appears to be reason. But their idea of reason is very different from the rationality of Socrates, who used his reasoning powers to bring his dialogue partners into a state of unknowing, or the rationality of Augustine and Aquinas, for whom reason became *intellectus*, opening naturally to the divine. Reason, for many people today, rules supreme and is the only way to truth. The danger of this secularization of reason, which denies the possibility of transcendence, is that reason can become an idol that seeks to destroy all rival claimants.

As anthropologist Ian Tattersall notes in his superb book, *Becoming Human*, science fiction writers who created the character of Spock in the *Star Trek* series "hit close to home when they invented that supremely rational being. For there is undeniably something bizarrely seductive in the notion of living unencumbered by all the emotional baggage that being human inevitably entails. After all, irrational behavior, propelled by obscure emotion, has lain behind most of the endless misery that the human species has inflicted on itself (and others) over the course of recorded history. Yet there's a flip side to this, of course, for none of us would wish to be an automaton, and a life without emotion would be a life without exhilaration, love, and joy."[27]

26. Caputo, "Atheism, A/theology," 283; cited in Armstrong, *Case for God*, 317.
27. Tattersall, *Becoming Human*, 239–40.

Part Two

The Circle and the Ellipse

> A person who works with his hands is a laborer;
> a person who works with his hands and his brain is a craftsman;
> but a person who works with his hands and his brain
> and his heart is an artist.
>
> —LOUIS NITZER, AMERICAN LAWYER

> Truth is not really a soul word;
> soul is often insight more than truth.
>
> —THOMAS MOORE, PSYCHOTHERAPIST

4

Understanding Religious Thought Elliptically

WHY ARE SO MANY adults indifferent to religion, even those who in their youth expressed enthusiasm and healthy curiosity toward matters of faith? What happened to our childhood wonder about the truth of biblical miracles, or the efficacy of prayer? Is this condition a byproduct of the loss of innocence, or is something wrong with the answers we received as children?

Rabbi Harold Schulweis, longtime spiritual leader at Valley Beth Shalom in Encino, California, wrote a practical guide titled *For Those Who Can't Believe* (1994) to answer these questions and to address the ambivalence and concerns of a generation that affirms: "I'm not the religious type, though I consider myself a spiritual person." While his target audience is Jewish, his approach is immensely helpful to Christians and to people of all faiths.

Rabbi Schulweis tackles head-on tough questions asked by people reared in faith traditions, questions such as "Where is God?" "Does God really hear prayer?" "Why does God call for our worship?" "Do miracles occur?" "Is there divine revelation?" "Is obedience to authority the hallmark of faith?" and "What is the role of conscience in the religion?" To each of these questions he brings the perspective of a sage, based on a methodological starting point that eliminates the problem underlying all such questions at their very source.

Most questions religious people ask become hurdles to faith because they are framed incorrectly from the start. The implication behind our questions, the deficiency in our thinking, is that something is true or false, literal or fanciful, revealed or invented, divine or human, particular or universal. The problem with either/or questions is that they promote either/or answers. Such dichotomous forms of thinking set a trap, for the structure of either/or thinking implies that the options presented exhaust all other alternatives: either the Bible is divine or it is human; either one believes there are proofs for God's existence or one is an atheist; if one religion is true, others are false, and so on. Either/or thinking is intolerant of religious pluralism, impatient with both/and resolutions, and dissatisfied with anything less than all-or-nothing answers. It accepts only absolute answers and dismisses uncertainty as a sign of unbelief.

I am fond of the question that has been making the rounds lately: "What is the opposite of faith?" Either/or thinking answers, "Disbelief!" Both/and thinking answers: "Certainty!" And the latter, of course, is the "correct" answer. Like Schulweis's book, the aim of this segment of my book is to present alternative responses to rigid, either/or approaches that narrow the possibilities for seekers at all stages of their journey, precritical, critical, and postcritical.

Children, Schulweis notes, are born philosophers. They possess the sense of wonder, out of which faith springs. Parents must pay particular attention to the early questions children ask and to the first answers they give, for these answers carry crucial consequence for spiritual understanding. The religious inquiries of our youth may well be the most important questions we ever ask, for they come from minds that are impressionable, that embrace both faith and doubt. Adults must learn to answer such questions as soon as they are raised, in ways that embrace adventure and ambiguity, and not with answers that are evasive or that stifle the imagination. Answers that define reality affect our self-understanding, our morality, and our morale. The poet Wallace Stevens wrote, "We live in the description of a place, not in the place itself."[1] Religion is the description of the place we inhabit.

When I teach a course on Christian theology, I draw an image of a circle and an image of an ellipse, and I explain how an elliptical approach to such concepts as the nature of God, an understanding of sin and salvation, and the relation between faith and reason, provides a more helpful result than approaches that rely on the model of a circle for theological understanding. A circle, of course, has a single center, and everything is determined by its relation to the center. The ellipse, by contrast, is a figure that can be described only in relation to two foci, which cannot be resolved into one.

As we saw earlier, some people are unable to think elliptically (dialectically) about the question, "Where is God?" so they eliminate the tension between immanence and transcendence by deciding in favor of one polarity, that of supernatural theism—a model that conceptualizes God as "out there" and totally separate from nature. This understanding of

---

1. Cited by Schulweis, *For Those Who Can't Believe*, 17.

Understanding Religious Thought Elliptically

God is reductionistic, for it allows for only one correct perspective on the presence of God; if God is "out there," God cannot be "here with us," or vice versa. The symbol of a circle takes us back to "either/or" thinking, a simplistic stance that settles on only one possibly correct answer.

The elliptical model, however, makes it possible to view God as simultaneously transcendent and immanent, for both views are biblical and both are essential to religion. The truth is in the polarity between the two foci; the truth is not one-dimensional but dialectical. When one polarity is emphasized to the detriment or exclusion of the other, religion becomes rigid, intolerant, and increasingly confrontational. This form of thinking characterizes the religious approach we have called the Precritical Paradigm.

The Postcritical (Progressive) Paradigm, guided by the holistic possibilities found in the dialectical model, places equal importance upon faith (as displayed in religious beliefs and practices, both corporate and private) and reason (as displayed in the disciplines of philosophy, science, religious studies, and other academic subjects) in the quest for knowledge and understanding of reality. It also values the antithetical anthropological perspectives suggested in the opening chapters of the book of Genesis—humans are made "in the image of God" in the first creation account (Genesis 1) and "from the dust of the ground" in the second creation account (Genesis 2)—and the tension created by these competing yet harmonizable views. Dialectical thought is simultaneously God-affirming and world-affirming. Advocates of the Postcritical Paradigm need not choose, indeed should not choose, one over the other.

If the transition from a circular to an elliptical model may be said to be characteristic of the Progressive Paradigm in theology, there is a curious parallel with what occurred in modern astronomy. Until the time of Kepler, it was universally held that the planets moved in circular orbits—this was based not on observation but on the notion that, since the circle was considered to be the perfect figure, God, being perfect, could not have designed the orbits of the planets in any other way. When Kepler discovered that the planets move in elliptical orbits, he changed the shape of the astronomical universe, and, in the process, the course of future theology.[2]

The following theological topics, many of them discussed earlier from a more limited, "circular" perspective (based primarily on the dictates of *logos*), will now be addressed from a more holistic "elliptical" perspective. My presentation incorporates the argumentation developed by Rabbi Schulweis.

---

2. Hendry, *Theology of Nature*, 128.

1. God: Near or Far?

As an ordained minister and college chaplain, I am often asked to preach at nearby churches, where I sometimes deliver a message to the children. Though children are generally attentive, occasionally one asks a question. Having heard that God dwells in heaven but also that the church is the house of God, children often wonder, "Where is God?" As a professor of religion, I am tempted to answer that "God is everywhere," but such an answer could be construed as an evasion. Children don't want God to be "everywhere" but rather to be "somewhere." The answer "God is everywhere" might satisfy in the short run, but may come to be interpreted eventually to mean that God is nonexistent.

"Location" questions, when applied to God, heaven, or hell, should not be answered dismissively or authoritatively. However, our answers can become opportunities to broaden ways of thinking about spiritual matters. Instead of responding with pat answers from orthodox belief systems, adults can appeal to children's religious imagination, inviting questioners to envision an authentically spiritual universe.

Rabbi Schulweis provides a helpful example from his own experience. One evening, following prayer with his seven-year-old-daughter, he responded to the question "Where is God" with a game. He asked her to touch his arm, which she did; then to touch his chest, then his nose, and so on. Finally he asked her to touch his love. She stopped momentarily, and then reached out to touch his chest and arms. He pointed out that she had already touched his chest and arms. "Now touch my love." She was unable to do so, though she smiled knowingly.[3]

The exercise was an introduction to a deeper understanding of faith. It enabled his daughter to learn that there are "things" in the world that are very real, things about which we care deeply, that cannot be touched, examined with the senses, or located in space. The "where" question was not dismissed as wrong; it simply did not apply to nonmaterial reality. The intent of the game was to prepare the ground for an understanding of the reality of nonmaterial, spiritual matters. The point was not to teach a dualistic perspective—that the universe is split into natural and supernatural realms—but to ground the power, mystery, and significance of transcendence in earthly love.

---

3. Schulweis, *Those Who Can't Believe*, 22.

2. Prayer: Vertical or Horizontal?

Prayer begins early in life. For some, it is the first religious act performed. While there are many forms of prayer, for most people prayer is petitionary; that is, it derives from something wanted, needed, or requested. Most of us were taught at an early age that God answers prayer. In the Bible we learn that when we are in need or in trouble, and we pray honestly, God hears and answers. And so we pray, sincerely. And if our prayer is noble, and not simply selfish, we expect God will answer in the affirmative.

As we grow up, we are troubled by ineffectual prayer; answers of conventional theology, such as "God said no" or "We can't know God's will," become troubling. At critical junctures in our lives, conventional answers raise storm clouds of doubt, and we wonder whether God answers prayer at all. We look at a world gone awry, where inequities and calamities befall innocent people, and we question God's justice and even God's reality.

One of the reasons why prayer has lost meaning for many is not spiritual ineptitude, but rather that the God to whom we had been taught to pray has been inadequate. Before one can raise new spiritual possibilities, one must become convinced of the bankruptcy of old theological paradigms. Note the problems with the Lord's Prayer, the model prayer recited by Christians in all times and places: "Our Father, who art in heaven, hallowed be thy name." The depth of our separation from the God of the past becomes very apparent when we face the startling fact that we, in our time, cannot possibly begin in the same place where Jesus assumed that his disciples could begin.

Jesus' answer, for example, assumed that God was a person who could be addressed as "Father." He also assumed that this divine being was external to life, or "in heaven." Furthermore, he assumed that this male deity delighted in our recognition of the sacredness of his name. In addition, he suggested that this theistic God enjoyed the flattery of his subjects. These are all aspects of a theistic belief system that is no longer valid.

If we examine Jesus anew, and understand in him what Episcopal Bishop John Shelby Spong terms "a portrait of the presence of God in human life that manifests itself in wholeness," we have a basis for a new understanding of prayer. God represents wholeness, and if this is what God is, prayer is the experience of meeting that God. According to this understanding, prayer is:

- being present with others, sharing love, opening life to transcendence. Prayer recognizes that there is a sacred core in every person that must not be violated;

- the conscious human intention to relate to the depths of life and love and thereby to be an agent of the creation of wholeness in another;
- the offering of our life and our love through the simple action of sharing our friendship and our acceptance. Prayer seeks the strength to give others the courage to dare, to risk, to be in a whole new way;
- the struggle for human justice. Prayer is our active opposition to those prejudices and stereotypes that diminish the personhood and the being of another;
- a call out of childish dependency into spiritual maturity;
- being present, sharing love, opening to new possibilities. Prayer is more than words addressed heavenward; it can never be separated from acting.[4]

When theism went unchallenged and God was perceived as a being external to life, then prayer became quite naturally an activity of withdrawal from this world. Quiet days, pilgrimages, retreats, all of this devotional activity represented acts of holiness, understood as moments when one withdrew from normal routines in order to meet the holy. My understanding of prayer is changing. As my pastor friend John Bristol used to say: "Prayer is more about advancing than about retreating." In this sense, prayer comes in my living and in engaging the lives of others. Prayer is that process of being open to all that life can be and then of acting to bring that fullness to pass. Prayer is entering into the pain or joy of another person. Prayer is what I do when I live passionately and wondrously and invite others to do so. The deity I worship is not a supernatural being who stands over against our world and who seeks through some invasive process to imprint the divine will on the life of my world. The deity I worship is rather part of who I am individually and corporately. So praying can never be separated from acting. There is no magic here. "Prayer is the recognition that holiness is found in the center of life, and that it involves the deliberate decision to seek to live into that holiness by modeling it and by giving it away."[5] Prayer is not an occasional activity but an essential part of our lives, central to the way we live. I believe this is what Paul had in mind when he urged his readers to "pray without ceasing" (1 Thessalonians 5:17).

---

4. Spong, *Christianity Must Change*, 143–48.
5. Ibid., 148.

By reconsidering the meaning of prayer, we become aware that prayer is not magic. Magic uses formulas and incantations with the hopes of influencing outcomes; the goal of magic is to produce results. That's not how prayer works. Praying for an "A" in class, for instance, is outside the domain of genuine prayer. We can pray for the means to achieve a desirable grade, such as for patience and discipline to study. That would be a responsible form of prayer. Irresponsible prayer, like magical thinking, invites false hope and false means to achieve its ends. It denigrates human knowledge and the competencies that are required to achieve the desired ends. Genuine prayer is concerned with "energizing the means so as to achieve ends of worth."[6] As Kierkegaard noted, "Prayer does not change God, but it changes the one that offers it."[7]

Prayer should no longer be viewed as asking God for things. Such an understanding presupposes a master-servant model, one that elevates God and lowers humans. According to that model, divinity gives and humanity receives. The Bible offers an alternative approach, a covenantal understanding of God. Covenantal prayer is a two-sided relationship in which both God and the petitioner are active and in which neither is passive.

Covenantal prayer becomes a form of self-examination. Understood this way, it is the self who is the target of prayer. Prayer is a way of discovering who we are and who we need to become; it is the constant search for the means of repair of the self and the world. When that occurs, prayers of dependence and acquiescence become prayers of interdependence and mutual responsibility. According to Paul Tillich, "In true prayer, God is both He to whom we pray and He who prays through us."[8]

Vertical, one-sided prayer, leads to placing the entire burden on the Other. Covenantal prayer, however, is horizontal; it involves both petitioner and God in an energizing partnership. If we wonder, "Does prayer move God?" the answer is: prayer moves God only if we who pray are moved to respond. If we pray and do not hear, if we pray and do not act, we become ensnared in magical thinking. To pray to God who brings peace on earth without lifting our voice or finger to struggle for peace trivializes the function of prayer for peace. This understanding provides new meaning to the plaque that hung prominently in the home of my missionary parents and read, "Prayer Changes Things." Where I once understood that prayer vertically, I now understand it to work horizontally. Prayer changes things

---

6. Schulweis, *Those Who Can't Believe*, 33.
7. Quoted in Fox, *Mystical Bear*, 15.
8. Cited by Schulweis, ibid., 39.

by first changing the petitioner. As the ideal of "David" was in the marble before Michelangelo carved it, so the ideal of the divine image is in our being before it is carved by prayer. The worshiper becomes "the sculptor who painstakingly carves his self after the divine image."[9]

Plotinus, the second-century AD philosopher acknowledged as the founder of Neoplatonism, advised, "Withdraw into yourself and if you do not like what you see, act as a sculptor. Cut away here, smooth there, make this line lighter, this one purer. Never cease carving until there shines out from you the Godlike sphere of character."[10] When Moses sought to know God's way and God's glory (Exodus 33:13, 18), what was revealed was "God's mercy, compassion, forbearance, goodness, truthfulness, loving kindness. These are the attributes of divinity to be humanly emulated. The imitation of God's attributes is the ambition of prayer."[11]

3. Miracles: True or False?

If there is no magic in prayer, then what do we make of the miracles in the Bible? How do we distinguish between magic and miracles?[12] Can we avoid the paradox of Rabbi Menachem Mendel of Kotzk, who maintained that "Whoever believes in miracles is a fool; and whoever does not believe in miracles is an atheist"?[13] Can we believe in miracles without being fools, or disbelieve them without losing faith? Once again, it is the framing of the question into an either/or alternative that forces us to choose. And since the options create conflict, we often compartmentalize religious and scientific assumptions, as if they dealt with different realities. To avoid getting caught in this dualistic trap, we need to examine how the word "miracle" is used and to what kinds of events it is applied.

Fundamentalists read the Bible literally, and that requires them to treat miracles literally. Passages dealing with creation, with the flood, with the Exodus, with the birth of Jesus, with the resurrection of Lazarus, with the end of history, all are interpreted verbatim. Nonfundamentalists might also read the Bible with reverence, but they are uncomfortable with the implausibility of its miracles. So to give the text credibility, many merely

9. Ibid., 42.
10. Cited by Schulweis, ibid., 42.
11. Ibid.
12. For my working definition of miracle, see page 19, n. 5.
13. Cited by Schulweis, ibid., 46.

Understanding Religious Thought Elliptically

replace literal scripture with literal science. But in so doing, they ruin its religious sense.

Biblical commentaries contain suggestions for modern readers who find themselves caught between natural or supernatural interpretations of the meaning of miracles. Some theologians focus on the moral significance of the event called miraculous. The Egyptian plagues, for instance, are viewed as a conflict between the morality of the Hebrew religion and the immorality of the Egyptians. Understood in that manner, the plagues can be seen as a drama of poetic justice. Sometimes the language used to explain events such as the revelation given on Mount Sinai or used in the Psalms and in the climactic passages in the book of Job to explain divine acts or divine intention is explained to be theophanic language, meaning that it speaks of divine presence poetically, for that is the only way such religious phenomena can be expressed.

Jewish and Christian commentators often interpret alleged miraculous events allegorically. Take for example the episode recorded in Exodus 17:11. There we are told that Israel prevailed in its battles with the Amalekites only when Moses's hand was raised, but was defeated when Moses let his hand down. A helpful explanation is that the passage refers to the faith of the people. As long as they remained faithful, they were victorious, but when they doubted and became discouraged, they were defeated. In this manner, supernatural accounts are viewed as parables with spiritual value. Not the medium but the message is to be heeded.

Whenever miracles are taken literally, so that divine intervention disrupts nature, we are caught between the horns of dualistic dilemma and forced to choose between science and religion, reason and faith. To avoid such conflict, and to ensure that biblical miracles not be read as contradictions to the natural order, biblical commentators encourage us to find divine wisdom and goodness in the reliability of the cosmos, not in occasional events deemed unnatural. "Faith is not dependent on miracles. Miracles depend on faith. And faith, far from blind, sees life's deeper truths."[14]

The philosopher Abraham Joshua Heschel frequently opened his evening lectures with an announcement that he had just experienced a miracle. He went on to explain to the puzzled audience that he had observed the setting of the sun. For Heschel, the miraculous is not to be looked for in the strange events in nature but in the ordinariness of existence. Rabbi Schulweis prefers the expression "sign-miracle" over the term

---

14. Ibid., 52.

"miracle," thereby affirming that miracles function as signs, hence their "sign-ificance." Miracles are pointers to that which makes an important difference in one's life or in the life of our community. The sign-miracles do not refer to something contrary to nature; they are not meant to violate reason or nature. Rather they compel us to observe the extraordinary in the ordinary, the marvel in the routine. Sign-miracles "are natural moments in our lives that we recognize as transforming."[15]

Conventional theology is apprehensive of both naturalistic and humanistic explanations of miracles. While a theistic bias predominates in the teaching of popular theology, we need to pay attention to insights that perceive and implement the miraculous in our daily lives. A well-known tale makes this clear. It is the account of a man stranded on the rooftop of his home, surrounded by floodwaters. He prays to God to be saved. A rowboat with rescuers comes by and offers him safety. He turns them away, confident that God will save him. A helicopter flies overhead and lowers it rope ladder. The pilot urges him to climb the ladder. He turns the pilot away, waiting for God to save him. The waters rise, and in disappointment the imperiled man protests to his maker: "I am a believing man and have always proclaimed my trust in you. Why have you, Lord, forsaken me?" A heavenly voice responds: "But my child, I sent you the men in the rowboat and you dismissed them. I sent you the pilot and you refused his help. Why have you forsaken me?" Faith is a way of seeing and a way of responding to what we see.

A famous rabbinic symposium clarifies this principle. Rabbi Akiba was challenged by the pagan Tineus Rufus: "Whose deeds are greater, those of God or of man?" Akiba replies, "Greater are the deeds of man." The pagan is surprised by Akiba's response. To provide evidence for his assertion, Rabbi Akiba brings forth sheaves of wheat and loaves of cakes. Akiba asks, "Which are superior?" Of course the loaves of cakes. Akiba's demonstration pointed out the error of dualistic thinking. Rufus presented Akiba with an either/or alternative: either God or man, either the deeds of God or the deeds of man, are superior. Rufus lacked awareness of the cooperative relationship between God and humanity. Akiba calls attention to the daily sign-miracles. In his tradition, breaking bread is as miraculous as dividing the sea. Similarly, wine, not grapes, represents the fullest expression of the holy, the covenant between people of faith and Nature's God.[16]

---

15. Ibid., 56.
16. Ibid., 60–61.

4. Revelation: Word of God or Words of Man?

Within the religious tradition, Schulweis finds meaningful what he calls a "theistic humanism," a perspective that provides a critical bearing on how humans understand their role in ethics, ritual, prayer, and the miraculous. If these are understood as interactive events between deity and humanity, what of the Bible? Is it the word of God or the words of man? Are the narratives in the Bible fact or fiction? Once again, such options force us into either/or thinking. They are motivated by a literalist approach that treats scripture in isolation from the filter of human interpretations. Such piety is based on a mindset that the more literal the interpretation of a text, the truer the faith; the more symbolic the interpretation, the weaker the faith. Actually, the converse is true, for it is literalism, not symbolism, which conceals the depth of the biblical text.

Consider what the story of Noah's ark loses when it is explained verbatim. The literalist, seeing divine judgment, misses the lesson of the human capacity for self-destruction. The literalist, seeing damnation, overlooks the ability of one person to save the world.

The literalism that counts the number of animals on the ark or searches for its actual location on Mt. Ararat turns moral saga into fantasy, and those who try to verify details of the story end up with a fairy tale. Challenging the truth of the Bible, detractors have faulted the text as providing unworkable dimensions and construction. Its capacity, they argue, was only a fraction of what was needed for the animals and their food supply, not to speak of their specialized requirements for housing. Such criticism misses the moral meaning of the account. The Bible is not a reporter's journal recording the details of actual events. Neither is the Bible a book of science nor a text of geology. The Bible is concerned with meaning, with the spiritual implications of an event, not with its physical cause and effect.

Hardly a verse in the Bible taken verbatim is exempt from embarrassment. That's true of almost any verse in the first eleven chapters of Genesis. Take the statement, "And God said, 'Let there be light.'" If God speaks, does God have a larynx? If God spoke these words on the first day of creation, how could light have been created before the fourth day, when the sun, the moon, and the stars were created? However, if the text is freed from a literal reading, we are able to see that the sun is deliberately introduced late in the biblical order of creation so as to combat the pagan worship of the heavenly light. So too the creation of the world through the agency of a spoken word sets the biblical view in opposition to the pagan view that traces the origin of the world to violent battles between primordial gods. To teach the Bible in a literal fashion is to leave religious people vulnerable to simplistic "scientific" diatribes.

To teach the whole of the Bible in terms of "true" or "false" judgments is to impose the wrong criteria on the scriptural text. We cannot properly ask whether the book of Psalms is true or false any more than we can ask whether poetry, painting, and music are true or false. Some of the narratives of the Bible record an account of an event that was literal, according to the mindset and historiography of its day; others reveal the spiritual effect of the event on people. To treat the truth of the Bible as if it were all literal recording or all figurative portrayal distorts its message.

Aside from problems created by the literal understanding of the Bible, many modern readers are offended by the questionable moral character of the heroes of the biblical revelation. It is clear that the Bible contains much behavior that is unethical. Why is this material included, and what can we learn from biblical heroes? The book of Genesis provides numerous examples. We may well be upset by God's favoritism in accepting Abel's offering and rejecting Cain's; by the aggressive conduct of Jacob who wrested the birthright blessings of Esau through subterfuge; by the folly of Jacob's offering a coat of many colors to his son Joseph, thereby initiating a cycle of sibling disasters.

Similar morally disturbing acts come to mind, such as the fairness of God's hardening of Pharaoh's heart; God's testing of Abraham's loyalty by commanding him to sacrifice his son Isaac; Sarah's resentment of Hagar and Abraham's casting out of Hagar and her son Ishmael; visiting the sins of the fathers upon the children; God's command through Samuel that Saul kill all Amalekite women and children in the ongoing war against Israel's traditional enemies; the senseless suffering of Job and his family in a heavenly wager between God and the Satan over Job's fidelity to God; the vicarious suffering of Jesus on the cross for the sins of others.

It is unnecessary to defend each and every act of the biblical heroes or of God's role in history. We need to keep in mind that the Bible does not moralize in the manner of a didactic text. In the narrative stories of Genesis, the Bible does not telegraph its moral messages. The Jacob and Joseph sagas are moral dramas that must be followed to their conclusion. The same Jacob who manipulated Esau to surrender the birthright later must wrestle with his angel of conscience, must have his name and character changed through his inner struggle, and emerge lame from the battle. Jacob, whose career started in deception, is in turn victimized by the trickery of Laban and later by the deception of his sons, who pretend that Joseph was devoured by a beast.

The Bible presents imperfect heroes. Without exception, they are fallible. When questionable episodes are viewed in the light of the entire biblical history, moral context is provided. At the conclusion of the story of Job, it is Job who is vindicated and not his friends, who "have not spoken of me what is right, as my servant Job has" (Job 42:7). The critique even of God's role in history is within the Bible itself, placed into the protesting voice of prophets such as Habakkuk: "O Lord, how long shall I cry for help, and you will not listen? Or cry to you, 'Violence!' and you will not save? ... why do you look on the treacherous, and are silent when the wicked swallow those more righteous than they?" (Habakkuk 1:2, 13). The prophets are not yes-men. The ideal prophet defends both the people against God and God against the people.

Given the fallible heroes of the Bible and even some shortcomings of God, in what sense is the Bible sacred? "If by sacred we mean that the Bible is inerrant, its heroes infallible, its morality complete, then," Schulweis notes, "its sacred character seems questionable. But the Bible is holy not because it is the final word but because it is the first word of an unending tradition."[17] A dramatic instance can be cited from the passage in Exodus 20:5, where the notion of inherited guilt and punishment extends "to the third and fourth generation of those who reject me." That teaching, however, is explicitly repudiated elsewhere in the Bible, including in Ezekiel 18:20: "A child shall not suffer for the iniquity of a parent, nor a parent suffer for the iniquity of a child; the righteousness of the righteous shall be his own, and the wickedness of the wicked shall be his own."

The Christian tradition, like the Jewish faith, does not end with the scriptures; its teachings are shaped by the conscience of later interpreters and by the religious commentaries of its masters.

5. Conscience: Voice of God or Voice of Man?

Søren Kierkegaard (1813–1855), the noted Danish Christian existentialist, made an important contribution to the life of faith in his formulation of three levels of existence or stages through which humans go in their ascent toward God. On the first level, which he labeled the *aesthetic stage*, individuals are ruled by their senses, in which case they can be called "sensual aesthetes." Such persons live solely for the present, and particularly for self-gratification.

17. Ibid., 73.

Aesthetes, characterized by the absence of either moral standards or religious faith, remain detached and uncommitted. Kierkegaard extends this attitude to include "the intellectual aesthete," the contemplative person who tries to stand outside of life and behold it as a spectator.

The aesthetic life, however, is not ultimately fulfilling, for it ends in boredom and despair. Aesthetes, recognizing that they are living inauthentically, find no remedy on this level. They must either remain there in boredom and despair or make a transition to the next level by an act of choice. Willing, not thinking, is the key. The act of choosing does not resolve the tension, for one must *either* remain at the first level *or* choose to move on. The antithesis remains.

The second level, called *the ethical stage*, requires that one abandon attitudes of selfishness and make commitments to others. Here moral standards and obligations are adopted, as dictated by reason. Cold detachment is left behind, for in this stage one embraces universal standards. The example Kierkegaard chose as the transition from aesthetic to moral consciousness is marriage, in which a person renounces the satisfaction of the sexual impulse according to passing attraction and enters the state of marriage, accepting all its obligations. This stage is meaningful and superior to the aesthetic level because it provides continuity and stability to life.

Whereas Kierkegaard believed sincerely in universal moral obligations, this stage is not the end or goal of existence. The problem with the ethical stage is that the ethical person remains committed to autonomy and self-sufficiency. The ethical hero recognizes self-sufficiency as sin, but believes he can overcome it by sheer willpower and ability. And therein lies the problem of the ethical stage. Eventually the ethical person comes to the awareness of an inability to fulfill the moral law and becomes conscious of guilt and estrangement from God. The ethical person is once more confronted with a choice: either to continue in one's effort to fulfill the moral law, or move to a higher stage, to a life of faith. This requires an act of commitment, which Kierkegaard called a "leap of faith." In his own life Kierkegaard had found that the previous stages were based upon the "illusion of humanism," resulting in failure to recognize his need for God.

The third and final stage, which he called *the religious stage*, entails a life of faith. This is final because it recognizes the existence of God and the need to relate oneself wholly to God. In each previous stage, Kierkegaard selected a figure from literature or history as an example. For the aesthetic stage he chose Don Juan, the classic figure from Spanish drama who lived solely for sensual pleasure and was unable to commit to a meaningful relationship with others. The ethical stage is typified by Socrates, who took his own life rather than compromise his moral standards. The example he selected for the religious stage was Abraham, whose trust of God and unwavering obedience led him to choose to sacrifice his only son Isaac, even in the face of absurdity, for to question God would be to place reason over faith.

Is such behavior justifiable or is it unethical? In selecting this example, Kierkegaard was not denying the validity of ethics. He stated that the individual who is called to break with the ethical must first be ethical, that is, must first have subordinated to universal morality. The break, when one is called to make it, is made in "fear and trembling" and not arrogantly or proudly. In this final stage, the ethical is not abolished but dethroned by a higher purpose or end, a phenomenon he described as the "teleological suspension of the ethical." The key to this final stage is not the commendable humanistic goal of universal duty to others, but the unqualified giving of oneself to God. If one doesn't go beyond the ethical, beyond moral obligation, one cannot properly say that one is related to God, or obedient to God. Ethical duty, he believed, must ultimately lead to God, but since it usually leads to humanity (i.e. to humanism), then this stage must be transcended. An absolute relationship to an absolute (God) requires a relative relationship to relative ends. And for Kierkegaard, everything other than God is relative.

In the nineteenth century Kierkegaard was a voice crying in the wilderness of a complacent civilization, for his one passion was to show what it meant to be a Christian. The church in his day was so institutionalized, he argued, that it was no longer Christian; in fact, it had become "impossible to be a Christian in Christendom."

Readers raised in evangelical Christian homes will recognize in Kierkegaard's thought much that characterizes their own belief. Here one finds an emphasis on the sovereignty of God and the lordship of Christ, in addition to the sinfulness of humanity and the need for a transcendent Savior. Kierkegaard is attractive to those who emphasize the centrality of relationship in religion, and the need for passion and commitment in their faith. The more one reads Kierkegaard, however, the stranger and less accessible he becomes. Let us explore his choice of Abraham as exemplar of the religious stage of life, and consider anew the command to sacrifice Isaac (Genesis 22).

Abraham was a man of faith, and like Abraham, Jews, Christians, and Muslims wish to be people of faith. Abraham heard God's voice and was prepared to sacrifice his son. Holding the knife in his hand to slay his son, he heard the angel of the Lord tell him to stay his hand and to slay instead a ram caught in a nearby thicket. What is this story asking of us, we wonder? What does it teach us about the life of faith? Does a literal reading of this story encourage religious extremism, even the killing of others?

On almost every level, the story is disturbing. It raises questions that border on the absurd. How could Abraham agree to such a command? Why did he not protest? How did he know the command was from God? And if he could be sure, how could God make such immoral demands of Abraham? How did Abraham decide which voice to obey, that of God or that of God's angel? Is God's word to be obeyed even when obedience is contradicted by reason?

How does religion resolve the dilemma of obedience to authority? Is faith the triumph of obedience over conscience? If so, what is the role of conscience in religion? How are modern people to understand the meaning of the Abraham story? The following interpretations of Abraham's faith reflect two divergent views of revelation.

1. Kierkegaard views Abraham as a religious hero, whose fidelity to God transcends his love of his son. In his willingness to sacrifice Isaac, Abraham passes the test of unconditional obedience. In the Jewish liturgy, Abraham is honored for his willingness to sacrifice the promised future of his people out of trust in God. In Christian theology, Isaac is viewed as a prefiguration of Christ and Abraham typifies God, who so loved the world that he gave his only son, sacrificing him vicariously as the perfect substitute for humanity. From that point of view, believers should obey the directives of divine authority without question. Conscience cannot be allowed to contradict the divine imperative.

2. The alternative interpretation of the biblical account emphasizes the revelation of the angel of the Lord. On this reading, the angel who stays Abraham's hand is a symbol of Abraham's moral conscience. "Abraham's acceptance of the voice of the Lord's angel over God's commanding voice expresses his faith in a moral God who could not will the death of an innocent."[18] Earlier in Genesis we read about God's threat against Sodom and Gomorrah, at which time Abraham challenged the morality of God's plan: "Will you indeed sweep away the righteous with the wicked?" (Genesis 18:23). Neither the biblical nor the theological tradition regards Abraham's rhetorical opposition to God's intention as a treasonable act against divine sovereignty. On the contrary, Abraham's dissent is grounded in God's goodness and fairness: "Shall not the Judge of all the earth do what is just?" (Genesis 18:25). Unlike Job's assault on God, who sought

---

18. Ibid., 81.

an intermediary to intercede between him and God (Job 9:33), Abraham sought no umpire; he "appeals to God against God in the name of God."[19]

What is needed today is not blind allegiance, such as might be commanded in the first approach, but individuals with the courage to pursue the heroic role of moral conscience in religion, whereby mortal authorities are challenged when they contradict fairness and goodness. Holy dissent against God and in the name of God is a unique Judaic feature, one that Christians and Muslims are exhorted to emulate. In the Bible, Moses is depicted as rising on several occasions to challenge God's decision, and each time Moses succeeded in overturning God's judgment (Exodus 32:32; Deuteronomy 9:19-20; 10:10). According to Schulweis, "Far from being considered acts of insubordination, these acts of dissent testify to the high status accorded to human conscience."[20] Although rebellion against God is certainly not condoned in the Bible, the name "Israel"—the name given to Jacob and to his posterity—is said to mean: "those who strive with God ... and win."

This understanding of the role of conscience in religion challenges traditional views of revelation. If conscience is the hyphen in the human-divine covenant, revelation becomes "a dialogue of reciprocal covenant, an ongoing process of listening and interpreting, of receiving and giving. Awareness of having entered the covenant makes it impossible to separate the divine and human element in the encounter of revelation ... The test of the believer is not whether he believes or whether he obeys, but what he believes and what he will not believe, what he obeys and what he will not obey."[21]

---

19. Ibid., 82.
20. Ibid., 85.
21. Ibid., 87-88.

5

Understanding God Panentheistically

THEOLOGY IS "TALK ABOUT God." And the majority of people who use the term "God," particularly in the Western world, have in mind a theistic concept of God, meaning an all-powerful and supreme ruler of the universe. Supernatural theism, by implication, includes the view that all finite things are dependent in some way on this ultimate reality, a reality generally described in personal terms. After all, imaging God as a personal being is very common in the Bible. It is also the natural language of worship and prayer, and there is nothing wrong with it in such contexts. A transcendent reality that does not possess at the very least those qualities that constitute the dignity of human beings, qualities such as intelligence, feeling, freedom, power, initiative, and creativity, could not adequately inspire trust or reverence in human beings. In this sense God would have to be "personal" to be God. It is doubtful whether believers could worship something that does not have at least the stature of personality.

While the idea of a "personal God" is beneficial in that it makes God relational and accessible to humanity, the extremes of this position, such as presented in the Hebrew scriptures, raise insuperable problems for people in the modern era. This God fights wars and defeats enemies, chooses people and works through them, sends storms, heals the sick, spares the dying, rewards goodness, and punishes evil. Many people have trouble intellectually with these anthropomorphic renderings of God and with the seeming irrationality of belief in a personal God. While only the most traditional believers and the most literal readers of scripture believe such things anymore, this deity remains the primary object and substance of the Christian church's faith. It is this understanding of God that is becoming meaningless to increasing numbers in the modern world.

While it is attractive to speak of intimacy with God and accessibility to God, religious philosophers have long warned against ascribing human

Understanding God Panentheistically

qualities and attributing human feelings to God. Still, the joy of familiarity with God and the need to recognize and be recognized by God override the philosopher's critique. There is, however, a critical flaw in this perspective: Once we conceive of God as a person like ourselves, God becomes open to criticism.

To protect God, apologists and theologians maintain that this way of thinking must be discarded. God is not like us, says Karl Barth; God is "Totally Other." Following this understanding, God is viewed as different not only in degree but also in kind. In using the model of Transcendence, whereby God is said to be all knowing, all powerful, and all good, we instinctively know that we are not referring to the same kind of qualities we understand when speaking of attributes in humans. Does this mean, then, that God cannot be said to be moral in the manner that we are said to be moral? If so, that raises deep resentments. We hear it in the outburst of the philosopher John Stuart Mill: "I will call no being good who is not what I mean when I apply the epithet to my fellow creatures, and if such a being can sentence me to hell, to hell I will go."[1] In his publication, *The Sins of Scripture*, Bishop Spong examines biblical moral principles attributed to the will of God and concludes that those who wish to base their morality literally on the Bible have either not read it or not understood it.

As Schulweis observes, "In elevating God to the level of transcendent lawgiver and judge, the human being is drawn increasingly subordinate to the will of God. An alienating dualism has intruded in the original picture, splitting the divine and the human, erecting a wall between God 'above' and nature 'below.' As a result, questions about prayer, miracles, and revelation are turned into forced either/or options. Prayer is either a unilateral response from God or a lonely human monologue; miracle is either God's intervention or human invention; revelation is either God's word cast down from above or a soliloquy from below."[2]

But what are the alternatives? Is atheism (a-theism) the only alternative to theism? Technically, of course, there are numerous options, including polytheism (the belief that there are numerous deities), pantheism (the belief that God is in everything for everything is divine), henotheism (the notion of worshipping a territorial god, conceived as one god among many), animism (the belief that nature is filled with spirits or souls, which must be worshipped or appeased), and panentheism.

---

1. Cited by Schulweis, *Those Who Can't Believe*, 132.
2. Ibid.

One can find historical traces of panentheism in both western and eastern orthodox theology, though the word itself was popularized by English philosopher Alfred North Whitehead (1861–1947). Panentheism is not the same as pantheism, the concept that "all things are God." Rather, pan*en*theism is the concept that "all things are *in* God." Panentheism views God not as a supernatural being separate from the universe, beyond nature and history, but as the encompassing Spirit around us and within us. According to this conception, God is more than the universe, yet the universe is in God. Viewed spatially, God is not "out there" but "right here." Whereas supernatural theism emphasizes God's transcendence—God's otherness, God as more than the universe—panentheism affirms both the transcendence and immanence of God. It does not deny or subordinate one in order to affirm the other. For panentheism, God is both more than the universe and yet everywhere present in the universe.[3]

In this regard, panentheism is located between traditional theism and pantheism. As David Ray Griffin describes it, panentheism "combines features of both pantheism, which regards God as 'essentially immanent and in no way transcendent,' and traditional theism, which regards God 'as essentially transcendent and only accidentally immanent.'"[4] Griffin's work helps to explain why panentheism isn't just pantheism with a new name: "Panentheism is crucially different from pantheism because God transcends the universe in the sense that God has God's own creative power, distinct from that of the universe of finite actualities. Hence, each finite actual entity has its own creativity with which to exercise some degree of self-determination, so that it transcends the divine influence upon it."[5]

Theologians in various traditions have offered different ways of defining and modeling this God-world relationship. According to the influential German evangelical theologian Jürgen Moltmann, in the panentheistic view God, having created the world, also dwells in it, and conversely the world which he has created exists in him. He writes of God "making space," a *nothing* (*nihil*) to which God gives being (*creatio*

---

3. Critics of process theology dismiss this way of viewing God as unbiblical and claim that it represents a return to Greek and Roman paganism. This mistaken understanding of panentheism leads Diogenes Allen to posit that the inspiration for Whitehead's God was Plato's *Timaeus*, in which Plato postulates a craftsman who took preexistent time, space, and matter and organized them, *Troubled Believer*, 48.

4. Griffin, *Reenchantment*, 141.

5. Ibid., 142. For additional information on the relationship between panentheism, process theology, and traditional Christianity see appendix A and Marjorie Suchocki's online explanation, "What is Process Theology?"

ex nihilo). "God does not create merely by calling something into existence . . . In a more profound sense he 'creates' by letting-be, by making room, by withdrawing himself."[6] Moltmann's language expresses the idea of the world, including humanity, as "enveloped by God without losing its true distinctiveness." Consonant with Moltmann's theology, Anglican theologian Arthur Peacocke writes that "God is best conceived of as the circumambient [i.e., surrounding] reality enclosing all existing entities, structures and processes, and as operating in and through all, while being 'more' than all. Hence, all that is not God has its existence within God's operation and Being."[7] Other panentheistic models have been suggested, but all reveal a common theme: the world is given existence, energy, life, nourishment, and continuous creation by the God in whom "we live and move and have our being" (Acts 17:28).

Fortunately there are alternatives to the concept of theism, for "theism" and "God" need not be the same. Supernatural theism is but one human definition of God. Panentheists affirm that "God" does not refer to a supernatural being "in heaven," apart from nature, but rather to the sacred at the center of existence, the holy mystery that is around us and within us. Panentheism affirms the centrality of mystery in the universe and the possibility of relating intellectually and experientially to that mystery. It is possible, then, to be an agnostic or even an atheist regarding the God of supernatural theism and yet be a believer in God in the way offered by panentheism.

In 1986 John F. Haught, one of our most insightful Christian scholars, wrote a short work titled *What is God? How to Think About the Divine*. Writing for skeptical individuals who question whether talk about God is obsolete, Haught proposed that we alter the way we think about God; instead of using personal terms to describe God—asking "who" God is—he suggests that we focus instead on "what" God is, focusing on the transpersonal or superpersonal aspect to God found in many religious traditions, aspects of deity that cannot be adequately represented in personalistic imagery. This approach is helpful ontologically as well as intellectually.

Ontologically, an examination of the transpersonal dimension of God's nature, that side of God's being that cannot be adequately represented in personalistic terms, may help us to make some sense of the "scandal" of the divine hiddenness. Intellectually, thinkers ask questions like "What is nature?" "What is history?" "What is the universe?" Those are the

---

6. Moltmann, *God in Creation*, 88–89.
7. Clayton and Peacocke, *In Whom We Live*, 146.

questions of inquiry, so in that intellectual environment it seems appropriate to ask also "What is God?" Haught's project isn't to demonstrate the existence of God, but rather to help us think about God, thereby arguing that a case can be made for taking seriously the possibility that God is.

The suspicion of God's existence that one finds in the writings of Nietzsche, Marx, and Freud is shared by many intellectuals today. Noting a serious question today among scientific thinkers, philosophers, and many other intelligent people as to whether the word "God" actually refers to any genuinely real dimension of our experience, Haught claims that talk about "God" may be little more that whistling in the dark or a cover-up for human weakness. Given the trite and personalistic ways the idea of God has been employed by many "religious" people, such suspicion is often justified. But the word "God" can mean much more than this.

Haught contends that the idea of God was not a theoretical construct invented by theologians but came to human consciousness spontaneously as the product of religious experience, as a response to the sense of the "sacred," a phenomenon Rudolf Otto termed the *mysterium tremendum et fascinans*. Originally described in the language of symbol and myth, this experience "was acted out in ritual and other kinds of human activity long before it became a topic of philosophical or theological discussion."[8] Modern reflection on God should utilize similar symbolic categories, ones that can be identifiable in the experience of all human beings and not simply "religious" people.

Building on the contributions of depth psychology, process theology, and the insights of important twentieth-century religious thinkers such as Whitehead, Paul Tillich, Paul Ricoeur, Bernard Lonergan, and Karl Rahner, Haught identifies five experiential human notions as the locus for conceptualizing deity: depth, future, freedom, beauty, and truth. While there is something undeniably "real" about each of these aspects of conscious existence, there is something elusive about them as well. Like our idea of God, such experiences are either bio-psychological phenomena that refer to nothing beyond themselves, or they point beyond themselves to a Source that grounds them—which Source is a God candidate.

Utilizing these five categories enables Haught to emphasize what he calls the "neuter" rather than the masculine and feminine images ordinarily evoked by religious symbolism, the "whatness" rather than the "whoness" of God. Considered the leading figure in the development of twentieth-century hermeneutics, German philosopher Hans-Georg

---

8. Haught, *What is God?*, 2–3.

Understanding God Panentheistically

Gadamer relates how his teacher, Martin Heidegger, once observed: "Who is God? That is perhaps beyond the possibilities of our asking. But what is God? That we should ask."[9] And Gadamer thinks that we should pay more attention to neuter expressions such as "the divine" or "the sacred," terms that occurs frequently in poetry: "I think the neuter is one of the most mysterious things in human language . . . To use the neuter—for example, "the beautiful"—expresses something of ungraspable presence. It is no longer "this" or "that," male or female, here or there; it is filling empty space . . . The neuter represents in a way the plenitude of presence, the omnipresence of something. Hence the divine is indeed an expression for such omnipresence."[10] Thus, while inadequate in itself, the neuter in our thinking of God is a helpful corrective to a one-sided personalistic understanding.

In selecting ordinary aspects of human experience, Haught demonstrates that humans react to concepts such as depth, future, freedom, beauty, and truth "in the same way that Rudolph Otto's *homo religiosus* reacts to the sacred. We experience these realities first of all as *mysteria*, that is, as incomprehensible, overwhelming, and majestic . . . Secondly, they are *tremenda*, in that they are terrifying in their demands upon us, and so understandably we shrink from them, fearing that we shall be lost if we surrender completely to them. But finally they are *fascinosa*, inasmuch as there is something ultimately fascinating, attractive, and satisfying about them. They have the same features Otto saw in the religious experience of the sacred,"[11] particularly when one examines these as dimensions that appear more as the horizon of our experience than as qualities or objects of our experience. As the geographical horizon is elusive since it recedes as we explore further, so God might be understood in part as the ultimate horizon of all our experience, always receding, encompassing, illuminating, but never falling within our comprehending grasp.

One of the most persistent aspects of the "problem of God" is that there is no unambiguous evidence in our ordinary experience of any providential, transcendent, divine presence. Many atheists and agnostics point to this and wonder how truly intelligent persons can be believers. But the point here is that the reality of God is no less capable of immediate validation than are the dimensions of depth, future, freedom, beauty, and truth. For God not to be accessible to our senses or our wishes should be

---

9. Cited in Haught, ibid., 8.
10. Cited in Haught, ibid.
11. Ibid., 5–6.

no more outrageous than that these dimensions are incapable of being brought under our comprehending control. God is not one object among others in our experience. Rather, God may be understood as the ultimate horizon that makes all experience possible in the first place. The sacred does not force itself into the range of objects or events that make up the content of ordinary experience. Instead, God may be viewed as the inexhaustible depth and ground out of which all our experiences arise.

Whitehead, whose philosophy is permeated by aesthetic considerations, has shown that an unduly narrow doctrine of perception, limited to the five senses, has dominated much of modern thought. Without denying that our senses do connect us with the real world, Whitehead emphasizes that the senses are inadequate to mediate the full complexity of the world, giving us only an abstract and narrow range of the universe. By distinguishing between the sharply defined region of sense data and the vaguer but deeper organic perception that lies beneath sensation, he provides a doctrine of perception that allows us to understand the "absence of God." God is necessarily hidden from the realm of sense objects simply because sense perception is too narrow to give us the deeper and more important aspects of reality. Furthermore, possessing something—comprehending God—eliminates the longing for it. The paradox of suspension between having and not having, knowing and not knowing, is the very condition that makes it possible for us to ask questions and to seek the truth. Religion, then, may be understood as the conscious rejection of the strong temptation to make truth—understood rationally and cognitively—the object of our mastery. It is a surrender to truth as the *mysterium tremendum et fascinans* in which alone our freedom and fulfillment lie. Wherever there is a sincere desire for the truth about ourselves, others, and the world there is authentic religion, even if it does not go by that name.

Whitehead encourages us to accept the "absence of God" as the necessary condition for the aesthetic intensity and significance of our lives. The name he gives to this ongoing quest is *adventure*. This is religion, in its pure, undistorted essence: religion is adventure. "The universe that we inhabit may itself be understood—and science supports this position—as an adventure. It appears to be a fifteen or twenty billion-year-old quest for more and more intense forms of ordered novelty . . . Religion must be seen as continuous with the universe's risk-filled episodes of adventure. Otherwise it is unrelated to the rest of reality."[12]

---

12. Ibid., 89–90.

Understanding God Panentheistically

Organized religions, insofar as they have allied with the status quo, with predictability and monotony, have displayed a keen antipathy toward adventure. Because they teach a doctrine of ultimate order, their teachings are easily perverted into divine sanctions for particular socio-political order. As such, religion feeds on our fear of adventure, losing its vitality whenever it forfeits the risk required by openness to novelty. A purely conservative religion, while manifesting an understandable passion for order, promotes the stagnation of monotony and the suspension of life's narrative story.

At its normative best, religion has provided the most adventurous component in the historical evolution of human consciousness. Its openness to novelty and the risk involved in this openness are evidenced in its great religious innovators and visionaries. In attempting to implant their vision, they and their followers have inevitably disturbed the monotony of the status quo. A truly adventurous religious spirit will always disrupt the cult of monotony while at the same time promising hope.[13]

The most important way of responding to the question "What is God?" is to say that essentially God is mystery. Haught's five metaphors, while helpful, do not exhaust and should not be substituted for that of mystery. Unfortunately, in a world where the methods and techniques of science have become dominant, the sense of mystery often leaves us feeling insecure. In the face of this eclipse of mystery, the very possibility of speaking meaningfully about God has likewise diminished. For that reason, it is essential today that leaders emerge to provide a sort of pedagogy of mystery.

The term "mystery" is often misunderstood simply as a gap in our knowledge, a temporary hiatus that might be closed as scientific consciousness advances. Thus the realm of "mystery" will allegedly be gradually diminished, and "knowledge" will take its place. As B. F. Skinner, the noted psychologist, has put it, the objective of science is to eliminate mystery. However, when "mystery" is understood in this way, namely as a gap to be replaced by scientific knowledge, it is little wonder that the word no longer functions to evoke a religious sense of the *tremendum et fascinans*. For in this case "mystery" is merely a vacuum that begs to be filled with our intellectual achievements rather than an ineffable depth summoning our awe and allegiance.

Haught encourages us to address the gaps in our present understanding and knowledge as "problems" rather than as "mysteries." "Problem"

---

13. Ibid., 91.

points to an area of ignorance that may be solved eventually by the application of human ingenuity. "Mystery," on the other hand, denotes a region of reality that, instead of growing smaller as we grow wiser and more powerful, can actually be experienced as growing larger and more incomprehensible as we solve more of our scientific and other problems. Mystery is the horizon that keeps expanding and receding into the distance the more our knowledge advances. In contrast to problems, mystery is incapable of any "solution." Whereas problems can be solved and eliminated, mystery becomes more prominent the deeper our questions go and the surer our answers become.[14]

For Haught, there are only two major "truths" that a genuine religious sense requires. All dogmas of religion are derivatives of these two truths: the first is that our lives are embraced by mystery, and the second is that this mystery is gracious. Keeping these two propositions before us "provides us with criteria to evaluate and criticize the actual religious lives of others and ourselves. For there is no doubt that religious traditions which have their origin in a decisive encounter with mystery and its graciousness can themselves deviate from their founding insights and end up participating in the eclipse of mystery. Religions can become entangled in the pursuit of domination or the legitimation of oppression and thus themselves become obstacles to the sense of liberating mystery. Hence they should constantly be evaluated in accordance with the criteria of mystery and its graciousness."[15]

While traditional theists have been one-sided in speaking of the remoteness of God from the ordinary realm of experience, mystics have emphasized the "nearness" of the sacred. In fact, because there is no contradiction between the absence and the nearness of God, God's absence may even be understood as essential for the sake of the nearness. By not intruding into or forcing itself upon the world and personal subjects, the divine mystery can be understood as caringly involved with the world. Concerned that the world not lose its integrity by being absorbed into the divine or diluted into an overbearing divine "presence," God may be seen to "withdraw" from the world and from persons in order to let them be. This withdrawal, this self-absenting of God, however, is not abdication but rather essential in order to give the world its autonomy and human

---

14. Ibid., 118–20.
15. Ibid., 127–28.

Understanding God Panentheistically

subjects their freedom. In this sense the absence and inscrutability of mystery may be understood as the other side of its intimacy with us.[16]

In our search for new ways to understand God, we have discovered that it is better if we no longer approach the topic by asking "Who is God?" On the basis of his own experience, Bishop Spong arrived at this conclusion as well. He learned that when human beings have personal gods, these look and act remarkably like human beings. For example, the Jewish God in the Hebrew scriptures was assumed to hate anyone that the nation of Israel hated, and with even greater zeal. The familiar Christian God acknowledged by Roman and later by European Christians not only blessed the imperialistic and colonial expansion of those empires and nations but also declared that the domination of the underdeveloped peoples of the world was the very will of the Christian deity. As supernatural theism is exposed to further scrutiny, humans can discern more clearly the process of "God creation" that they have always pursued. The attributes humans have claimed for God are but human qualities expanded beyond human limits. The following examples make this clear: Humans are mortal; God became immortal. Human life is finite; God became infinite. Human life is limited in power; God is omnipotent. Humans are limited in knowledge; God is omniscient. Humans are natural (of this world); God is supernatural. "When we unravel the theological doctrines of the ages," Spong writes, "the makeup of God becomes quite clear. God is a human being without human limitations who is read into the heavens. Humans disguised this process by suggesting that the reason God was so much like a human being was that humans were created in God's image. However, we now recognize that it was the other way around. The God of theism came into being as a human creation. This God too was mortal and is now dying."[17]

To get beyond the limitations of the past, Spong found it necessary to pose the religious questions by looking at the human experience in a different way. What Haught argues theoretically, Spong argues existentially. Having found the "who" question fruitless, Spong asks "what" questions, attempting to cast the Christian experience in nontheistic images. Going to the scriptures, he discovered numerous helpful images. One ancient Hebrew word for God, for example, is *ruach*. Literally, the word means "wind," a natural and even an impersonal concept, an experienced "what," not a "who." The wind or *ruach* was observed not as a being, but as a vitalizing force. Among the Hebrews the *ruach* or wind of God was said to

---

16. Ibid., 130–31.
17. Spong, *Christianity Must Change*, 49.

have brooded over the chaos in the story of creation in order to bring forth life (Genesis 1:2). Slowly this *ruach* evolved and became personalized and was called "Spirit." The *ruach* or wind of God was not external. It rather emerged from within the world and was understood as its very ground, its life-giving reality. This *ruach* was also thought to be connected in some way to human *nephesh* or breath, also understood as an impersonal concept. Breath was a force that wells up from within each of us and was thought in some sense to be identical with human life. *Nephesh* would later be translated as "soul" or "spirit." Therefore, in Jewish thinking, spirit was conceived of externally as the wind, the *ruach*, and internally as the breath of life itself, the *nephesh*.[18]

Marcus Borg, in a chapter titled "Imaging God: Why and How it Matters,"[19] also examines the variety of images of God in the biblical and Christian traditions and discerns therein two primary "models": (1) the "*monarchical model*," which clusters images of God as king, lord, and father (this approach leads to what Borg calls a "performance model" of the Christian life); and (2) the "*Spirit model*," which clusters images of God that point to intimate relationship and belonging (this model leads to a "relational model" of the Christian life).

Both models, Borg discovered, are found throughout all periods of Christian history, though the first is more common. From roughly the fourth century—when Christianity became the dominant religion of Western culture—through the present, the monarchical model has dominated. But alongside it, as an alternative voice, the Spirit model has also persisted. These models reflect two different voices within the Christian tradition.[20]

---

18. Ibid., 59–60.

19. Borg, *God We Never Knew*, 57–83.

20. In his seminal work, *Original Blessing*, Dominican scholar Matthew Fox approaches spirituality from the panentheistic tradition, thereby distinguishing between the fall/redemption paradigm and creation spirituality. The former, akin to Borg's "monarchical model," is dualistic and patriarchal. It begins its theology with sin and original sin, and it generally ends with redemption. Unlike creation spirituality, this spirituality does not teach believers about creativity, about justice-making and social transformation, or about the God of play, pleasure, and delight. This tradition has proven unfriendly to artists, prophets, or women. Because this tradition considers all nature "fallen" and does not seek God in nature, it is both silent toward science and hostile to it. Fox describes spirituality as a way of life characterized by four paths: (1) Befriending Creation: The Via Positiva; (2) Befriending Darkness: The Via Negativa; (3) Befriending Creativity: The Via Creativa; and (4) Befriending New Creation: The Via Transformativa.

The monarchical model portrays God as male, as all-powerful, as lawgiver, and as judge. Images of God in this model suggest that God is distant. Within this model, humans have offended divine majesty and deserve judgment. But because God loves his subjects, God creates a way for his people to escape the punishment they deserve: through appropriate sacrifice and true repentance. In the royal theology of ancient Israel, atonement was institutionalized in temple rituals. In the Christian version of the monarchical model, the king's (Lord's) love is seen especially in Jesus. Because God loves us, he sends his son into the world to die on a cross as the sacrifice that makes our forgiveness possible.[21]

The Spirit model, as used in the Bible, is broader than the specific Christian doctrine of "the Holy Spirit," which sees the Spirit as one aspect of God. In the Bible, Spirit is used comprehensively to refer to God's presence in creation, in the history of Israel, and in the life of Jesus and the early church. While the monarchical model also affirms that God is Spirit, of course, and that affirmation can be a source of confusion that limits our understanding of God, there is a difference. When Spirit is assimilated to the monarchical model, God is not Spirit but a spirit—that is, a spiritual being out there, not here. But when Spirit is set free from the monarchical understanding, Spirit retains the suggestive meanings associated with breath and wind: God is the encompassing Spirit both within and outside us.[22]

In addition to wind and breath, the Bible provides other non-anthropomorphic images, such as rock (meaning a place of refuge and safety). Additional non-masculine images include mother, wisdom, lover, and shepherd. These metaphors for the Spirit affect our root image of God in quite obvious ways: (1) they emphasize *the nearness of God* rather than the distance implied by the monarchical model, thereby suggesting the language of relationship; (2) they utilize *both male and female metaphors* (as well as some that are neuter), rather than the exclusively male images of the monarchical model; and (3) they include *both anthropomorphic and nonathropomorphic images*. Taken together, both models suggest that the relationship to God is personal, even as God is more than a person. The sacred is not simply an inanimate mystery but a presence. Using an ancient biblical analogy, these metaphors lead to a covenantal understanding of the divine-human relationship, which emphasizes belonging and connectedness. This model is intrinsically dialogical.[23]

---

21. Borg, *God We Never Knew*, 63–64.
22. Ibid., 72.
23. Ibid., 75–76.

Beyond Belief

The Spirit model of God affects the meaning of a number of central Christian teachings. It does so by changing the framework in which things are seen. Borg provides four examples:

> 1. *Creation looks different.* According to the monarchical model, God's creation of the world is understood as an event in the distant past involving the creation of a universe separate from God. The Spirit model depicts God's creation as an ongoing activity: in every moment God as Spirit (as the nonmaterial "ground" of all that is) is bringing the universe into existence.
>
> 2. *The human condition looks different.* Our central problem is not sin and guilt, as it is within the monarchical model, but "estrangement," meaning that humans are separated from that to which they belong. Our problem is blindness to the presence of God, separation from the Spirit that is all around us and within us and to which we belong.
>
> 3. *Sin looks different.* For the monarchical model, sin is primarily disloyalty to the king, seen especially as disobedience to his laws. The Spirit model addresses "sin" is more profound ways: for the metaphor of God as lover, sin is unfaithfulness; for the metaphor of God as the compassionate one who cares for all her children, sin is failure in compassion. Thus sin remains, but as betrayal of relationship and absence of compassion. Repentance also remains, only now it does not require sacrifice and contrition but a turning and returning to that to which we belong. Judgment also remains, only now not as the threat of eternal judgment but rather as living with the consequences of our choices. To remain estranged from God is to remain unsatisfied and unfulfilled.
>
> 4. *God as king and lord looks different.* God as Spirit is glorious, radiant, and splendid, like the splendor of a king. In the Spirit model, God as king and lord is the subverter of systems of domination, not the legitimator of domination systems.[24]

The images of God associated with the Spirit model dramatically affect how we think of the Christian life. Rather than God as a distant being with whom we might spend eternity, Spirit—the sacred—is right here. Rather than sin and guilt being the central dynamic of the Christian life, the central dynamic becomes relationship—with God, the world, and each other.

24. Ibid., 77–78.

The mystics of every religious tradition, following the Spirit model rather than the monarchical model, have always spoken out against specific definitions of God. The Western mystics appear to have assumed that a personal God was only a stage, and an inferior one at that, in human religious development. The mystical portrait of God was first imaginative, and then ineffable. It involved an interior journey, not an exterior one. In the mystical tradition no one can claim objectivity for his or her insight. Each person is called to journey into the mystery of God along the pathway of his or her own expanding personhood. Every person is thus capable of being a theophany, a sign of God's presence; but no one person, institution, or way of life can exhaust this revelation. God, for the mystics, is found at the depths of life, working in and through the being of this world, calling all nature to its deepest potential. It is a God concept better approached if we move first from a "who" question to a "what" question, and then from our perception of God to our experience of God.

Academic theologians, in addition to mystics, were among the first to become aware of the Western world's enslavement to traditional theistic concepts, which no longer held power or meaning. The demise of theism began in the breakdown of biblical literalism in Germany in the early 1800s. The publication of *The Life of Jesus* in 1835 by David Frederich Strauss brought the mythical and legendary aspects of the gospel stories to public attention. Julius Wellhausen furthered this study with his four-document theory of the formation of the Pentateuch in his landmark volume, *Prolegomenon to the History of Ancient Israel* (1878). From biblical studies, the anti-literalist movement impacted theology, as it became apparent that the theological doctrines of antiquity could no longer be based on the literal texts that once supported them. Considered by many to be the dominant New Testament scholar of the twentieth century, Rudolf Bultmann carried this study to a new level by making us aware that the gospel material was encased within the mythology of antiquity and thus could not be interpreted literally. The theistic understanding of God was part of that mythology. Bultmann suggested that if we could demythologize those texts, the insights of a saving truth could still be found.

Alfred North Whitehead, who began his professional life as a mathematician, laid out the theological framework for perceiving God not as divine being external to the universe, but as a divine process coming into being within the life of this world. This conception of God as existing with all of reality, not prior to it, became known as process theology. Dietrich Bonhoeffer called the world to something he named "religionless

Christianity," suggesting in his letters, written from prison as he awaited his execution by the Third Reich, that Christians need to live in this world "as if there were no God." His death as a martyr prevented him from conceptualizing further the implications of his hypothesis, but a religionless—perhaps even a nontheistic or godless—Christianity appeared on the horizon of his thinking.

Paul Tillich, himself a refugee from Nazi Germany, proposed as far back as the 1930s and 1940s that Western Christians should abandon the external height images in which the theistic God had historically been perceived, replacing them with internal depth images of a deity not apart from us but the very core and ground of all that is. This God was not a person, but rather was the mystical presence in which all personhood could flourish. This God was not a being but rather the power that called being forth in all creatures. This God was not an external, personal force that could be invoked but rather an internal reality that, when confronted, opened us to the meaning of life itself.[25] Tillich, who believed that the word "God" had been distorted by the inadequate images of the past, was convinced that those images must die before the word "God" could ever be used again with meaning. He urged a moratorium on the use of the word "God" for at least a hundred years.

Following Tillich, Bishop Spong provides a model that integrates the Christian doctrine of the Trinity with this understanding of God. The meaning of God, according to his conception, is understood as (1) the source of life, (2) the source of love, and (3) the ground of being. He finds in this triune understanding a portrait of God embodied in Jesus of Nazareth, a whole human being who lived fully, who loved lavishly, and who had the courage to be himself under every circumstance.

So the call of this internal God found in our depths becomes primarily a call into being, a call that is not unique to religion. It is a call that refocuses what has been known as the religious dimension. In this scenario, the task of the church becomes less that of indoctrinating or relating people to an external divine power and more that of providing opportunities for people to touch the infinite center of all things and to fulfill all their potential. This understanding of God places a premium on the church's vocation to oppose anything that prevents us from the fullest expression of our humanity.[26]

---

25. Spong, *Christianity Must Change*, 64.
26. Ibid., 66.

We are learning that "meaning" is not external to life but must be discovered in our own depths and imposed on life by an act of our own will. We are being made aware that life is not fair and will not necessarily be made fair either in this life or in any other. So we have to decide how we will live now with this reality. One thing is certain: the journey of faith must go forward.[27]

---

27. One of the most expansive books for understanding the divine-human relationship is *How to Know God*, written by world-renowned author and spiritual leader Deepak Chopra. For a summary of Chopra's seven levels in the divine-human relationship, consult appendix B.

6

Understanding God's Relationship with an Evolving Creation

THE DOCTRINE OF CREATION is central to all biblical faith traditions. The doctrine affirms that God created all things, meaning that the world and everything in it depends on God for its existence. Whereas prominent Greek thinkers such as Plato and Aristotle virtually ignored origins, accepting the explanation that matter, and therefore the world, was eternal, the Bible presents an external force that created and continually sustains the cosmos.

In the Bible, however, the doctrine of creation does not stand alone but depends upon and elaborates on the redemptive activity of God in history. In the Old Testament creation is viewed in the light of Israel's covenant faith; in the New Testament creation is viewed in the light of Jesus Christ and the "new creation" that through him became a historical reality. In both Testaments the doctrine emphasizes the sovereignty of God, the goodness of creation (that the cosmos and everything in it is characterized by design, that is, by a divinely decreed order), the supreme position of honor and responsibility that God has given to human beings, and the divine purpose that undergirds and controls history from its beginning to its consummation.

Creation faith, particularly as affirmed in the historic creeds of Christianity, represents a repudiation of metaphysical dualism, which might suggest that the created world is evil, and a repudiation of metaphysical randomness, which might suggest that life is essentially meaningless. Creation faith is what American Christians overwhelmingly affirm when they profess: "I believe in God the Father almighty, maker of heaven and earth."

In the past four centuries, remarkable changes have occurred in the field of science, including what is known about the motion of the heavens, elementary substances, and origins of the cosmos and of the human race. New conceptions of the cosmos led to new views concerning God and God's relation with the world. Modern Christians essentially regard science as a good gift and appreciate its benefits. Yet when science addresses religious concerns such as human origins or divine sovereignty, many Christians feel they need to choose between the competing claims of religion and science. In such situations conventional Christians favor the claims of religion.

Twenty-first-century cosmogonies present several alternatives, namely the choice between a universe closed to influences from God and a universe open to influences from God.[1] If the universe is held to be closed in the sense proposed by scientific materialists, then what is observable is solely the result of "natural laws" upon pre-existent matter and/or energy. No guidance or design is needed. The other major alternative is that the universe is open to God's influences, which may be overt or subtle.

An Open Universe: Alternatives

Under the alternative of an open universe, various options exist, differing principally on how one understands the role of God during the creative process:

1. *Creationism* affirms the biblical view that God created the world in the manner described in the first chapter of Genesis. Proponents of this view disagree over the precise nature and duration of the creation. Three options exist, each affirming the notion of biblical inspiration: (a) the *literal chronological view* interprets the Hebrew word *yom* (translated "day") in Genesis 1 as a literal twenty-four period. In addition, each "day" is understood chronologically, so that during the first twenty-four hours of time God created light, in the second day the firmament, and so forth until the completion of creation after six literal days. The Genesis 1 narrative, therefore, is understood simply as history. (b) The *figurative chronological view* interprets the word *yom* figuratively, as an indeterminate length of time. The chronology of the days remains the same, but the days themselves are lengthened. This position, first proposed in the nineteenth century in response to new scientific discoveries regarding the age of the earth, attempts to harmonize geological research and scripture. Exponents of this view argue that the period of six "days" could extend to

---

1. A cosmogony is an account of the generation of the universe; it represents a model of history, a hypothesis about the past that cannot be tested by experiment and therefore remains a conjecture.

four billion years or more. (c) The *figurative topical view*, also known as "the framework hypothesis," asserts that Genesis 1 is a literary work using poetic elements to arrange creation by topic, not by sequence or chronology. Thus the order of the Genesis 1 account is figurative, as is the use of the term "day." According to this view, the pattern of six days contains two sets of triads. The first triad (days 1, 2, 3) establishes three spheres or realms, and the second triad (days 4, 5, 6) names various subjects that inhabit those realms. A direct parallelism or correspondence is portrayed between days 1 and 4, 2 and 5, and 3 and 6. The topical structure of the narrative is as follows:

Spheres	Subjects
Day 1. Light (Gen. 1:3–5)	Day 1. Light Bearers (Gen. 1:14–19)
Day 2. Sea, Sky (Gen. 1:6–8)	Day 5. Fish, Birds (Gen. 1:20–23)
Day 3. Land, Vegetation (Gen. 1:9–13)	Day 6. Land Animals, Humans (Gen. 1:24–31)
Day 7. Sabbath (Gen. 2:1–4a)	

According to this third option, the function of the creation narrative is to focus on the centrality of the Sabbath and on worship. The text is only secondarily about creation, which should be understood as unfolding according to a meaningful pattern.

Each view has advantages and disadvantages, but all maintain a high regard for biblical authority. All three views affirm God as the creator and sustainer of the universe.

2. *Theistic evolution* accepts the reality of evolution and posits God's guidance. This view also has several variants: (a) *progressive creation* holds that God produced and subtly controlled the universe through all the major steps of a cosmogony. In this view God continually directed the course of the cosmos while forming and filling it, making use of and guiding processes designed by God. (b) *Theistic macroevolution* maintains that God originally created matter and its laws and later created humans in his image. Except for those two acts of creation, the universe has developed according to secondary causes as though it were a closed system.[2]

The idea of theistic evolution has a long-standing support in the Christian tradition.[3] In his work *On the Literal Meaning of Genesis*, written

---

2. Rice, "Cosmology of Modern Science," 106–7.

3. The phrase "theistic evolution" is used to characterize the views of a wide range of thinkers. In my estimation the phrase is flawed, in part because "theistic" is a rather pale adjective to refer to the God of Christian faith: it places too much emphasis on

early in the fifth century, Augustine (354–430) set out to provide a doctrine of creation based on his interpretation of the Genesis creation accounts. While God brought everything into existence in a single moment of creation, the created order should not be viewed as static, inasmuch as God has endowed it with the capacity to develop. Augustine used the image of a dormant seed as an analogy for this process. Within the original created order God embeds seminal principles (*rationes seminales*, meaning "seed-bearing reasons"), which will grow and develop at the right time.[4]

Earlier Christian writers had noted how Genesis 1 spoke of the earth and the waters "bringing forth" living creatures, and had concluded that this pointed to God's endowing the natural order with a capacity to generate living things. Augustine took this idea further, arguing that God inserted into the world dormant powers, which were actualized at appropriate moments through divine providence. Augustine argued that Genesis 1:12 implies that the earth has received the power or capacity to produce things by itself. "Where some might think of creation in terms of God's insertion of new kinds of plants and animals ready-made into an already existing world, Augustine rejected this as inconsistent with the overall witness of scripture. Rather, God must be thought of as creating in that very first moment the potencies for all kinds of living things that would come later, including humanity . . . For Augustine, God created a universe that was deliberately designed to develop and evolve."[5]

Thinking theologically, one suggestion—endorsed particularly by a number of modern theologians with backgrounds in physics—is that somehow God's design is built into the process at the quantum level.[6] This position is said to go back to Darwin's great American supporter, the Harvard botanist Asa Gray, who in 1860 argued that the raw material on which selection works—what we today would call "mutations"—is directed by God. Selection, as it were, weeds out the unneeded and inadequate. Modern thinkers may not want to assign change directly to God's intervention, in the sense of violating the regular course of nature. However,

---

the transcendence of God and lacks the depth we will examine more fully in this chapter. I am also uncomfortable with the label "creationist" because in the public mind "creationist" is usually seen as opposed to "evolutionist." Perhaps a better phrase is "evolutionary creationism," for it best conveys (1) the belief that the God of biblical faith has empowered the universe and life with the ability to evolve, and (2) the belief that God continuously creates through these evolutionary processes.

4. McGrath, *Christian Theology*, 218.
5. Ibid., 219.
6. Ruse, *Can a Darwinian Be a Christian?*, 86–87.

they argue that quantum indeterminacy leaves room for God to act in a positive fashion.

The mutations that are needed are caused by quantum-level effects, but such changes do not stand out because they are averaged by non-needed or nondirected changes. As philosopher Michael Ruse explains, "Suppose one needed a positive change at time t. Overall, quantum theory might tell you that you will get five positive changes and five negative changes, but that we cannot predict which will be positive or negative on any particular occasion. There is nothing to stop God from putting in the positive change at time t, so long as God allows it to be masked by the other nine positive and negative changes. Laws are not being violated and special directed laws are not needed, but direction is involved nevertheless."[7]

This suggestion, however, is very much a "God of the gaps" kind of argument: if one cannot think of an explanation for how things work, then search for a way to fit God into the spaces where understanding fails. The problem with such a simple solution is that if God can slip in to produce the right quantum event when a mutation leading to humankind is needed, why can God not likewise slip in to prevent the wrong quantum event when a mutation causing great pain and unhappiness is about to occur? If God gets credit for producing intelligence, why should God not also get blamed for producing sickle-cell anemia?

The more compelling Augustinian option says that, no matter why things are as they are, the fact is that humans evolved and did so by the will of God, in conjunction, no doubt, with all sorts of random factors. God did not impersonally plan all things beforehand and then let them happen, but God is actively involved in seeing that things occur as they should. The laws and the events, random or not, are God laws and events, which God foresaw and intended the end result. Therefore God deserves credit.

There are, of course, costs to the solution, costs that must be paid by any Augustinian. In the first place, the whole question of freedom—particularly the freedom of the human will—is thrown into doubt. Does God control everything to such an extent that things had to happen, no matter what anything in creation wanted or intended? Or does one want to argue that free will came into play only when humans finally appeared?

In the second place, there is the question of evil and pain. Even if we attribute a great deal of evil to the actions of free humans, there still remains natural evil or pain. If God so controls things that humans appeared despite the improbability, then is God also responsible for such things as

---

7 Ibid., 87.

bad mutations? Is God responsible for those earthquakes and floods and other natural calamities that take so many innocent lives? Making God responsible at one level seems to entail making him responsible at other levels as well.[8]

Many Christians today find it difficult to accept the notion that creation and evolution belong together. The belief that such are opposing and conflicting concepts has become so ingrained in the minds of many that it is hard to conceptualize how the God of the Bible may work out his creative purposes through an evolutionary process. Believers have been taught that they must choose between creation and evolution. However, many distinguished scientists and theologians are inviting us to see that this is a false choice and asking us to consider instead a both/and alternative.

The eminent biologist Theodosius Dobzhansky (1900–1975), who immigrated to the United States from the Soviet Union, did important work in the field of population genetics and was instrumental in the development of the Modern Synthesis of evolutionary theory. He was also a practicing Russian Orthodox Christian. "It is wrong," he wrote, "to hold creation and evolution as mutually exclusive alternatives. I am a creationist *and* an evolutionist." In that article he presented a tribute to paleontologist Pierre Teilhard de Chardin, another Christian who embraced evolution and who influenced him spiritually: "There is no doubt at all that Teilhard was a truly and deeply religious man and that Christianity was the cornerstone of his worldview. Moreover, in his worldview science and faith were not segregated in watertight compartments, as they are with so many people. They were harmoniously fitting parts of his worldview. Teilhard was a creationist, but one who understood that the Creation is realized in this world by means of evolution."[9]

Were Dobzhansky and Teilhard the only Christians in the sciences who brought evolution and creation together, one might choose to dismiss them, but in fact they are among many scientists, here in the United States and elsewhere, who have done so, including many evangelical Christians. What these men and women are doing is hardly new. Beginning in the thirteenth century, theologians adapted their understanding of creation to the Aristotelian-Ptolemaic model of an earth-centered circular cosmos, so different from the ancient Hebraic model. Later, after struggling with the Copernican and the Newtonian models, theologians eventually found ways to accommodate their thinking to that cosmology as well. The current reflections

---

8. Ibid., 91–92.
9. Dobzhansky, "Biology Makes Sense," 125–29.

on God's action in an evolving creation—the universe of Darwin and Einstein—stand very much in this tradition of faith seeking understanding.[10]

Unfortunately, many Christians are unaware of this history. They are also unaware that the work of understanding creation and evolution together flourished in Darwin's day. During the latter half of the nineteenth century many prominent evangelical and reformed theologians and scientists in both the United Kingdom and North America concluded that evolutionary science is not in conflict with Christian faith in creation.

During the decades following the publication of *The Origin of Species*, Darwin enjoyed the support of many Anglican clergy, including leading educators and theologians. Theologian Aubrey Moore described Darwin as one who, "disguised as a foe, did the work of a friend," for thanks to him Christianity must now understand that "God is everywhere present in nature."[11] The prominent Calvinist theologian James Orr (1844–1913) was among many who accepted evolution while disagreeing with some aspects of Darwin's own interpretation of the process: "Assume God—as many devout [Christian] evolutionists do—to be immanent in the evolutionary process, and His intelligence and purpose to be expressed in it; then evolution, so far from conflicting with theism, may become a new and heightened form of the theistic argument. The real impelling force of evolution is now from within."[12]

This re-evaluation of the ancient doctrine of God's immanence in creation became a theme in the writings of biologist Asa Gray (1810–1888) and geologist James Dana (1813–1895). Both were active churchman, committed to traditional Christian doctrine. Gray, America's foremost botanist, was a friend of Darwin's. From his extensive studies of American flora he abandoned separate creation and found in natural selection a convincing explanation for the great variety of plant species. Dana, a leading American geologist, began as a progressive creationist, but came in time to accept evolution, seeing natural selection as a natural law or method that pointed beyond nature to a Lawgiver. Both scholars rejected the notion of evolution as materialistic and aimless. Holding to "a strictly scientific Darwinism," they were convinced that evolution did not contradict belief in design and purpose in nature.[13]

---

10. Schneider, *Science and Faith*, Essay VII: "Theologies of an Evolving Creation."
11. Cited in Peacocke, "Biological Evolution," 357.
12. Cited in Livingstone, *Darwin's Forgotten Defenders*, 142.
13. This topic is addressed in chapter 14 and in the Conclusion, in the segment titled "The Issue of Purpose."

Understanding God's Relationship with an Evolving Creation

Likewise, thinkers in the reformed tradition were relating theology and science in a positive way. These included Presbyterian philosopher James McCosh (1811–1894), who became president of Princeton University in 1868, and Presbyterian theologian Benjamin B. Warfield (1851–1921), a professor at Princeton Seminary. McCosh devoted himself to developing a natural theology that incorporated evolution. Warfield, a highly respected thinker, was an orthodox Calvinist and perhaps in his era the most articulate promoter of biblical inerrancy; yet, he saw no conflict between scripture and science when it came to understanding evolution as an expression of God's creative activity. "I am free to say, for myself," he wrote, "that I do not think there is any general statement in the Bible, or any part of the account of creation, either as given in Gen. I & II, or elsewhere alluded to, that need be opposed to evolution."[14] Warfield could say this because, following Calvin, he held that scripture did not need to be interpreted literally when it referred to nature. Furthermore, "the findings of science could be enlisted to help discover proper interpretations of scripture."[15]

Like other theologians sympathetic to evolution, Warfield read deeply in the field and kept abreast of developments. And like his colleagues Gray and Dana he distinguished between "evolution" and "Darwinism," meaning by the latter a wholly materialistic process, and accepted the former while rejecting the latter. "To his understanding of God and nature Warfield applied the concept of concurrence, expressed by the Latin word *concursus*. He first had used *concursus* to explain how the Bible could be the inspired work of the Holy Spirit and at the same time the work of its human authors. The same is true, he said, of Nature, God's other 'Book': it operates by secondary causes, the so-called laws of nature, which include evolution, with which God, the Primary Cause, endowed the universe at the beginning of creation, while concurrently it is guided, governed, and sustained by God's superintendent Providence."[16] These men were among the most influential of a large number of nineteenth-century churchmen who integrated a scientific understanding of Darwinian evolution with a comprehensive theological worldview anchored in conservative Christianity. It is ironic that at the very time when the discovery of DNA and research in molecular biology were providing much more compelling evidence for evolution, the movement known as Young Earth Creationism and its Intelligent Design variant have persuaded many people in North

---

14. Cited in Livingstone, *Darwin's Forgotten Defenders*, 118.
15. Noll and Livingstone, "Hodge and Warfield on Science," 64.
16. Schneider, *Science and Faith*, Essay VII: "Theologies of an Evolving Creation."

America that evolution and creation are opposed to one another and that evolution is an atheistic philosophy that leaves no room for God.

Contemporary theology has put forth a variety of new models of God's relationship to the creation, yet all agree on one thing: God is to be understood not as intervening from outside the creation to perform creative acts, but instead as interacting with every creature within the creation itself. As Roman Catholic theologian Denis Edwards puts it, the Triune God "is present to every creature in its being and becoming."[17] God's presence pervades every part and particle of the universe from its beginning in the Big Bang to the emergence of each new living species.

A Fully-Gifted, Self-Organizing, Freely Creating Universe

Understanding God to be the source of all created reality, physicist Howard J. Van Till formulated his principle of a "robust formational economy" to emphasize that God has given the physical universe a role in its own creation. The evidence science has gathered from nature, he asserts, may lead a believer to conclude that God has "thoughtfully conceptualized and fully gifted" the creation from its initial formation. These divine gifts have made it possible "for the creation to organize and transform itself from elementary forms of matter into the full array of physical structures and life-forms that have existed in the course of time." One must understand "creation" not as "the imposing of form . . . but the giving of being, a uniquely divine act."[18] According to this perspective, God has endowed the creation from the beginning with all of the capacities to become the universe we experience.

A similar view can be found in the writings of the nineteenth-century Anglican minister Charles Kingsley, an associate of Darwin, who concluded that the universe made by God was also a universe able to make itself. Many people are troubled by the notion that the universe enjoys a "free process," as Anglican quantum physicist and theologian John Polkinghorne put it, just as human beings enjoy free will. Is it possible to reconcile God as Primary Cause with a process as random as genetic mutation? One way lies in seeing the interplay between chance and natural selection as a secondary cause. Arthur Peacocke, who pioneered in DNA research as a physical chemist before he became an Anglican priest, uses the language of Lutheran eucharistic theology to describe the universe as a sacrament of God's presence: God

---

17. Edwards, *The God of Evolution*, 32–33.
18. Van Till, "The Fully Gifted Creation," 188.

works "in, with, and under" the processes of the natural order. Far from being a threat to a notion of a creating God, "the processes unveiled by the biological sciences," he states, "are God-acting-as-Creator . . . God is the ultimate ground and source of both law ('necessity') and 'chance.'"[19]

Roman Catholic theologian Elizabeth Johnson puts it this way: "God uses chance, so to speak, to ensure variety, resilience, novelty, and freedom in the universe, right up to humanity itself. Absolute Holy Mystery dwells within, encompasses, empowers through the evolutionary process, making the world through the process of things being themselves, thus making the world through chance and its genuinely irregular character. If God works through chance, then the natural creativity of chance itself can be thought of as a mode of divine creativity in which it participates."[20] Thus evolution through the interplay of chance and natural selection can be understood to be the very process that God intends and works for within the creation. The universe as creature *participates* in the creativity of its Maker.[21]

These models of God's relationship with an evolving creation do not answer the obvious question, "just *how* does God act?" Behind the question lies the understandable human desire to be able to point to God's "fingerprints" in natural processes, or to find a link where God's creative activity could be identified. While Intelligent Design advocates claim that they are able to do so, a claim which may well be a major reason for the popularity of this new movement, most theologians take the position of Polkinghorne that "divine action will always be hidden."[22]

The Vulnerable God

Alfred North Whitehead characterized God's relationship to the world as that of a "Persuasive Lover," and Haught, Peacocke, and others have offered variations on Whitehead's theme. The love relationship is an apt metaphor, for love is the fundamental and most intimate of relationships. Two additional qualities make this analogy particularly attractive: (1) that the essence of love is persuasive rather than coercive, and (2) that the experience of the beloved is to flourish and grow and emerge into fullness of life as a result of being loved. If this is so in human experience, then in a much more profound way God's unconditional love for the creation must

19. Peacocke, *Theology for a Scientific Age*, 360–63.
20. Johnson, "Does God Play Dice?, 363, 365.
21. Schneider, *Science and Faith*, Essay VII: "Theologies of an Evolving Creation."
22. Polkinghorne, *Quarks, Chaos and Christianity*, 72.

be such as to invite the creation into ever more complex levels of being. To accomplish this, the God of infinite love freely accepts the integrity of nature, its processes and its laws, thereby inviting the world through the complex interplay of all of its elements to emerge into more novel forms and greater beauty through the evolutionary process.[23]

Many Christians are likely to be uncomfortable with the notion that the Creator may be something less than the omniscient, omnipotent God of classical theology, who exercises absolute power over the creation at every moment of its existence. Yet the notion of a vulnerable, self-limiting God is itself biblical. An important passage has proved to be illuminating in this respect: in the letter to the Colossians (1:17) it is said of Christ that "in him all things hold together." Yet, of this same Christ Paul writes in his letter to the Philippians (2:5–8) that "though he was in the form of God, [he] did not regard equality with God as something to be exploited, but emptied himself, taking the form of a slave, being born in human likeness . . . he humbled himself . . ." The Greek noun for "emptying" is *kenosis*. The concept of kenosis has become important in the thinking of many theologians today. Applied to God's relationship with an evolving creation, it suggests that God graciously removes absolute power over the creation in order to allow the world to experience its possibilities. Kenotic theology invites the believer to think of God's relationship to the creation in a way that brings out love's humility. Reflecting on St. Paul's words that "love is patient" (1 Corinthians 13:4), Moltmann notes:

> God acts in the history of nature and human beings through his patient and silent presence, by which he gives those he has created space to unfold, time to develop, and power for their own movement. We look in vain for God in the history of nature . . . if what we are looking for is special divine interventions. Is it not much more that God waits, and awaits . . . that 'he is patient and of great goodness' (Ps. 103:8)? 'Waiting' is never disinterested passivity, but the highest form of interest in the other. Waiting means expecting, expecting means inviting, inviting means attracting, alluring, enticing. By doing this the waiting and awaiting one keeps an open space for the other, gives the other time, and creates possibilities of life for the other. This is what the theological tradition called *creatio continua* [continuous creation].[24]

---

23. Schneider, *Science and Faith*, Essay VII: "Theologies of an Evolving Creation."
24. Moltmann, "God's Kenosis," 149.

Understanding God's Relationship with an Evolving Creation

Creation as kenosis is, in the words of Polkinghorne, "the work of Love." In kenotic theology it is God's love, not God's power, that is almighty. This almighty and unconditional love empowers the creation to explore and unfold its evolutionary possibilities.

The notion of an evolving creation, however, brings into sharp relief a matter that has always challenged Christian theology, the troubling question of theodicy: how a benevolent and loving God can allow so much physical and natural evil in the world. If evolution is creation, what sense can one make of all the brutality and destruction of life in the universe over billions of years? How does the theologian who takes this view justify God's allowing a process that has led species into dead ends, deaths, and extinctions on a massive scale?

As John Schneider notes, "One way to address this tragic question is to look for an answer in the idea of a loving, self-emptying, vulnerable God. Just as in human affairs love must allow the beloved freedom to make mistakes and even fall into tragedy, so God's love for his autonomous creation must take the risk of allowing evolution to lead individuals and species to suffering, death, and extinction. Such vulnerability is not weakness, but strength—the strength of love."[25]

Some theologians have found an answer to theodicy in the Theology of the Cross that comes out of the Lutheran tradition of the Protestant Reformation. George Murphy, an ordained minister in the Evangelical Lutheran Church of America with a doctorate in physics, sees in the cross of Christ God's answer to the suffering of the natural world as well as human sin and suffering. Through the Son's humbling himself and being obedient even to death upon the cross (Philippians 2:8), God accepted and endured a violent act of suffering. The passion of Christ is "a claim that God suffers with the world from whatever evil takes place."[26]

Holmes Rolston, distinguished philosopher and theologian widely recognized as the father of environmental ethics, emphasizes our continuity with the rest of the biological world and at the same time reconciles evolutionary morals with a Christian ethic of self-sacrifice. In both cases, in the life we are called to live as followers of Jesus and in the biological realm, there is an analogy with the self-sacrificing character of God. Describing nature as "cruciform," Rolston teaches us to see the work of God not in the predator but in the prey. The universe is not a paradise but a theater where labor and suffering drive us to make sense of things. The whole

---

25. Schneider, *Science and Faith*, Essay VII: "Theologies of an Evolving Creation."
26. Murphy, *The Cosmos in Light of the Cross*, 87.

natural history is somehow God's doing, including suffering, which, "if it is difficult to say simply that it is immediately from God, is not ultimately outside of God's plan and redemptive control. God absorbs suffering and transforms it into goodness."[27] So Rolston suggests that, in faith, the secret of life is seen to lie not in natural selection and the survival of the fittest; rather, "the secret of life is that it is a passion play."

The cruciform creation "is, in the end, deiform, godly, just because of this element of struggle, not in spite of it. There is a great divine 'yes' hidden behind and within every 'no' of crushing nature."[28] While God rescues from suffering, Christian faith never teaches that God avoids suffering in the achievement of the divine purposes. Seen in the paradigm of the cross, God too suffers, not less than creatures, in order to gain for them a fuller life.

Roman Catholic theologian John Haught also views evolution and the immense suffering experienced in the creation in the light of the cross: "Reflection on the Darwinian world can lead us to contemplate more explicitly the mystery of God as it is made manifest in the story of life's suffering, the epitome of which lies for Christians in the crucifixion of Jesus. In the symbol of the cross, Christians discover a God who participates fully in the world's struggle and pain . . . Evolutionary biology not only allows theology to enlarge its sense of God's creativity by extending it over measureless eons of time; it also gives comparable magnitude to our sense of the divine participation in life's long and often tormented journey."[29]

Evangelical Protestant theology has tended to focus upon the cross as an act of atonement for human sinfulness. However, the New Testament makes clear that in the suffering of the cross, God in Christ enters into a redemptive relationship with the entire cosmos, the whole creation that is "groaning in labor pains," awaiting its release (Romans 8:19–25). Through Christ "God was pleased to reconcile to himself *all things* . . . by making peace through the blood of his cross" (Colossians 1:20). In Christ's passion God identifies with the struggles and tragedies of the evolving creation. If, as in panentheism, God "in the beginning" makes a space to let a world be, so, in Paul's vision, in the end God will take this evolving world into God's self, "so that God may be all in all" (1 Corinthians 15:28).[30]

---

27. Rolston, "Does Nature Need to be Redeemed?," 218–20.
28. Murphy, *Reconciling Theology and Science*, 70–72.
29. Haught, *God After Darwin*, 46.
30. Schneider, *Science and Faith*, Essay VII: "Theologies of an Evolving Creation."

Part Three

A New Understanding of Jesus and the Gospels

The intellect often demands proof that it is on solid ground. The thought of the soul finds its grounding in a different way. It likes persuasion, subtle analysis, an inner logic, and elegance. It enjoys the kind of discussion that is never complete, that ends with a desire for further talk or reading. It is content with uncertainty and wonder.

—Thomas Moore, psychotherapist

The most beautiful emotion we can experience is the mystical. It is the sower of all true art and science. He to whom this emotion is a stranger . . . is as good as dead. To know that what is impenetrable to us really exists, manifesting itself to us as the highest wisdom and the most radiant beauty, which our dull faculties can comprehend only in their most primitive forms—this knowledge, this feeling is at the center of all true religiousness.

—Albert Einstein, physicist

7

Understanding the Sacredness of Scripture

A PANENTHEISTIC UNDERSTANDING OF God requires a re-examination of Christian theology in its entirety, a task I leave to more capable commentators. Part three addresses three topics, scripture (chapter 7), Jesus and the gospels (chapter 8), and the doctrines of resurrection and eternal life (chapter 9), utilizing early Jewish-Christian methods and perspectives that harmonize with panentheism.

Christians have always affirmed a close relationship between the Bible and God, just as other religions affirm a close connection between the sacred and their holy scriptures. Foundational to reading the Bible is a decision about how to view its origin. Does it come from God, or is it a human product?

Acknowledging the obvious human element in the Bible, modern Christians generally take a both/and stance regarding biblical authorship: the Bible is both divine and human. This approach, upon further review, is problematic and only compounds the confusion. When the Bible is seen as both divine and human, we have two options. One is to say that it is all divine and all human. That may sound good, but no one maintains such an unworkable tension. The other, more typical option is to attempt to separate the divine parts from the human parts—as if some of it comes from God and some is a human product. The parts that come from God are then given greater authority than the others. However, who's to say which parts are divine, and which human? The Bible does not come with footnotes that say, "This passage reflects the will of God; the next passage does not." So those who take the entire Bible as divine are consistent, but they might be consistently wrong.

How, for instance, does one understand the Ten Commandments? Most Christians who think of the Bible as both divine and human would say that the commandments come from God. Does that mean that they are equally authoritative? If so, all Christians should worship God on Saturday, since that is the day clearly in mind as the day of worship. There is biblical evidence that the sanctity of the Sabbath was in effect among the Israelites prior to the revelation of the commandments to Moses on Mount Sinai (cf. Exodus 16:22–30). And if the Ten Commandments are divinely inspired, why are they written from a male point of view (for instance, they prohibit coveting your neighbor's wife but say nothing about coveting your neighbor's husband)? Furthermore, the commandments against stealing, adultery, murder, bearing false witness, and so forth are simply rules that make it possible for humans to live together in community. Biblical scholarship affirms that the pattern upon which these commandments are based is a treaty pattern invented by the Hittites, a powerful empire that predated Moses and came to an end prior to the time of Moses. Divine genius is not required to come up with rules like these. This is not to say that the Ten Commandments are unimportant, but rather that their origin is human.[1]

The perspective I am advocating does not see the Bible in its entirety as divine in origin, or some parts as divine and some as human. It is all human, the product of two faith communities, each with its own understandings of inspiration. As such, it contains ancient Israel's perceptions and misperceptions, just as it contains the early Christian movement's perceptions and misperceptions. Thus any and every passage of scripture involves interpretation. We who read it must discern how to hear and value its various voices. Reading the stories of creation or the stories of Jesus' birth literally involves an interpretive decision equally as much as does the decision to read them metaphorically. There is no such thing as a noninterpretive reading of the Bible. As we read the Bible, then, we should ask not, "What is God saying?" but "What is the ancient author or community saying?"[2]

To read the Bible properly, it is necessary to get beyond the superstitious and mystical aura that believers have used to safeguard scripture through the centuries. At least part of the problem lies in the excessive claims made for these scriptures. The Bible is not the word of God in any literal or verbal sense. It never has been! The gospels, for instance, are not static but reflect changing theological perspectives. Nor are they the words of eyewitnesses, as has so often been claimed. Most eyewitnesses to the life of Jesus were long dead before the gospels were recorded.[3] The gospels

---

1. Borg, *Reading the Bible*, 26–27.

2. The meaning of a biblical text, of course, is not confined or restricted to what the ancient author or community said. The task of interpretation is more than historical; it involves contemporizing the message and its application.

3. Conservative New Testament scholar Richard Bauckham disagrees, taking

Understanding the Sacredness of Scripture

were also shaped by the events of their own time, perhaps even more dramatically than the events of the time in which Jesus actually lived. For example, the capture and destruction of Jerusalem by the Roman army in AD 70 is a powerful reality in the background of the gospel narratives. The same can be said for the events that led to the expulsion of Jewish Christians from the synagogues by AD 90 and to the eventual dissolution of Christianity from Judaism. Seeing the gospels in a proper historical perspective is a critical first step into biblical knowledge.[4]

Next, when we read the texts of the New Testament, we need to be prepared to discover that there is an enormous gap between the claims that have been made for Jesus in the life of institutional Christianity and the record that was actually contained in the Bible. Most believers, for example, have never been told that there are no camels in the biblical story of the wise men and no stable or stable animals in the story of Jesus' birth. They are not aware, either, of the expanding claims made for Jesus in the gospels themselves. The earliest gospel says nothing about the virgin birth of Jesus, an account that did not appear in Christian history until the eighth or ninth decade, when the gospels of Matthew and Luke were written. The same is true of the narratives that speak of a physical bodily resurrection of Jesus. They, too, were late additions to the Christian story. Perhaps more important is the fact that the divine nature of Jesus or the interpretations of Jesus as the incarnation of God was also a late-developing reality.

To trace the expanding claims made for Jesus in the New Testament, one must begin with Paul, the first author of any part of the New Testament. In the epistle to the Romans, written about AD 58 (some twenty-eight years after the death of Jesus), Paul began to develop explanations for his experience of Christ. God, he says to the Christians in Rome, had "declared" Jesus to be "Son of God with power according to the spirit of

---

great pains to convince his readers that the gospels are based on eyewitness accounts. Despite exhaustive investigation, the argumentation in his monumental book *Jesus and the Eyewitnesses* (2006), while impressive, is narrow, nuanced, and based largely on conjecture. His methodology runs counter to most all recent New Testament scholarship, including the findings of source criticism, form criticism, and redaction criticism. Such findings have demonstrated that the traditions in the gospels are the products of a long and complex history that was fluid, varied, and largely uncontrolled by any centralized hierarchy. The first generation of Christians, while relying on the guidance of apostles and other followers of Jesus, had a mostly charismatic approach to leadership, in expectation of an imminent new age that would transform known history. The gospels were recorded during a period when that sense of urgency and imminence was waning and when eyewitness reports at best were questionable.

4. Spong, *Christianity Must Change*, 72–73.

holiness by his resurrection from the dead" (Romans 1:4). We need to take note of three key ideas here. First, according to this early Pauline statement, God declares or designates Jesus to be "Son of God." There is no sense here of divine equality or of what later came to be called incarnation. Next, Paul states that God made this declaration according to the "spirit of holiness." The Holy Spirit was not yet viewed as a separate and distinct aspect of God. Third, this designation of Jesus as God's divine son took place by his "resurrection from the dead." So for Paul it was the Easter experience, which came after the crucifixion, which constituted the basis for the God claim that he was making about Jesus. Paul seemed not to know of a divinely initiated virgin birth, for this belief is not mentioned in any of his letters. In this early strata of theological thinking we find a point of view that later came to be called "adoptionism." This means that late in his career it was Paul's understanding that God had adopted Jesus into the being of God. In Paul's mind, this adoptive status was not conferred upon Jesus until the resurrection.

Some ten years after Paul had written his epistle to the Romans and some forty years after the conclusion of Jesus' earthly life, the gospel of Mark came into existence. Here, for the first time in Christian history, the biographical details of Jesus' life were chronicled in written form. In the first verse, Mark informed his readers of his purpose for composing this book: "The beginning of the good news of Jesus Christ, the Son of God." He took Paul's earlier words and adapted them to his purpose in an interesting way. He accepted two parts of Paul's earlier declaration, but gave to them narrative form. Later in the chapter he took Paul's words, that God had declared Jesus to be God's son, and described just how it was that this declaration occurred. The voice of God spoke from heaven, Mark declared, and said of Jesus, "You are my Son, the Beloved; with you I am well pleased" (Mark 1:11). Next, Mark took Paul's idea that this declaration came by way of the "spirit of holiness" and created a specific setting. He wrote that the heavens tore apart, enabling the "Spirit" to descend on him "like a dove," that is, in a very physical way (Mark 1:10). Up to this point Mark seemed to be following the Pauline script closely, but he made a profound change, changing the moment in which this declaration took place. Whereas Paul had made the declaration occur at the time of the resurrection, Mark put it into his opening story of Jesus' baptism. He did so in order to demonstrate that the power of God was at work throughout the life of Jesus. He could not do that if Jesus had become the Son of God only at the time of the resurrection.

Understanding the Sacredness of Scripture

By the time Matthew wrote, some ten to twenty years after Mark, Matthew began his story of Jesus' life with the narrative of his birth, thereby moving all of Paul's original symbols about Jesus' divine designation back into the story of his nativity. God still declared Jesus to be the Son of God, for Matthew, only this declaration was now placed into the mouth of the angel who appeared to Joseph in a dream. Matthew went on to say that this divine nature was preordained by the prophet Isaiah, but the status was nonetheless still accomplished, even for Matthew, by the Pauline "spirit of holiness," though by Matthew's time that concept had become the more explicit "Holy Spirit." This Spirit was not yet fully distinct as a separate part of the triune God, for the Spirit in Matthew's birth narrative actually appeared to function as the male agent in conception. We must remember that of this moment in Christian history, no story of the coming of the Holy Spirit as a separate power, either at Pentecost (Luke) or at Easter (John) had yet been written.

Luke, writing five to ten years after Matthew, changed Matthew's details a bit but essentially left the story line intact. Luke's annunciating angel was, for example, far more specific than Matthew's. Luke's angel had a name, Gabriel (Luke 1:26). This divine creature appeared, according to Luke, in person, not in a dream, and it was Mary, not Joseph, who was the recipient of this angelic revelation. Mary's baby was designated by this angel as both "the Son of God" (Luke 1:35) and "Son of the Most High" (Luke 1:32). Clearly, Jesus was God's son from conception in this third gospel, and Paul's "spirit of holiness" was now becoming specific.

The fourth gospel, written during the last decade of the first century, omits any narrative about Jesus' birth and declares that Jesus was said to have shared in God's identity prior even to his conception and birth. So preexistence became a category in which Christians could now talk about Jesus. So, for John, there was no time in all history when Jesus was not God's son. By the start of the second century, Jesus' identity with God was now complete, providing the concept of the incarnation its primary biblical focus.

What we see here is one grand theological story, designed to capture the imagination; the migration of Paul's early affirmation had finally reached its limits. God had declared Jesus as the divine son, indeed as a part of who or what God is; that designation had been accomplished by the spirit of holiness, a character in a divine story that had grown rapidly, first into the Holy Spirit and then into the very essence of God. Finally, the origin of the Son's designation had journeyed backward in time, from the resurrection to the baptism to the conception to the origins of the creation itself.[5]

From this example, and many others like it, we come to see an essential feature of the Bible as a whole: its essentially narrative framework. We have examined images of Jesus and discovered that, just as they shape our image of the Christian life and worldview, so does our image of scripture. We have noted that both Jesus and his followers were rooted in Judaism, the sacred traditions of Israel (the Old Testament) having shaped their ways of seeing, thinking, and speaking.

Story Theology

In our effort to see the significance of scripture, we are greatly aided by a relatively recent emphasis in biblical and theological scholarship. In the 1970s and 1980s, a movement known as story theology called attention to the centrality of "story" in Jewish and Christian scriptures.[6] This theme can be seen in three features of the Bible: (1) the narrative framework of the Bible as a whole, which on a grand scale can be considered as a single story beginning with paradise lost in the opening chapters of Genesis and concluding with the vision of paradise restored in the book of Revelation; (2) the presence of literally hundreds of individual stories in the Bible; and (3) finally, the centrality in scripture of a small number of "macro-stories"—the primary sources of the religious imagination and life of ancient Israel and the early Christian community.

Story theology not only emphasizes the centrality of story in the biblical tradition, but also criticizes much of Christian theology and modern historical scholarship for having obscured this feature. Theology has typically focused on extracting a core of meaning from a story, which is then expressed conceptually. The story as story is lost. Modern historical study of the Bible has also deemphasized the story, either by searching for the underlying history or by an analytical approach that often loses the story by focusing on its fragments. In both cases, the story as story disappears.

Story theology seeks to recapture the narrative character of scripture. Though it is a recent movement, its approach is very ancient, for the Bible largely originated in story. The story of Israel originated in and was carried by storytelling, as were the gospels, their traditions about Jesus having been transmitted as stories long before they became texts.

---

5. The preceding example is adapted from Spong, ibid., 73–82.
6. The following is adapted from Borg, *Meeting Jesus Again*, 119–37.

Understanding the Sacredness of Scripture

As a genre, religious stories function in a particular way. Unlike religious laws, which address behavior, and unlike theology and doctrine, which address understanding and belief, stories appeal to the imagination. The great stories of the Bible model the religious life. And it is with life, rather than belief, that we are here concerned.

At the heart of scripture lie three macro-stories that have shaped the Bible as a whole and have imaged our understanding of Jesus and the religious life in a particular way. Two of the stories are grounded in the history of ancient Israel: the story of the exodus from Egypt and the story of the exile and return from Babylon. The third, the priestly story, is grounded in an institution, namely, the temple, priesthood, and sacrifice. As the three formational stories of the Hebrew Bible, they shaped the religious imagination and understanding of both ancient Israel and the early Christian movement.

1. The *exodus story* is essentially a story of bondage, liberation, journey, and destination. For the slaves, life in Egypt is marked by oppression. The story moves through the plagues and the liberation itself, but does not end with leaving Egypt. Liberation frees the people from the lordship of Pharaoh by transporting them to a transitional phase in their journey: the wilderness sojourn. That phase lasts forty years, but the destination is the Promised Land.

As a story about us, what is it saying? The story images the human condition as bondage. Our problem is that we live in Egypt, the land of bondage. The account requires us to ask, "To what am I in bondage, and to what are we in bondage?" The answer is we are in bondage to cultural messages about success, gender roles, and the good life; we are in bondage to voices from our own past and to addictions of various kinds. The solution, of course, is liberation. But liberation is not the end of the story. Rather, the way out leads to a journey through a wilderness, a place of freedom but also of fear and anxiety. The wilderness is a place of encounter, where we are nourished by the sacred. The journey takes a long time—forty years—a metaphor for a lifetime. Its destination is God, but God is the one who is known on the journey. It is a journey outward as well as inward. Most of us—unless our name is Caleb or Joshua—will die en route to that Promised Land, as did Moses.

2. Like the exodus story, the *story of exile and return* is grounded in a historical experience, when, after Jerusalem was destroyed by Babylon in 587 BC, many of the Jewish survivors were forced into exile in Babylon. There they lived as refugees for some fifty years, separated from their

homeland and under oppression. Next to the exodus, this experience was the most important historical event shaping the life and religious imagination of the Jewish people.

What does this image about the human condition tell us? What is life like in exile? It is an experience of separation from all that is familiar and safe. It usually involves powerlessness, marginality, and victimization. Like the metaphor of the exodus story, this story has psychological as well as cultural-political dimensions. It reminds us of the Garden of Eden story in the book of Genesis, since we too live outside the garden, east of Eden. The solution is a journey of return. The story speaks of God aiding and assisting those who undertake the journey (Isaiah 40:28–31).

3. The third story, the *priestly story*, is grounded in an institution. Within this story, the priest is the mediator who makes us right with God by offering sacrifice on our behalf. Unlike the previous stories, this one leads to a different image of the religious life. It is not primarily a story of bondage, exile, and journey, but a story of sin, guilt, sacrifice, and forgiveness. How does this story image the human condition? We are primarily sinners who have broken God's laws, and who therefore stand guilty before God, the lawgiver and judge.

All three stories shape the message of Jesus, the New Testament, and subsequent Christian theology. In a still-classic work on the atonement, *Christus Victor* (1931), the Swedish theologian Gustaf Aulen identified three main understandings of the death and resurrection of Jesus in the history of Christian theology.

1. The first image understands the central work of Christ as *victory over "the powers"* that hold humans in bondage, including sin, death, and the devil. Like the exodus story, this image sees the human predicament as bondage and the work of Christ as liberation.

2. Aulen calls the second major understanding of the death and resurrection of Christ the "substitutionary" image, which pictures the death of Jesus as a *sacrifice for sin* that makes God's forgiveness possible. This image, associated with the priestly story, did not become dominant in the church until the Middle Ages.

3. A third understanding of Christ's death and resurrection portrays Jesus not as accomplishing something on our behalf or defeating forces of evil, but as *revealing God's love or compassion*. This understanding, with some modification, can be correlated with the exile story, for it is the way of insight or enlightenment that embodies the way of return, a disclosure of

the internal spiritual process that brings us into an experiential relationship with the Spirit of God.

All three stories were important for Jesus, the early Christian movement, and subsequent Christian theology, but only one of them—the priestly story—came to dominate the popular understanding of Jesus and the Christian life to the present day. Despite the power and positive meaning in this model, suggestive of Jesus' love and forgiveness, this image, when it becomes isolated from the others or the dominant understanding of religious life, can produce severe distortions: (1) it leads to a static understanding of the Christian life, making it into a repeated vicious cycle of sin, guilt, and forgiveness; (2) it creates a passive understanding of culture and of the Christian life, thereby losing the sense of life as a process of spiritual transformation; (3) it leads to an understanding of Christianity as primarily a religion of the afterlife, emphasizing belief now for the sake of salvation later; (4) it presents God primarily as lawgiver and judge, picturing God's love as conditional and placing grace within a system of requirements; (5) this story has merit when understood metaphorically, but taken literally, it seems nonsensical; (6) this story works only when people feel guilt, which should not be the central issue in our lives.[7]

The macro-stories, when taken together, are holistic. They share four powerful elements:

- all understand something profound about the human condition, that life involves suffering and alienation;
- all make powerful affirmations about God, portraying God as intimately involved with human life;
- all are stories of hope, new beginnings, and new possibilities; and
- all are stories of a journey. This includes the priestly story, for taken in context with the others, the priestly story means that God accepts us just as we are, whatever our place on the journey.

These stories, all taken from the Hebrew scriptures, have powerful application in Christianity as well. In addition, the New Testament has a journey story of its own, that of discipleship. The initial clue is the meaning of the word "disciple," which does not mean to be "a pupil of a teacher," but rather a "follower after somebody." Discipleship in the New Testament, of course, is a journeying with Jesus. To follow Jesus means being on the road with him; it means undertaking the journey from the life of conventional

---

7. Ibid., 130–31.

wisdom to the alternative wisdom of life in the Spirit. Journeying with Jesus can involve denying him, even betraying him. Journeying with Jesus also means to be in a community, to become part of the alternative community of Jesus. And discipleship involves becoming compassionate, compassion being the defining mark of the follower of Jesus. Compassion is the fruit of life in the Spirit and the ethos of the community of Jesus. This understanding, unlike the conventional moralistic images of the Christian life, presents a transformist, dynamic understanding of the Christian life, where everything old passes away and where everything new becomes better (2 Corinthians 5:17).

The Bible in the Postcritical Paradigm

The Bible represents the heart of the Christian tradition, providing Christians their identity, their sacred story. Of course, Christianity is ultimately centered in God, but it is the God of whom the Bible speaks and to whom it points. Despite its formational nature, the Bible has become a stumbling block for many Christians today. In particular, many are leaving the church because the Precritical Paradigm's way of reading the Bible—with its emphasis on biblical infallibility, historical factuality, and moral and doctrinal absolutes—ceases to make sense to them.

The Postcritical Paradigm provides an alternative to biblical literalism. Utilizing three adjectives—*historical*, *metaphorical*, and *sacramental*—it describes how scripture should be understood. These three approaches apply as well as to the creeds and other normative Christian teachings.[8]

1. To speak of *the Bible as a historical product* is to see that it is a human product, not a divine product. Not "absolute truth" but relatively and culturally conditioned, the Bible uses the language and concepts of the cultures in which it took shape. It tells us how our spiritual ancestors saw things, not how God sees things. The Bible is not verbally inspired, since the emphasis is not upon words inspired by God but on people moved by their experience of God.

For the Postcritical Paradigm, describing the Bible as sacred scripture and therefore as "holy" is to value the historical process known as canonization. The documents that make up the Bible were not "sacred" when they were written, but over time were declared sacred, meaning that

---

8. The following points are adapted from Borg, ibid., 43–60.

they became the most important documents for that community, providing its foundation and shaping its identity.

2. Much of the language of the Bible is metaphorical: one-third of the Old Testament is poetry or semi-poetical literature. To speak of *the Bible as metaphor* is to emphasize that this language should not be interpreted literally. Metaphor does not mean that the Bible is not true, but rather that it is not primarily concerned with facticity. The Bible does contain history, but even when a text contains historical memory, its meaning is more than (not less than) literal. For example, although the exile in Babylon in the sixth century BC really happened, the way the story is told gives it a more than historical meaning. As we noted earlier, it became a metaphorical narrative of exile and return, providing images of the human condition and its remedy. In other cases, as the Genesis stories of creation, there may be little or no historical factuality. Though these stories are not literally factual, they are profoundly true.

Because the gospels combine memory and metaphor, some of these accounts, when literalized, become literally incredible. The story of Jesus changing water into wine at the wedding in Cana (John 2:1–11) illustrates the point. A literal reading of the story emphasizes the spectacular event as a sign of Jesus's identity, "proof" that he was divine. A metaphorical reading of this story yields a different meaning. It notes the story's literary context in John's gospel as the opening scene of the public activity of Jesus. It seems to be John's way of saying: "Here in a nutshell is what the story of Jesus is about."

The story begins: "On the third day, there was a wedding." The phrase "on the third day" evokes the resurrection, the Easter story at the end of the gospel. The imagery of a wedding banquet helps us view the ministry of Jesus as a celebration at which the wine never runs out and the best is saved for last. Here we have a pointer to the sacramental nature of the Christian life and to the belief that Jesus is God's best.

A metaphorical reading of the gospels provides rich meaning for Christians in all times and places; a literal reading misses all of this, emphasizing belief in the miraculous elements rather than on its meaning for a life of faith. Metaphorical language is *a way of seeing*. To apply this to the Bible means that in addition to its metaphorical language and metaphorical narratives, the Bible as a whole may be thought of as a "giant" metaphor. "Thus the point is not to believe in the Bible—but to see our lives with God through it."[9]

---

9. Ibid., 57.

3. To speak of *the Bible as sacrament* is to say that it mediates the sacred. If a sacrament is a physical vehicle or vessel for the Spirit, the Bible is sacrament in the sense that it is a visible human product whereby God becomes present to us.

For the Postcritical Paradigm, "the Bible—human in origin, sacred in status and function—is both metaphor and sacrament. As metaphor, it is a way of seeing—a way of seeing God and our life with God. As sacrament, it is a way that God speaks to us and comes to us."[10] Thus the Bible is a two-way bridge, a path to the divine and a way to connect to our deepest self. Like a backboard in the game of basketball, scripture is a means to an end, not an end in itself.

---

10. Ibid., 59.

8

Understanding the Jewishness of Jesus

As a biblical scholar, I affirm the following six assertions with certainty:

1. Christianity arose as a sect of Judaism;
2. Jesus, his followers, and the earliest leaders of Christianity, were all Jewish;
3. Every book of the New Testament, including the writings attributed to Luke, was written from a Jewish perspective;
4. Christianity originated as a Jewish eschatological movement;
5. Jesus envisioned his mission in a quasi-prophetic manner;
6. Around the end of the first century AD the overall focus of Christianity shifted dramatically, to the point of severing its relationship with Judaism. By this time the majority of Christians were gentiles who mistrusted Jews and held disparaging attitudes toward Judaism.

At the heart of Christianity stands an affirmation that is without parallel in the monotheistic tradition: "Jesus is Lord." This statement, believed by scholars to be an early Christian creed, contains a striking confession, indicating that the first followers of Jesus viewed him as an extraordinary human, one whose influence exceeded that of human rulers (the imperial Ceasars) as the power and authority of God exceeds that of humans. Eventually they equated him with God.

C. S. Lewis, a former atheist who converted to evangelical Christianity and gained fame as an apologist for traditional Christianity in the mid-twentieth century, famously argued that three options—and three alone—are available for people in thinking about Jesus Christ: either he was a liar, a self-deceived lunatic, or else he was what Christians have traditionally affirmed, Son of God and Lord of all. Despite my appreciation for Lewis and his distinctive writings, I find these options inadequately narrow and woefully misguided, for Jesus does not fit any of these categories. They emerge from the perspective of the Precritical Paradigm, from reading the gospels as if they were straightforward historical documents.

Such a reading distorts the image of Jesus, for it focuses exclusively on his deity, emphasizing the miraculous—especially the virgin birth and the physical bodily resurrection. Concentrating on the saving significance of Jesus' death (that he died for our sins), this approach concludes that Jesus and Christianity are the only way of salvation. Furthermore, it places head knowledge—belief—at the center of Christianity, stressing that to be a Christian requires affirmation that all of the above is factually true.

Modern scholarship discounts such narrow understanding of Jesus and views literalistic interpretations of scripture as misleading. So we need to rethink our understanding of Jesus. Who was he, and what, from the historical records, can we infer about him?

Despite belonging to the Jewish peasant class, he was minimally literate, in that he undoubtedly went to school in the synagogue in Nazareth, where the emphasis would have been on reading and writing, with the Torah as the primary text. He became a woodworker, which, in terms of social standing, placed him at the lower end of the peasant class, more marginalized than a peasant who still owned a small piece of land.

At some point in his life Jesus embarked upon a religious quest. He probably underwent what William James calls a "conversion experience," not, of course, from paganism to Judaism, for he grew up Jewish. Conversion, as James defines it, need not infer a change from one religion to another, or from being nonreligious to being religious. It can refer to a process of internal transformation, whether sudden or gradual, which led him to undertake his ministry. Influenced by a fiery preacher known as John the Baptist, in his late twenties or around the age of thirty he embarked on his career. Mark dates the beginning of Jesus' ministry to John's arrest, which suggests that, with his mentor in prison, Jesus stepped in to carry on.

So what was the adult Jesus like, and what did he come to understand about himself and his mission? All understandings of Christianity rely ultimately on two assessments: Jesus' self-understanding and the early church's conceptualizing of that self-understanding. Let us start with the obvious: Jesus was deeply Jewish. Not only was he Jewish by birth and socialization, but he remained a Jew all of his life. His scripture was the Jewish Bible. He did not intend to establish a new religion, but saw himself as having a mission within Judaism. He spoke as a Jew to other Jews. His early followers were Jewish.

Understanding the Jewishness of Jesus

Jesus became a gifted teacher. His verbal gifts were remarkable. His language was most often metaphorical, poetic, and imaginative, filled with memorable short sayings and compelling short stories we call parables. He was clearly exceptionally intelligent. Like the classical prophets of ancient Israel, he performed symbolic actions: on one occasion he staged a demonstration in the temple, overturning the tables of the money changers and driving out the sellers of sacrificial animals. There was a radical social and political edge to his message and activity, as he challenged the social order of his day and indicted the elites who dominated it. He must have been remarkably courageous, willing to continue what he was doing even when in lethal danger. He was a remarkable healer: more healing stories are told about him than about anybody else in the Jewish tradition. He attracted a following, which means he was quite compelling about him. He also attracted enemies, especially among the rich and powerful. Unlike the founders of the world's other major religious traditions, his public ministry was brief, lasting at most three or four years. Living only into his early thirties, he was then crucified on charges of sedition. At his crucifixion the Romans placed an inscription on his cross that read, "Jesus of Nazareth, King of the Jews," thereby issuing a warning to his followers that Roman rule would not tolerated insurrection.

Though it is hard to believe, some Christians are unaware of the Jewishness of Jesus, or, if they are aware, either downplay it or obscure that reality with later Christian anti-Semitism. The separation of Jesus from Judaism has had tragic consequences for Jews throughout the centuries, and any faithful image of Jesus must take with utmost seriousness his rootedness in Judaism. If we fail to understand Jesus as a Jewish figure teaching and acting within Judaism, we will misunderstand his mission.

As a result of reading the New Testament, filtered through the creeds of later Christendom, Christians have arrived at an understanding of Jesus that is quite different from the sketch presented above. That understanding might be summarized under the phrase "Christian messiah," an exalted status that includes such titles of Jesus as "Son of God," "Word of God," "Wisdom of God," "Lamb of God," "Light of the World," "Bread of Life," "Alpha and Omega," and "firstborn of all creation." These may not convey what Jesus of Nazareth thought or taught about himself, but they came to summarize what New Testament Christians believed Jesus to be.

The gospels, as the rest of the New Testament, are products of developing traditions of the early Christian communities in which they were written. As such, they contain two types of information: *history remembered*, meaning some of the things reported in the gospels really happened and reliably represent Jesus as a figure of history, and *history metaphorized*, meaning some of the tradition is not literally true but represents the revised understanding of the communities themselves following Easter. Biblical scholarship distinguishes between these two understandings of Jesus by speaking of "the Jesus of history" and "the Christ of faith." Marcus Borg, in his writings, substitutes the phrase "the pre-Easter Jesus" for the historical Jesus and "post-Easter Jesus" for the "Jesus" of Christian tradition and experience. The latter includes both "the canonical Jesus" we meet on the surface level of the New Testament and "the creedal Jesus" we encounter in the classic Christian creeds of the fourth and fifth centuries. For Borg both pre- and post-Easter understandings of Jesus are valid, the first as the community's memory of the historical Jesus and the second as the community's testimony of Jesus. In other words, after his death, Jesus the Galilean Jew became in the experience and language of his followers "the face of God" and ultimately the second person of the Trinity.

This conceptual transformation may be viewed as a three-fold process; early Christian thinking about Jesus began with (1) experience and then moved through (2) metaphorical expression to (3) conceptual formulation. In the beginning was experience, that of the disciples and others of Jesus. The primary cause of the transition from the pre-Easter to the post-Easter Jesus was the Easter experience, expressed by the early Christian conviction that "God raised Jesus from the dead." Though the gospel stories portray this as occurring literally, "the core meaning of Easter is that Jesus continued to be experienced after his death, but in a radically new way: as a spiritual and divine reality."[1]

The Easter experience led to a transformed perception of Jesus among his followers. In the sixty or seventy years after Jesus' death, when the traditions found in the New Testament took shape, Jewish Christian communities searched the Hebrew scriptures, finding a large number of metaphors or images that related to Jesus and his significance, images such as servant of God, lamb of God, light of the world, bread of life, Lord, door, vine, shepherd, messiah, savior, great high priest, sacrifice, Son of God, Son of Man, Wisdom of God, and Word of God. Over time, these metaphors became the subject of intellectual reflection and conceptualization. Some, ultimately, became doctrine. This process produced the post-Easter Jesus—the "Christ of faith"—of Christian tradition.

---

1. Borg, *God We Never Knew*, 93.

Jesus and Jewish Eschatology

As a first-century Palestinian Jew, Jesus belonged to a world where religion (theology) and politics went hand in hand. The theology was Jewish monotheism, a doctrine forged through centuries of subjugation and persecution, going back to the Babylonian exile. First-century Jews held their monotheism passionately. Theirs was not an abstract theory about the existence of one God. They believed their God, Yahweh, was the only God, and that all others were idols. A corollary of monotheism was "election," the belief that the Jews had been chosen by this one God, making what happened to Israel of universal significance. Many Jews of Jesus' day believed that God was about to vindicate them, understanding this act as having global implications, as the means of divine judgment and/or mercy upon the rest of the world.

Monotheists, who believe in one God and in their status as God's elect people, while currently suffering oppression, would also believe the present state of affairs temporary. Monotheism and election thus give birth to eschatology, a perspective that views history as purposeful and therefore as moving toward a climactic resolution or restoration, at which time everything would be made right. First-century Jewish eschatology claimed that Yahweh would soon act within history to vindicate his people and to establish permanent justice and peace. This belief included the great promises of forgiveness articulated by biblical prophets, notably Isaiah, Jeremiah, and Ezekiel. The so-called post-exilic writings spoke of a restoration still to be described, a liberation they described as a new exodus.

In keeping with this understanding, it follows that Jesus of Nazareth might have viewed his mission as prophetic, announcing, like John the Baptist before him, God's coming kingdom. But Jesus, it seems, went beyond John's verbal role, embodying in his person and his ministry the presence of that kingdom. For Jesus, the all-encompassing rule of God was near, which when it came in its fullness, would restore Israel's role as "light to the nations" and challenge evil in all its manifestations, political, social, and economic. The coming kingdom of God was not a new sort of religion, a new moral code, or a new soteriology (a doctrine about how one might go to heaven after death). Nor was it a new sociological analysis, critique, or agenda. It was about Israel's story reaching its climax, about Israel's history moving toward its decisive moment.[2]

---

2. Borg and Wright, *Meaning of Jesus*, 31–35.

Beyond Belief

E. P. Sanders, in his classic text *Jesus and Judaism*, maintains that before the outbreak of the War of the Jews against Rome in AD 66, "common Judaism" held the following hopes for the future: the restoration of the tribes of Israel; the conversion, destruction, or subjugation of the gentiles; the renewal of Jerusalem, including a new or rebuilt temple; and the purification of God's people and their worship.[3] Whatever one makes of his idea of a common Judaism, surely the beliefs Sanders highlights were widespread among Jesus' contemporaries, as was apocalyptic eschatology in general. According to Sanders, Jesus was an apocalyptic prophet standing in the tradition of Jewish restoration theology. He shared the beliefs common in Judaism, together with this prevailing understanding of Israel's story and hope. Having established the essential Jewishness of Jesus on this topic, Sanders finds primitive Christianity to be a movement in continuity with Jesus' hopes and expectations: "The most certain fact of all is that early Christianity was an eschatological movement."[4]

Biblical support for that contention can be found in the well-known fact that, with the exception of Philemon, 2 John, and 3 John (all three of which are brief and nearly devoid of theology), apocalyptic eschatology or some obvious trace of it appears in all first-century Christian documents. For instance, 1 Thessalonians, the earliest extant Christian writing, is full of apocalyptic expectation. As A. T. Robinson recognized, this letter is a "challenge" for anyone who denies that Christianity began amid apocalyptic enthusiasm.[5] Since Jesus was the point of origination for what became Christianity, one might reasonably infer that he was an apocalyptic figure. If within a year or two of Jesus' death Paul persecuted the followers of Jesus because of their eschatological proclamation, that leaves precious little time in which the followers of a noneschatological Jesus could have developed an entirely new eschatological perspective without a precedent in the preaching and actions of Jesus. The conclusion seems obvious: Eschatology was pervasive at the beginning of the Christian movement because it was central to Jesus and his mission.

This understanding of Jesus as "eschatological Jewish prophet" announcing the inbreaking of God's culminating kingdom is controversial in current biblical scholarship in part because of a debate on the meaning of the term "eschatology," typically defined as "the study of last things." In addition to the idea of "the end of the world," much emphasized by

---

3. Sanders, *Jesus and Judaism*, 279–303.
4. Sanders, "Jesus: His Religious Type," 6.
5. Robinson, *Jesus and His Coming*, 104–17.

current evangelical Christians but essentially a non-Jewish view,[6] at least three biblical possibilities can be maintained:[7]

1. An *apocalyptic* meaning, in which eschatology truly signifies a time in the future when the course of history will be changed to such an extent that one can speak of an entirely new state of reality; it concerns a cosmic cataclysm and a new age followed by utopian bliss. This view is generally associated with "end-time" events such as the coming of a messianic age, the vindication of Israel or the elect, and sometimes a last judgment and resurrection of the dead. This is not what I believe Jesus had in mind, though biblical memory suggests that he seemed to envision the occurrence of something cataclysmic.

2. An *historical/political* meaning, in keeping with the spirit of the Old Testament pre-exilic prophets, who spoke of the "Day of the Lord" (a day of judgment) as referring to an event or a cluster of events within history, such as the military conquest of Israel or Judah by a foreign empire. Here "end" means "an end of statehood" and newness "a restoration of statehood."

3. A *teleological* meaning, understanding the concept of eschatology in the sense that the "end" it envisions is associated with ultimate purpose, hope, or an ideal vision. This view seems to capture what Jesus meant when he came proclaiming the good news of God, saying, "The time is fulfilled, and the kingdom of God has come near; repent, and believe in the good news" (Mark 1:15). That kingdom, surely, concerned the final destiny of the Jewish people.

What adds to the biblical confusion is that various understandings of eschatology lie superimposed one upon another in the New Testament. There were some within the early church who clearly expected the "end of the world" in their generation, including the resurrection of the dead, the last judgment, and the "new heavens and new earth." Where did this expectation arise? Was it grounded in Jesus' own expectation or should the church's expectation of the "last things" be understood as a post-Easter development, a deduction based upon the Easter event itself?

---

6. Jewish eschatologies did not typically involve "the end of the world." The disappearance of the material world is not part of the expectation. The exception may be 2 Peter 3:10–12.

7. G. B. Caird, in *Language and Imagery of the Bible*, 243–71, examined the variety of uses given to the concept of "eschatology" by modern scholars and discovered seven different senses in which the term is used.

As is well-known, "resurrection" in Judaism was an event expected at the end of time. To some within the early church, the fact that Jesus' resurrection had occurred was an indicator that the general resurrection must be near: Christ was the "first fruits" of those to be raised from the dead (1 Corinthians 15:23). Moreover, first-century Christians did not think about the imminent coming of the kingdom or talk about the end of the world in a general way. Rather, they spoke of the imminent end of the world only in connection with the return of Jesus. It is important not to exaggerate the extent to which the early church was an "end-time" community. Despite the explicit statements affirming an imminent end, it is not clear that this was an essential expectation (except, perhaps, in the book of Revelation). Though the letters of Paul and the gospel of John contain explicit references to the end, clearly the emphasis of both authors is on the present rather than on the future, acknowledging the present as the time when the reality of God can be known in a decisive way.

The belief in two ages, a characteristic of Jewish eschatology, is found in the thought of the apostle Paul. In his writings, the present evil age is giving way to the coming age of justice and peace, so that the end of the one is the beginning of the other. It is not altogether clear to which of the three categories of biblical meaning this view belongs. Defining and cataloguing such a concept involves a mixture of subjective and objective evaluation. How, for instance, do we understand Isaiah's vision in Isaiah 35:1–10? Read literally, it describes a complete reversal of nature, a final kingdom of justice and peace such as envisioned in the first meaning of "eschatology" above. Read contextually, however, the vision applies to the restoration of Zion (the Kingdom of Judah) and can be viewed as an example of the second meaning of eschatology above. Such an understanding, read through Paul's "two-age" understanding of eschatology, applies in the present and can refer to the third meaning of eschatology, namely to the spiritual newness Christian believers are experiencing as the result of the death and resurrection of Christ. We recall the well-known reference in 2 Corinthians 5:17, where, according to Paul, the Christ-event itself signifies the passing of the old age and the inception of the new: "everything old has passed away; see, everything has become new!"

Some scholars, particularly church-based theologians concerned to extricate Jesus from error and from the troubling possibility that his expectations were disappointed, have toned down or reinterpreted many of the eschatological prophecies in the gospels and thereby disassociated Jesus from failure as a prophet. The British scholar C. H. Dodd ingeniously read the Synoptic texts so that they give us "realized eschatology," meaning that we should view the kingdom as having already come in Jesus' ministry. John Dominic Crossan dissociates Jesus from a large number of biblical traditions about him and from the violent expectations of John the Baptist, occasioned by the last judgment. Crossan's Jesus hopes instead for a utopian future of justice and egalitarianism, a future inaugurated not by the last judgment but by social renewal. N. T. Wright passionately promotes a Jesus who used eschatological metaphors to prophesy what actually came to pass in the first century: his own resurrection, the coming of the church, and Jerusalem's violent demise.

Dale Allison, professor of New Testament and Early Christianity at Pittsburgh Theological Seminary, disagrees, arguing persuasively that Jesus placed himself as the central figure in the eschatological end-time drama. For Allison, the historical Jesus was not a poet speaking metaphorically about judgment; rather he lived and thought apocalyptically. Citing profusely from the gospels, Allison concludes that Jesus envisaged, as did many other Jews in his time and place, "the advent, after suffering and persecution, of a great judgment, and after that a supernatural utopia, the kingdom of God, inhabited by the dead come back to life, to enjoy a world forever rid of evil and wholly ruled by God. Further, he thought that the night was far gone, the day at hand."[8] The belief of early Christians in the imminence of the end, according to Allison, originated not from the church's post-Easter expectations, but with Jesus himself.

This is not to say that Jesus was an apocalyptic extremist, or that he had only eschatology on his mind. Part of the reason that Jesus so fascinates and inspires is that he embodied in his own person the extremes of human experience. On the one hand, Jesus announced and made real the eschatological presence of the God of Israel: Satan has fallen like lightning from heaven and the demons are being routed; the lame walk and the blind see; lepers are cleansed and those in poverty are cheered with good news; the long-awaited kingdom of God has arrived; the bridegroom is here; the old world is gone; the new world has come.

That, however, is only half of the story. Paradoxically, the joyful Jesus is familiar with sorrows and acquainted with grief. He has nowhere to lay his head; respected leaders assail his teachings and behavior; John the Baptist, whom he hails as more than a prophet, is arrested and beheaded; his own companions misunderstand him, betray him, and abandon him. Pagan soldiers whip him, mock him, and nail him to a cross of execution. His end is physical torment and mental anguish, loss of life and loss of

---

8. Allison, *The Historical Christ*, 95.

Beyond Belief

meaning. So the tradition gives us a Jesus who "knows how to laugh loudly and to wail miserably, a Jesus who knows the presence of God and the absence of God."[9]

If Jesus had pretended to know only the blessings of the future age, we should turn our backs on him, for we would know his faith to be a hopeless flight from the pain of living. And if he had focused exclusively on the tribulation to come, we would dismiss his hope as inconsequential, the distance between him and God as too great. But by announcing not only tribulation present and future but also salvation present and future and then by living into both, Jesus commends himself to us.

Marcus Borg represents a growing number of modern scholars who challenge this understanding of Jesus, envisioning instead a non-eschatological Jesus, whose role, if interpreted prophetically, should be limited to that of a social prophet engaged in radical social criticism. According to this model, Jesus was a counter-cultural revolutionary who opposed the domination systems of his day both in person and through an alternative community of disciples, chosen to represent the New Israel of God. In Borg's view the kingdom of God represents a this-worldly social vision—a vision that empowers Christians and defines the church's ongoing role in society— rather than an other-worldly eschatological vision imposed from above and occasioned by a church raptured from this earth, an interpretation popular in many American fundamentalist and evangelical circles today.

Viewing Jesus as a deeply Jewish but non-eschatological figure, Borg challenges another vital element in the popular image of Jesus, namely that Jesus understood himself to be the messiah. According to Borg, the pre-Easter Jesus consistently pointed away from himself to God; his message was theocentric, not christocentric, meaning that he was centered in God and not in messianic pronouncements about himself. On the basis of these two denials of popular but what he considers erroneous images of Jesus, Borg suggests five models in the Jewish tradition that accurately portray the self-understanding of the historical (pre-Easter) Jesus:[10]

1. Jesus as *mystic*: Like Moses, Elijah, and the prophets, Jesus was a "Spirit person," a "mediator of the sacred." This notion, which he calls the most crucial fact about Jesus, means that Jesus was one of those persons in human history to whom the sacred was, to use William James's terms, firsthand religious experience rather than a secondhand belief;

---

9. Ibid., 117.

10. Borg, *God We Never Knew*, 89–90. A fuller discussion is found in Borg and Wright, *Meaning of Jesus*, 60–76.

2. Jesus as *healer and exorcist*: The evidence that Jesus performed paranormal healings is very strong; in fact, more healing stories are told about him than about any other figure in the Jewish tradition. While admitting that psychosomatic factors may sometimes have been involved, Borg avoids usage of the term "miracle" in connection with Jesus, since the latter requires accepting a supernatural interventionist model of God. "Interventions, no. Marvels, yes."[11]

3. Jesus as *wisdom teacher*: Using provocative saying and memorable parables, Jesus taught a subversive and alternative wisdom. Conventional Jewish wisdom was based upon the dynamics of retribution, that is, rewards and punishments. Unlike conventional wisdom teachers, who pass on and sometimes elaborate the received traditions or conventions of a community or group, Jesus invited hearers into a different way of seeing—God, themselves, and life itself. His wisdom teaching invited people to live in the Spirit, to walk a path of transformation centered in the Spirit.

4. Jesus as *social prophet*: Like the social prophets of the Hebrew Bible (Amos, Micah, Jeremiah), Jesus criticized the economic, political, and religious elites of his time. Advocating an alternative social vision grounded in the compassion of God, he was often in conflict with authorities. In speaking of the kingdom of God, he used a political metaphor that contrasted existing kingdoms: the kingdom of God is what life would be like on earth if God were king, rather than Herod and Caesar.

5. Jesus as *movement founder*: Jesus brought into being a Jewish renewal or revitalization movement that challenged and shattered the social boundaries of his day, a movement that eventually became the early Christian church. Although his public activity was very brief, Jesus formed an embryonic group whose inclusiveness and egalitarian practice embodied his alternative social vision.

It is not pedagogically acceptable to commingle eschatological and noneschatological perspectives of Jesus. Either his mindset was eschatological or it was not, and for that reason modern scholarship does not allow fence-sitting on the matter. There is no question in my mind that Jesus was clearly driven by current Jewish eschatological expectations and that he organized his ministry around those conceptions. As an eschatological prophet, however, he brought the entire package of prophecy to bear on

11. Borg and Wright, *Meaning of Jesus*, 67.

Beyond Belief

his task, meaning that through his work and ministry he believed he was inaugurating and embodying the works of the kingdom.

The kingdom need not be seen as a strictly "end-time" phenomenon, however, for in a spiritual sense the kingdom is found in whole nowhere, but in part everywhere. Jesus' first sermon, as recorded in Luke 4:18–21, singles out the marks of the kingdom. In that passage Jesus takes the scroll of the prophet Isaiah and finds the place where it is written: "The Spirit of the Lord is upon me, because he has anointed me to bring good news to the poor. He has sent me to proclaim release to the captives and recovery of sight to the blind, to let the oppressed go free, to proclaim the year of the Lord's favor." After reading he said, "Today this scripture has been fulfilled in your hearing." This passage reveals the manifesto of Jesus, who understood himself as embodying the hopes of the long-awaited Jubilee, which decreed the emancipation of land, slaves, and debts at the end of the seventh sabbatical, an appropriate image of what current Judaism envisioned as the coming reign of God. According to Luke's gospel the kingdom Jesus envisioned is already here, "within us" or "in our midst" (Luke 17:21). While the kingdom was embryonically present in Jesus, it cannot be said to have been fully present in him. As Jesus made clear in his parables, the kingdom is an expanding (unfolding) phenomenon. Like yeast in dough, the kingdom must grow continuously until all is leavened (Matthew 13:33; Luke 13:21). Every age must announce its coming and commit fully to its hopeful vision. In every age, all who seek the kingdom are its citizens and every messenger is holy.

Whether we depict Jesus eschatologically, noneschatologically, or as the culmination of both mindsets, in every respect Jesus was a Jewish figure of his day.

The Jewishness of the New Testament

Once we understand the Jewishness of Jesus, as well as the Jewishness of Mary his mother, of the apostles, of Paul, and even the Jewishness of all the biblical heroes of the Bible, the next step is to study the Bible—not only the Hebrew scriptures (Old Testament) but the Bible in its entirety—from a Jewish perspective, since every author in the entire Bible was Jewish by birth, and the sole exception, Luke, was a gentile proselyte to Judaism.

The starting point for this understanding of scripture requires knowing how the Jewish people wrote sacred narratives. That information will help us understand how to interpret the narratives found in the Christian

Understanding the Jewishness of Jesus

gospels and in the book of Acts. If these Christian writings are primarily Jewish works, then they cannot be understood apart from the Jewish context, the Jewish mindset, the Jewish frame of reference, the Jewish vocabulary, and even the Jewish history that shaped and formed those writers.

In recent times a small group of biblical scholars, spearheaded by the British New Testament scholar Michael D. Goulder and popularized in America by Bishop John Shelby Spong, have argued that the gospels need to be read as *haggadah*—as edifying fiction—in the midrashic style of the Jewish sacred storyteller, and not as objective descriptions of literal events.

The exegetical methodology termed midrash can be traced back to the return of the Israelite people from their exile in Babylon under the favorable rule of the Persians, beginning with the reign of Cyrus in 539 BC. Since the context in which the Torah had been written was much different from that of the postexilic period, and because there were so many variations of the Israelite religion due to external cultural influence during this period, the religious authorities felt a need for ongoing adaptation and explanation so that the observance of the Torah could be ensured. There developed two basic types of midrashic literature, *halakhic* and *haggadic*. While the former elucidated the Torah in legal terms, the latter was concerned with homiletic and narrative commentary. With the fall of the temple in AD 70, the rabbinical scribes took these oral traditions and began transferring them into writing, a process that culminated in the Talmudic writings. Building on this tradition, Jewish exegetes continued to produce a vast and rich written and oral reinterpretation of the Hebrew scriptures.

Thus, in the extensive history of Jewish life and literature, there developed a need for commentary and reinterpretation of traditional texts in light of the ever-changing present situations. Midrash, therefore, is the hermeneutical act of rereading and expanding a text in the form of a new narrative to update the existential meaning. Midrash is both a literary genre and a hermeneutical method, used to explain the deeper meaning of a biblical text. In this sense, midrash performs the function of recontextualizing an already existing text so as to enlarge and enhance its significance in and for the currently existing situational context. Such an approach is not concerned with historic accuracy but with meaning and understanding.

By way of example, consider the biblical notion that God parts the waters to rescue his people. At the Red Sea, parting the waters was the sign that God was with Moses (Exodus 14). Later, when Jewish writers of antiquity interpreted God's presence to be with Joshua after the death of Moses, they repeated the parting of the waters (Joshua 3). As Bishop Spong notes,

> When Joshua was said to have parted the waters of the Jordan River, it was not recounted as a literal event of history; rather it was the *midrashic* attempt to relate Joshua to Moses and thus demonstrate the presence of God with his successor. The same pattern operated later when both Elijah (2 Kings 2:8) and Elisha (2 Kings 2:14) were said to have parted the waters of the Jordan River and to have walked across on dry land. When the story of Jesus' baptism was told, the gospel writers asserted that Jesus parted not the Jordan River, but the heavens. This Moses theme was thus being struck yet again (Mark 1:9–10), and indeed, for a similar purpose. The heavens, according to the Jewish creation story, were nothing but the firmament that separated the waters above from the waters below (Genesis 1:6–8). To portray Jesus as splitting the heavenly waters was a Jewish way of suggesting that the holy God encountered in Jesus went even beyond the God presence that had been met in Moses, Joshua, Elijah, and Elisha. That is the way the *midrashic* principle worked. Stories about heroes of the Jewish past were heightened and retold again and again about heroes of the present moment, not because those same events actually occurred, but because the reality of God revealed in those moments was like the reality of God known in the past.[12]

According to Spong, we are not reading history when we read the scriptures. "We are listening to the experience of Jewish people, processing in a Jewish way what they believed was a new experience with the God of Israel. Jews filtered every new experience through the corporate remembered history of their people, as that history had been recorded in the Hebrew scriptures of the past."[13]

The same holds true for the gospels. Scholars as far apart on the ideological spectrum as Marcus Borg, John Dominic Crossan, and Robert Gundry agree that many of the narratives in the gospels should be read metaphorically, that is, as symbolic narratives created to illustrate a particular meaning. Starting with the birth narratives in Matthew and Luke and extending to narratives such as the wedding feast at Cana (John 2:1–11) and Peter walking on the water (Matthew 14:28–31), all should be viewed as parables rather than as recorded history. From one point of view, these scholars are not telling us anything new, for Christians have always allegorized scripture, finding meaning in texts they no longer viewed as historical. But Borg and like-minded scholars are saying something more.

12. Spong, *Liberating the Gospels*, 36–37.
13. Ibid., 37.

Understanding the Jewishness of Jesus

They are not claiming that we must, for modern reasons, reinterpret the old texts in new ways, against their authors' original intentions. Instead they contend that the texts were never intended to be understood literally in the first place. As Crossan notes: "When I looked at the so-called nature miracles of Jesus... those stories screamed parable at me, not history, not miracle, but parable. They shouted at me: 'It's a parable, dummy.'"[14]

Roger David Aus, urging that the gospels contain large tracts of *haggadah*, which their Jewish-Christian authors knew to be true only in a less-than-literal sense, has written to similar effect: "It is one of the tragedies of the Christian church that the number of its Palestinian Jewish members dwindled so rapidly after the very successful missionizing of the Gentiles. The latter soon made the former into small sects such as the Palestinian Ebionites. Early Palestinian and later even Hellenistic Jewish Christians, however, could have conveyed to Gentile Christians the nature of Jewish *haggadah*, and the centuries-old Gentile Christian debate about the 'historicity' or 'facticity' of *haggadic* sayings or narratives [in the canonical gospels] would have been basically unnecessary."[15]

The first generation of Christians, the vast majority of whom were Jewish, undoubtedly saw *haggadah* at work in the gospel tradition, recognizing certain Jewish antecedents present therein and noting that the authors were filtering their experience of Jesus through the corporate remembered history that had been recorded in the Hebrew scriptures of the past. The confusion of tongues at Babel (Genesis 11:1–9) is surely related to the overcoming of that confusion of tongues at Pentecost (Acts 2). The story of Pharaoh seeking to kill the Jewish boy babies in Egypt (Exodus 1:22) is surely connected to the story of Herod seeking to kill the Jewish boy babies in Bethlehem (Matthew 2:16–18). The story of Moses, who, after meeting God on the mountain, had his face shine so brightly that it had to be covered (Exodus 34:29–35), is surely related to the story of Jesus being transfigured so that he too shone with an unearthly radiance (Mark 9:2–8). The account of the Palm Sunday procession (Mark 11:2–10) is surely related to the story in Zechariah (9:9–11) where the king came to Jerusalem, lowly and riding on a donkey.[16]

"As long as the Gospels were read and interpreted only by gentile people," Spong notes wryly, "either these ancient Hebrew connections were unknown or it was assumed that these were nothing but Old Testament

---

14. Crossan, *A Long Way*, 167–68.
15. Aus, *Death, Burial, and Resurrection*, 291.
16. Spong, *Liberating the Gospels*, 33–34.

foreshadowings of the life of Christ. To believe that these texts are actual anticipations of Jesus meant that Christians had to believe that these verses had been placed into the texts of antiquity by the holy God so that hundreds of years later people would see in Jesus' literal fulfillment of these expectations proof of his divine nature."[17] This distorting, anti-Jewish way of reading the gospels continued unchallenged for centuries. The price that Christians paid for this unquestioning prejudice was "the loss of the essential meaning of the Gospels. For the truth found in the Gospels could be revealed only by reading these texts through a Jewish lens."[18]

The second and third generations of Christians, who tended to be gentiles, read these Jewish antecedents in the gospel story with a deeply prejudiced anti-Jewish bias that distorted the message of these books. The reasons for this developing bias are cultural and political. The Jewish War against Rome from AD 66 to 70, resulting in the fall of Jerusalem, with its destruction of the temple and the priesthood, raised the price of an uneasy accommodation between Jewish and gentile Christians and resulted, over the next twenty years, in a separation so total and hostile that the Jewish Christians were finally expelled from the synagogues.

Prior to the fateful year 70, Judaism tolerated varieties of opinions within its fold, pluralism always being a byproduct of security. Between years 30 and 70, Jewish followers of Jesus continued worshiping in the synagogues. These people, not yet called Christians, were called the "followers of the way" (Acts 9:2; 19:9, 23; 24:22; cf. 11:26). Before the fall of Jerusalem, it was quite clear that Jesus was being incorporated by Jewish people into their faith story. During that period, within the synagogues, Jewish Christians were at best an enriching new tradition and at worst a minor irritation. But when the survival of this faith tradition was at stake, their level of toleration dissipated perceptibly. Acrimony grew between Jews committed to Jesus and traditional Jews who claimed orthodoxy for their convictions, tying their claims to the belief that the God they worshiped could be found only in the unchanging completeness of the Torah. This shift into a survival mentality set the stage for heightened negativity to develop. After the fall of Jerusalem, many followers of Jesus, both Jewish and gentile, began to interpret the Roman defeat of the Jews and the loss of the temple as God's punishment of traditional Jews for their rejection of Jesus. Thus the stage was set for hostility. Echoes of this rising hostility can be found overtly in the gospels, particularly in Matthew (21:43; 23:31–38; 27:25). As rhetoric

17. Ibid., 34.
18. Ibid., 35.

heightened, the lines around what Jews could tolerate within Judaism tightened considerably so that Jewish Christians, offended by this increasing hostility, began to move more and more into gentile circles.

From that point on, fewer Christians wished to identify with the rigidly orthodox survival mentality that began to characterize Judaism, while fewer Jews wanted to see any aspect of the Jesus tradition left within their faith traditions. The final break occurred in the late 80s, when orthodox Jewish leaders revised their regular worship traditions to include "anathemas" against all who deviated from strict orthodox standards. This revision resulted in the excommunication of Jewish Christians from synagogue life and ultimately from Judaism. Because the gospel of Matthew was written during the expulsion and the gospel of John shortly thereafter, the fourth gospel's blatant negativity toward orthodox Jews (John 8:44) and its descriptions of exclusion from the synagogues reflect that final fracture (John 9:22; 12:42). By the start of the second century the expelled Jewish Christians faded into increasingly Hellenized and gentile circles, and thereafter Jewish Christians ceased even to think of themselves as Jews, while those who claimed Jewish identity became more firmly entrenched in their tradition. "The common ground between Jews and Christians, once so powerful, became nonexistent. This hostile negativity toward Jews and all things Jewish has remained dominant in Christianity to this day."[19]

The gentile reading of the gospels was challenged less and less, until the new way of reading the Hebrew scriptures became viewed as orthodoxy. That created finally the long historical period during which the gospels were cut away from their essential Jewishness. Ignorance joined with prejudice first to distort truth and understanding and then finally to lose altogether the original meaning of the gospels. This ignorance imposed on the gospel texts a non-Jewish literalness that their Jewish authors would never have understood or appreciated. Somewhere around the year AD 140, the status of the gospels as Jewish descended so low that a man named Marcion actually sought to remove the Hebrew God, every gospel except Luke, and anything else Jewish from Christianity. He failed officially, but succeeded, far more than Christians would recognize, unofficially. As a result of that unofficial success, the gospels were for centuries covered with a negativity to all things Jewish.

An example of this Christian negativity toward things Jewish is the way Christians use the Old Testament even to this day. The primary value the Hebrew sacred story has for most Christians lies in the assumption that the

---

19. Ibid., 53.

meaning of the Old Testament is exhausted once its task of pointing to and being fulfilled by the New Testament has been accomplished. The prophets were thought to be similar to fortunetellers who served as divine predictors of future events, primarily concerning the life and mission of Jesus.

In the early years of the Christian church, as Christianity spread westward, a spirit of anti-Jewish hatred developed and became so pervasive that the very idea of the gospels as the products of Jewish authors and as a Jewish gift to the world seemed both incomprehensible and even revolting. The Christian church locked itself into certain basic assumptions by which it lived and to which it admitted no challenge. Among these assumptions was that the Bible, especially the gospels, were objectively true, that they described events of literal history, and that one could confidently assert that all they contained did in fact happen just as written. This mentality produced a comfortable feeling of security enduring for centuries, until the Enlightenment, which gave birth to rationalism and modern science.

The fact we must acknowledge is that Christianity was not born as a Western religion. A Western mentality has been imposed on this Middle Eastern understanding of the Bible. This mentality, concentrating on an external world, is rooted in time, space, and objectivity. It always seeks to answer historical questions, such as "Is this real?" "Is this objectively true?" Guided by these questions, the Western mind has rarely embraced the truth found in myth, legend, intuition, or poetry. Western questions always require a "yes" or "no" answer. Only begrudgingly will Western mentality admit hesitantly to something. A hesitant "yes" answer is a compromise with both honesty and courage that only postpones the inevitable, while a "no" answer removes spirit, mystery, and meaning from any objective consideration. Thus in the post-Christian contemporary world the "yes" answer produces the passion of the religious right; the hesitant "yes" answer nudges conservatives toward liberalism; and the "no" answer produces the secular humanists, who want to be free of all things religious. We need a better alternative, for there is little hope and little future for the Christian faith in any of these.[20]

If we read the gospels through Western eyes, we end up with Western questions: "Did it really happen?" or "Is it true?" Jewish people, on the other hand, did not relate to sacred history as if it were an objective description of literal events. Instead of asking whether something actually happened, they asked, "What does it mean?" "Why was this image chosen to convey this insight?" Modern readers of the gospels, if they wish to

---

20. Ibid., 18–19.

remain true to the intentions of the Jewish originators of that tradition, need to abandon their Western concern about facts while focusing instead on entering the experience lying behind the description in the biblical text.

9

Understanding the Resurrection and Eternal Life

IN ORDER TO MAKE sense of the cross, the doctrine of salvation, and the doctrine of the afterlife, we need to begin with Easter, for Easter is central to Christianity. Whatever Easter was, it had incredible power. Before the Easter experience Jesus' followers forsook him and fled. After the Easter experience, they were willing to die for their conviction because whatever their understanding of God, it had to include Jesus of Nazareth. This shift in God consciousness revolutionized the theology of a group of Jewish people so dramatically that the world has never been the same. In addition, the Easter event led Jewish Christians to create Sunday, a new holy day, different from yet fulfilling the notion of the Jewish Sabbath.

The continued experience of God's presence in this community of faith was so real that in time even this experience was redefined. Through this definition the concept of the Holy Spirit and later the doctrine of the Trinity became the very cornerstone of the Christian faith. No matter how one understands the meaning of Jesus' resurrection and the message of Easter, there must be about it something real enough to account for these measurable effects.[1] But what really happened, and what does it mean?

When we examine the gospel accounts, which describe in some detail the event we call the resurrection, we find that the literal truth of the Easter narratives raises more questions than it answers. And so we dare to ask whether Paul and the authors who write about the resurrection, writers we call Mark, Matthew, Luke, and John, assumed the literal objective quality of the Easter stories as they described them. Is it possible, we must ask, to affirm the reality of the Easter experience without taking literally the details of the resurrection moment? This is a crucial and necessary

---

1. Spong, *Liberating the Gospels*, 278.

Understanding the Resurrection and Eternal Life

distinction. Were the gospel stories of Easter written to capture a literal description of something that actually happened? Can Easter be real without this kind of objectivity? Is it possible, as we discussed earlier, that the loss of a Jewish *haggadic* perspective toward sacred stories resulted in a distortion of the intended message?

When we look at the story of Jesus' life as the gospel writers portray it, particularly when they deal with the birth and death of Jesus, can we think that they intended their words to be understood literally? They were not writing history or biography. They were trying to interpret a life-changing experience that had been very real to them, but all they could use were limited human words. The gospel writers signaled this weakness of vocabulary to their readers by exaggerating their language to the point at which their words became literally absurd. The entire gospel narrative is illustrative of this, but it reaches a climax in the stories of Jesus' birth and death. "None of the details can be read literally, since they are so lacking in rational credibility."[2]

Symbolic language is obviously present in the story of Jesus' birth. Do virgins conceive? Do angels sing to shepherds? Do stars wander through the sky so slowly that magi can follow them? Would wise men travel with symbolic interpretive gifts for a newborn child, including myrrh as a sign of what that baby's eventual death would accomplish? Even in the first century these things would be recognized as the stuff of fairy tales, not unlike narratives of those who seek a pot of gold at the end of the rainbow.

The gospel narratives go on to relate accounts of Jesus walking on water, transforming five loaves of bread into enough food to feed multitudes, and even raise people from the dead. The narratives then culminate in tales describing the final events in Jesus' life. Were the graves of the "saints in Jerusalem" really opened by Jesus' death so that the bodies of those long deceased ones could rise up, be resuscitated, and walk the streets of that city in the sight of many (Matthew 27:52)? Were these ever meant to be literal stories, even in the first century, or is there something else going on in these narratives that we miss because we have for so long been taught to read them as historical?

Did the risen Jesus miraculously appear out of thin air to the two people on the road from Jerusalem to Emmaus and then just as miraculously disappear into thin air after they had recognized him in the sacrament of the broken bread (Luke 24:13–35)? Did the risen Jesus walk through locked doors and barred windows to get into that upper room

2. Spong, *Eternal Life*, 174.

Beyond Belief

to join his disciples at the time of the evening meal on the first day of the week following the crucifixion (John 20: 19-23)? If people really believed that Jesus could do that, why would the stone in front of the tomb have been a problem and thus why was angelic help needed to remove it?[3]

Once we get beyond the simple inadequacy of human language to describe the realm of the divine, we must then face the absolute contradictions present in the biblical texts of Easter. How many angels were at the tomb? Was it one, as Mark and Matthew state, or were there two angels, as Luke and John assert? Where were the disciples when the reality of Easter first dawned on the disciples? Mark and Matthew indicate that they were in Galilee. Luke directly contradicted this understanding, insisting that every appearance of the risen Christ occurred in Jerusalem or in its environs. Did the women see the risen Lord at the tomb at the dawn of Easter? No, said Mark; yes, said Matthew; no, said Luke; yes, said John, but it was not "the women" but only one woman, and her name was Mary.[4]

Was the resurrected body of Jesus physical? Matthew seemed to think so when he portrayed the women taking hold of the feet of Jesus (Matthew 28:9). Luke portrays Jesus as eating fish in the presence of the disciples and as inviting the disciples to handle him, claiming that a spirit does not have flesh and bones (Luke 24:39-43). Such descriptions sound quite physical. But in the Emmaus road account this body could appear out of thin air and disappear into thin air. John had the same internal conflict in his text. John's Jesus could walk into a locked room, but once inside he also offered his physical wounds for inspection (John 20:19-25). "Everywhere one turns in the biblical texts of Easter there is confusion, for assertions made in one gospel are contradicted in another."[5]

Next, we examine the order of resurrection appearances as given in 1 Corinthians 15:1-6. The first witness was Cephas (Peter), then the twelve, then five hundred witnesses, and last of all, Paul. In Mark, the first gospel to be written, there is no mention of an actual appearance of the risen Jesus. This gospel announces an anticipated reunion in an unspecified future (Mark 16:1-8). Matthew, writing more than twenty years after Paul, states that the first appearance was not to Cephas, but to the women in the garden. Later he describes an appearance to the eleven, not to the twelve, but he never relates an account of a moment when an appearance to Peter might have occurred (Matthew 28). Luke does affirm that Peter was the

---

3. This is a partial list taken from the discussion in Spong, ibid., 174-77.
4. Spong, *Liberating the Gospels*, 280-82.
5. Ibid., 283.

first (Luke 24:34); second in his listing, however, was not the appearance to the twelve, as Paul had asserted, but to an unknown man named Cleopas (Luke 24:13), who was traveling with a friend on the road to Emmaus. Only after this episode, according to Luke, did Jesus appear to the disciples (Luke 24:36). John, the last gospel to be written, mentions that the risen Christ appeared first to Mary Magdalene, and only second to the disciples, but not to all twelve, since both Thomas and Judas clearly were absent. No source in the biblical tradition corroborates Paul's mention of an appearance to five hundred brethren or to James.[6]

Ask yourself, if you are still confined to the literal sense of the story, why it was that though the Christian community attached great weight to the resurrection, no two accounts of it were alike? Also note why the described events are seen as taking place at the dawn of the day, and why the resurrection takes place privately and not publicly. Are we dealing, in these ancient biblical narratives, with a different level of reality and a different kind of language? How does one explore and seek to make rational sense out of experiences that occur at the edges of life? Do these questions not give us a clue that these writers were trying to say something that stretched ordinary human language beyond its normal limits? Surely these writers were aware that they were describing an internal, profoundly real and reorienting psychic and mystical experience that had altered human consciousness and, therefore, human history. Should we expend time and energy looking for proofs of the literalness of these details so that we can, first, convince ourselves that they are true, and then pass on that understanding to the next generation? Can our fear of death ever be transcended by these literalistic approaches? In each of the above-cited examples I would argue that the words were not, and were never intended to be, literal descriptions of real happenings, and that to treat them as if they were is to distort them.

So we revisit the question of how to read the resurrection accounts. What really happened, and what does resurrection mean?

Let's begin with the concept of resurrection itself, a widely misunderstood concept. According to biblical scholars, a crucial distinction must be made between two words that are often confused: resuscitation and resurrection. Resuscitation is used when someone believed to be dead comes back to life. Resuscitation involves resumption of previous existence. Such a person needs to eat and drink and sleep and will eventually die. Resurrection in a biblical context is a very different notion, for resurrection does

6. Ibid., 280–81.

not mean resumption of previous existence but entry into a new kind of existence. Resuscitation involves something happening to a corpse; resurrection need not. While resurrection could involve a corpse, it need not. Easter, therefore, is about resurrection, not resuscitation.[7]

How is this distinction important to Christianity? Doesn't the resurrection of Jesus involve physical resurrection? Not necessarily. The earliest New Testament discussion of the resurrection of Jesus is provided by Paul in 1 Corinthians 15. In the last half of the chapter, Paul addresses the question of what the resurrection body is like: "How are the dead raised? With what kind of body do they come?" (1 Corinthians 15:35). As Paul responds to that question, he uses an analogy from nature that emphasizes both continuity and discontinuity. The physical body is to the resurrection body as a seed is to a full-grown plant. The seed becomes the plant (continuity), but the full-grown plant looks radically different from the seed (discontinuity).

Then Paul distinguishes between two kinds of bodies; the translators use the terms "physical body" and "spiritual body" to translate what in the Greek language means literally "a body animated by soul" and "a body animated by spirit." According to what Paul says in the immediate context, the "body animated by soul" is what we typically mean by a physical body (he uses such expressions as "flesh and blood," "perishable," "of the earth," and "of dust"). The "body animated by spirit," on the other hand, is none of these things. While not all Christians agree, one possible conclusion that we can draw here is that the chapter strongly suggests that the resurrection body is not a physical body. If that is what Paul meant, it explains much of the confusion in the biblical record about the resurrection. It helps to explains why, for instance, Paul does not ground his resurrection belief upon an empty tomb. In fact, since Paul nowhere even mentions the empty tomb, scholars believe this explanation was not yet part of the record. According to this understanding, finding the corpse of Jesus would not disprove the resurrection, since Paul does not conceptualize resurrection in a bodily sense. It also helps to explain some of the contradictory information in the gospels, including whether the post-resurrection appearances involved visions of Jesus or actual physical sightings, as well as how the resurrected Jesus was said to be able to eat while having a body that could vanish at will.

To explain belief in the resurrection, we return to the threefold process we described in chapter 8 to construct theological meaning: (1) first

---

7. Borg, *Meaning of Jesus*, 131.

Understanding the Resurrection and Eternal Life

comes experience, then (2) metaphorical expression, and finally (3) conceptual formulation. In the beginning was experience. The early Christian conviction that "God raised Jesus from the dead" is so widespread in the New Testament that it has been called the earliest creed.[8] The first Christians, like the apostle Paul, had a firsthand experience of Jesus as a living spiritual reality after his death. In the book of Acts, Paul's "Damascus Road" experience is described three times. This experience was clearly a vision. The same can be said of the reference in 1 Corinthians 15:8, where Paul includes himself in a list of those to whom the risen Christ appeared; the language suggests a visionary experience. The core meaning of Easter is that Jesus continued to be experienced after his death, but in a radically new way, as a spiritual and divine reality.

A closely related factor is that the early church was charismatic, meaning that the first Christians experienced what they believed to be the Spirit of Jesus in their midst. At Pentecost the first Christian community experienced the Spirit as tongues of fire and a great rushing wind. The book of Acts as well as Paul's letters "portray Spirit-filled communities in which ecstatic experiences were common. These experiences were linked to Jesus, though the terminology for doing so was still fluid. Sometimes the risen Jesus is spoken of as the giver of the Spirit; sometimes the Spirit is spoken of as the Spirit of Jesus, or the Spirit of Christ; and sometimes Spirit, God, and Christ seem to be used interchangeably. Such fluidity of terminology is not surprising in the early decades of a new religious movement. Behind this fluidity lies a common conviction, however: the experience of the Spirit was understood as the abiding presence of Jesus."[9]

Christianity was evolving, a process requiring metaphorical and conceptual development, a process akin to what modern theologians call "remythologization." The Easter experience produced a transformed perception of Jesus leading to "the canonical Jesus" of the New Testament and "the creedal Jesus" of later Christianity. During the hundred years after Jesus' death in which New Testament traditions took shape, Christian communities used many metaphors or images (mostly drawn from the Hebrew Bible) to speak about Jesus and his significance, images such as Suffering Servant, Son of God, messiah, savior, great high priest, and Word of God. Over time, these metaphors became the subject of intellectual reflection, some of which became doctrine.

---

8. Borg, *God We Never Knew*, 92.
9. Ibid., 94.

Beyond Belief

Christians also built upon Jewish apocalyptic expectation that the world was about to end. Many Jews believed the final sign of the end would be the arrival of the messiah and the resurrection of the dead, and Christians from the very beginning believed the resurrection of Jesus was that sign, the "first fruits" of that expected apocalyptic resurrection (1 Corinthians 15:20). Some Jews even expected the end would shortly follow the death of the messiah (Daniel 9:25–27). Such a process produced the "Christ of faith" of Christian tradition.

In his book *Resurrection: Myth or Reality?* Bishop Spong argues that a considerable length of time must be placed between the events of Good Friday and the experience of Easter.[10] The reality of Easter, whatever it was, broke into the consciousness of the disciples after they had fled to Galilee. So Easter was not originally a Jerusalem phenomenon at all, but a Galilean one. Thus Easter may well have been the experience that finally interpreted the crucifixion for the earliest Christians, but it should not be located historically in the same moment of time. It took time for Christians to process their experience of the death of Jesus, time to metaphorize and conceptualize it.

To understand what happened at Easter and what it meant to the earliest Christians, we must entertain the possibility that while the experience of Easter was profoundly real, the biblical descriptions of that moment are both mythological and even legendary. In addition, we need to consider the possibility that the resurrection narratives found in the gospels, like so many other details of the Jesus story, are midrashic interpretations of an "event" that human words could never really capture.

The symbol of three days for the period of time between the death and resurrection of Jesus can be quite instructive in this regard. The biblical symbol is radically unstable if literalized. The gospels use a wide array of expressions, including "after three days," "on the third day," "three days and three nights," and on the "first day of the week," to speak of the Easter event. That is not a consistent record of counting chronological time, nor should it be understood that way. The expression, rather, was a symbolic measure familiar to the Jews. For the Jews, when the end of the world came, all life would die in the climactic battle of Armageddon. Then the still of darkness and death would reign over the earth for three days. Finally, at dawn, after three days, the kingdom of God would descend from the sky to inaugurate the reign of God on earth. That dawning would usher in the first day of the new creation. It is not difficult to

---

10. Spong, *Resurrection: Myth or Reality?*, particularly chapters 19 and 20.

envision how Jewish Christians might take this symbolism and relate it to the end of Jesus' life, applying the post-Armageddon darkness to his death on the cross (Mark 15:33) and the symbolic three days in Jewish mythology to the time between his death and resurrection. Of course, as time passed, it was misunderstood by those gentile Christians who read the text literally without understanding the Jewish symbolism embedded in the phrase "three days." Gentile readers would not have been aware of the Jewish tradition concerning the end of the world. This mythological interpretive language was later thought by non-Jewish Western gentiles to be a literal description of what happened, something the gospel writers would not have imagined.[11]

Jesus was crucified; that is history. "When it was noon, darkness came over the whole land until three in the afternoon" (Mark 15:33); that is mythology (compare Amos 8:9–10). The symbol of three days in the tomb is also interpretive mythology. The followers of Jesus, known as the Way, soon combined the reality of their experience of Jesus with the hopes, dreams, aspirations, and legends of the Jews. "The Risen Christ would come to his Temple in glory. That was a hope vested in the Son of Man since Maccabean times, from the time of the book of Daniel (c. 165 BC). The veil in the Temple would be split from top to bottom. That was a detail that Matthew added to the developing legend (Matthew 27:51). It symbolized that when the perfect sacrifice was offered, the barriers that kept human beings from approaching God were obliterated. It was once again a powerful interpretive image, but not a literal one."[12]

Matthew added an earthquake to his resurrection story (compare Zechariah 14:5), as he had to the moment when Jesus died. For the Jews an earthquake frequently accompanied a divine revelation. Matthew also adds an account of a general resurrection of the dead (Matthew 27:51–53), a tale adapted from the tradition, drawing both from Ezekiel 37 (the vision of the valley of dry bones) and Zechariah 14:4–5 (which foretells the splitting of a mountain, mentions an earthquake, and prophesies the appearance of "the holy ones"). That too is interpretive rather than history.

The farther removed in time are the resurrection accounts from the experience itself, the more the mystery and wonder have been replaced by objective accounts and physical proofs. Converted one to six years after the crucifixion, Paul gives us no narrative details, saying only that Peter was the first to see the resurrected Jesus and that, according to his own

---

11. Spong, *Liberating the Gospels*, 297–98.
12. Ibid., 299–300.

list, he himself was the last (1 Corinthians 15:1–8). Mark, writing in the late 60s or early 70s, has Jesus appear to no one; rather, a messenger informs the disciples that Jesus is alive and will go before them into Galilee. Matthew, writing in the early 80s, says that the disciples did see Jesus in Galilee, but what they saw was not a resuscitated Jesus but a glorified being who appears instantaneously, as though traveling on the clouds, spelling out the mission that his disciples must embrace in the words we now call the Great Commission. Luke, writing in the late 80s, and John, writing in the 90s, make the resurrected Jesus so physical that they portray him as eating, walking, talking, teaching, interpreting scripture, and offering his body for inspection to demonstrate its physical, resuscitated nature. As the stories grew, they became simultaneously more supernatural and miraculous yet more physical and objective.[13]

Using metaphor, legend, midrash, and tradition, we move from experience to meaning. The Easter story of Jesus' resurrection was thus not an action that occurred in history, though when embraced, its effects were historical. It was not an event that occurred three days after the crucifixion. It was rather a window through which the timeless reality of love could be seen, understood as the love of God incarnate in Jesus of Nazareth.

The truth of Jesus cannot be captured by any human tale, for his life was and is of God, and the life of God can never be entered with the words and stories of human beings. The essence of Easter goes actually far beyond angels, tombs, messengers, and apparitions. All of those traditions and legends developed well after the primal experience of Easter had broken into the human consciousness. He was crucified. That is the one objective historical truth in the creeds. All else in the creeds is but commentary on who it was who was crucified and what his life meant and means. Death could not contain him.

So it was "in accordance with the scriptures" that he was raised. That text was the original invitation to seek the truth of Jesus in symbol and story. For it is not the description of the experience of Easter, but the experience itself, that beckons us. The experience of Easter is timeless; the description is always time-bound and therefore transitory. The Jewish way into that experience was to search the timeless scriptures, locating a meaning provided in the symbols and the stories of their sacred past. But that discovery could be actualized only if these stories and symbols remained open-ended, only if they were vehicles through which one journeyed into the mystery, the wonder, and the wordlessness of Life.

13. Spong, *Eternal Life*, 181–82.

Understanding the Resurrection and Eternal Life

What was it that the gospel writers were trying to convey? What did "experiencing Jesus alive" mean to them? Although we can never penetrate this curtain of mystery for certain, we know that something happened to their understanding of God. Something also happened to their understanding of Jesus. In the process, something happened to the disciples' understanding of themselves. These changes were objective and real with distinct and recognizable consequences. The Jesus-experience, which called and empowered them to live, to love, and to be in new ways, now defined them. The spirit present in Jesus was the power of his life calling them into a newly expanded consciousness that moved them away from fear of life and fear of domination by a vindictive external God to a recognition that the divine and the human were not separate, since the human was the vessel in which the divine lived.

Paul said in Galatians (1:16) that God had been revealed "in" him, though the English translators, still under the influence of supernatural theism with its external deity, translate the Greek preposition *ev* not as "in," as normally understood, but by the word "to," so that readers might view the revelation as coming to him from the external deity instead of being "in" him, "where all consciousness-shifts are inevitably located."[14]

Having examined the Easter event and the topic of the resurrection, our theological journey brings us finally to consider the subject of "eternal life." When Jesus was quoted in John's gospel as saying that he had come to give others life, and give it abundantly (10:10), he was speaking of eternal life as a present reality. He was divulging his grandest teaching: We already have eternal life. Jesus affirmed it and his immediate followers confirmed that the kingdom of God was a present reality, here and now (Luke 17:21). The human quest for eternal life is not based on the claim that one might live after death, but rather on an awareness that self-conscious human life already shares in the eternity of God. Eternal life is experienced in the present to the degree that one is in communion with that life-enhancing power of love we call God. Meister Eckhart, the medieval mystic, claimed that the highest parting for humans comes when "for God's sake we take leave of God." While we cannot be sure what Eckhart had in mind, one way to construe his enigmatic expression is to shift our image of God from one who is external to recognizing that we are a part of who God is. To embrace this recognition is to experience what the Bible calls "eternal life."

---

14. Ibid., 184.

Part Four

Reconciling Science and Religion

> Science without religion is lame,
> religion without science is blind.
>
> —ALBERT EINSTEIN, PHYSICIST

The only way in which the present split between religion and science could be mended would be through the acceptance by science of the fact and value of religion as an organ of evolving man, and the acceptance by religion that religions must evolve if they are not to become extinct, or at best turn into outdated living fossils struggling to survive in a new and alien environment.

—SIR JULIAN HUXLEY, EVOLUTIONARY BIOLOGIST; HUMANIST

10

Science and Religion: Three Views

ABOUT A CENTURY AND a half ago Charles Darwin's remarkable theory of evolution came into the Western world, says Andrew Dickson White, "like a plough into an anthill."[1] The religious and intellectual worlds of the nineteenth century, not prepared for Darwin, went scurrying in a variety of directions. Even now, at the start of a new millennium, religious believers are still reeling from the shock Darwin apparently delivered to many traditional beliefs.

Thoughtful, modern Christians find themselves caught in a web of questions, affected by the findings of contemporary science, many of them without adequate resolution. What is the place of religion in an age of science? Has science made religion intellectually implausible? Can one believe in God today? If so, what views of God are consistent with the scientific understanding of the world? Need we any longer hold that the world is created by God? Are humans really intended to be here? Has biology shown that life and mind are reducible to chemistry, thus rendering illusory the notions of soul and spirit? How can the search for meaning and purpose in life be fulfilled in the kind of world disclosed by science? These questions make up the so-called "problem of science and religion," one of the most fascinating, important, and challenging controversies of our time. They remain very much alive in our society and continue to evoke an interesting range of responses.

For many centuries in the West, the Christian story of creation and salvation provided a cosmic setting in which individual life had significance. It allowed people to come to terms with guilt, finitude, and death. It provided a total way of life, encouraging personal transformation and reorientation. Since the Enlightenment, the Christian story has had diminishing effectiveness for many people, partly because it has seemed

---

1. Cited by Haught in *Responses to 101 Questions*, 5.

inconsistent with the understanding of the world in modern science. Much of humanity has turned to science-based technology as a source of fulfillment and hope. Technology has offered power, control, entertainment, and the prospect of overcoming our helplessness and dependency. However, for all its benefits, technology is limited and cannot provide the promised personal fulfillment or social well-being.

The idea of evolution, a central topic of concern in this final section, is not necessarily troublesome to religious people, although it forces religious people to rethink their answers to many of life's big questions. Awareness that things change cumulatively over time and that life in some way "evolves" is longstanding and widely acknowledged in the Christian tradition. Rather, it is Charles Darwin's version of evolution that has been so disturbing.

Theologian John F. Haught offers the following explanation. Darwinian evolution is troublesome because (1) it offers a whole *new story of creation*, one that seems to conflict with the biblical accounts; (2) its notion of natural selection appears to diminish, if not eliminate, *the role of God* in creating the diverse forms of life; (3) its theory of human descent from "lower" forms of life appears to question age-old beliefs in *human uniqueness and ethical distinctiveness*; (4) its emphasis on the prominent *role of chance* in evolution seems to destroy the notion of *divine providence*; (5) it seems to rob the universe of *purpose* and human life of any permanent significance; and (6) for many Christians, Darwin's account of human origins seems to conflict with the notion of *original sin* or the "Fall," and therefore removes any need for a savior.[2]

Theology is only now coming to grips with Darwinian evolution. Even in the West, where many religious thinkers have given at least theoretical assent to Darwinian science, only a few have ever taken a long and deliberate look at it. And even those who claim to have faced up to the theory of evolution have often edited out some of its most objectionable features. When they have not rejected Darwinian ideas outright, theologians have mostly ignored them, content to nod at the platitude that "evolution is God's way of creating."[3]

To a great extent, theologians still think and write almost as though Darwin had never lived. Their attention remains fixed primarily on the human world and its unique concerns. The nuances of biology or of cosmology have not yet deeply affected current thinking about God and

---

2. Ibid.
3. Haught, *God After Darwin*, 1.

God's relation to the world. Although the ecological crisis has brought the natural world back into view for many sensitive people today, the story of nature's evolution is still not a consuming interest for most religious scholars, let alone for the general population of religious believers.[4]

Scientific skeptics, of course, decided long ago that the only reasonable option Darwin leaves us is that of a totally godless universe. According to American philosopher Daniel Dennett, Darwin's theory of evolution by natural selection is a "dangerous idea," particularly threatening to religious believers because it challenges any hope that the universe is here for a reason. Evolutionary science is said to contradict traditional religious intuitions that life and human existence were planned from all eternity. Dennett's depiction of evolution follows closely that of the well-known British zoologist Richard Dawkins, who has argued that blind chance and natural selection working over long periods of time can alone account for life's creativity.

That theology survives at all after Darwin is to some evolutionists a most puzzling anachronism. If atheism is the logical corollary of evolutionary science, then the day of religion and theology is surely over. But such a judgment is hardly warranted. As it turns out, an appreciation of Darwin's revolution, with its troubling picture of life and its origins, may considerably deepen and widen our understanding of God.

Utilizing the notion of "a hierarchy of explanations," namely that most phenomena can be explained from numerous levels that make sense at their own level, we will take an approach that in this universe, as in all of life, various explanations can coexist without contradicting or competing with one another. Take cellular DNA, for example, one of the richest instances of complexity we can find in nature; as Haught explains: "DNA can be understood quite well at the level of chemistry. At another level, DNA can be understood by the geneticist in terms of its hereditary properties, features that don't interest chemistry as such. And at a still higher level, DNA can also be interpreted by the Darwinian biologist as the fundamental unit of natural selection. Each of these levels can enrich our understanding of life. The evolutionist, moreover, does not have to be an expert in the 'lower' levels (for example, biochemistry) in order to understand the role DNA survival plays in the origin of species. There is a legitimate autonomy in each of the sciences."[5]

Accepting the idea of a hierarchy of explanations, the famous Harvard biologist Ernst Mayr nevertheless claims that Darwinian evolution

---

4. Ibid., 2.
5. Haught, *Responses to 101 Questions*, 58.

provides the "ultimate" explanation of life. Similarly Dawkins accepts in principle the notion of a hierarchy of explanations. Nevertheless he too resorts to a singular explanation, arguing that gene-survival is all that is going on when evolution brings about complex instances of design. Superfluous is any recourse to allegedly "higher" or deeper levels of explanation. Noting their inconsistency, Haught argues that theology can also legitimately claim its place, at another level of the hierarchy, in the explanation of life. To do so should not intrude competitively into the various levels of scientific explanation, as Dennett and Dawkins maintain, as though theology provides a "better" explanation. Rather, when theology claims that the ultimate explanation of evolution is divine creativity, it should do so without in any way disturbing the integrity of the various sciences. "Theologically speaking, the fact that God wants the universe to unfold in an extravagantly creative way does not abolish the chemical, genetic, and evolutionary accounts of life."[6]

Science and Religion: Contemporary Models

What philosopher Alfred North Whitehead stated in 1925 still holds true today: "When we consider what religion is for mankind, and what science is, it is no exaggeration to say that the future course of history depends upon the decision of this generation as to the relations between them. We have here the two strongest general forces . . . which influence men, and they seem to be set one against the other—the force of our religious institutions, and the force of our own impulse to accurate observation and logical deduction."[7]

Examining the spectrum of contemporary views, Ian Barbour identifies four distinct ways in which science and religion can be related to each other:[8]

1. Conflict—the conviction that science and religion are fundamentally irreconcilable;

2. Independence—the claim that there can be no genuine conflict since religion and science are each responding to radically different questions;

3. Dialogue—an approach that affirms interaction and looks for possible "consonance" between the disciplines, especially for ways in which science shapes religious and theological understanding;

6. Ibid.
7. Whitehead, *Science and the Modern World*, 181–82.
8. Barbour, *Religion and Science*, 77–105.

4. Integration—a perspective that highlights the ways in which, at a deep level, religion supports and nourishes the entire scientific enterprise.

John Haught reduced the options to three distinct types: opposition, separation, and engagement.[9]

Opposition (Conflict)

Many scientific thinkers are quite certain that religion can never be reconciled with science. They question how one can be a scientist and honestly be religious at the same time, at least in the sense of believing in God. Science seems to provide the only reliable path to knowledge. Many people view science as objective, universal, rational, and based on solid observational evidence. Religion, by contrast, seems to be subjective, parochial, emotional, and based on traditions or authorities that disagree with each other. Religion, they argue, cannot demonstrate the truth of its ideas in a straightforward way, whereas science can. Religion, without providing any concrete evidence of God's existence, requires faith. Science, on the other hand, is willing to test its hypotheses and theories. Religion cannot do this in a way that is satisfactory to an impartial witness, skeptics claim, so there must be a "conflict" between the scientific and the religious ways of understanding.

Within the Opposition camp there are several viewpoints, unanimous in their claim that religion and science are irreconcilable and mutually antagonistic in their assessment of which option provides an ultimate explanation of reality. They can be examined under two broad categories: scientific materialism, also known as "scientism" (characterized by a mindset in which the scientific method is the only reliable path to knowledge), and biblical literalism (characterized by a mindset in which religious faith and scripture always trump evidence). While both represent the opposite ends of the theological spectrum, they share various characteristics in common. Both believe that there are serious conflicts between contemporary science and classical religious beliefs. Both seek knowledge with a sure foundation—that of logic and sense data, on the one hand, that of infallible scripture, on the other. They both claim that science and theology make rival literal statements about the same domain—the history of nature—so that one must choose between them. Both represent a misuse of science. The scientific materialist starts from science but ends

---

9. Haught, *God After Darwin*, 24.

up making broad philosophical claims. The biblical literalist moves from theology to make claims about scientific matters. Both fail to respect the differences between the two disciplines. The idea that science is locked in eternal combat with religion is an understandable reaction to the common practice of confusing their respective roles.

The next position, separation, explores a major alternative to the two extremes of scientific materialism and biblical literalism.

Separation (Contrast)

One way to avoid conflicts between science and religion is to view the two realms as totally independent and autonomous. Each has its own domain and its characteristic methods. Proponents of this view say there are two jurisdictions and each must tend to its own business and not meddle in the affairs of the other. The task of science is *descriptive*, answering "what," "how," and "what is" questions, whereas the task of religion is *prescriptive*, dealing with questions of value, purpose, destiny, and ultimate origin, in other words, answering "who," "why," and "what ought to be" questions.

Because it keeps distinctions clean, the separatist approach appeals to theologians and scientists alike. On the surface, at least, it allows the substance of theism to remain untouched by evolution, while at the same time it forbids religion and theology to intrude into the business of science. The distinction, however, appears shallow. Can religious thought remain utterly unaffected by evolution? Do not the randomness, struggle, and impersonality of the evolutionary process decisively refute theism, as the scientific skeptics have argued? Can we separate our theological convictions from what seem to be the spiritually devastating implications of evolutionary science?[10]

If science and religion were totally independent, the possibility of conflict would be avoided, but the possibility of constructive dialogue and mutual enrichment would also be ruled out. Life, on the whole, cannot be so neatly divided into separate compartments, since it is experienced in wholeness and interconnectedness.

In the end, any adequate treatment of science and religion requires that, without giving in to temptations to conflate them anew, as occurred in the West during premodern times, we focus on ways in which they concretely affect each other.

---

10. Ibid., 28.

Engagement (Contact)

A third, more harmonious option, views science and religion as interdependent; both are needed, and both are here to stay. It is my contention that the time for ambivalence, suspicion, and animosity is over. Our world can no longer afford an adversarial stance between them. We have too many other battles to fight, too many common foes to defeat. Starting from an attitude of respect and collegiality, science and theology need to engage fully with one another, beginning with conversation and, using the language of love, move to infatuation and then to passionate embrace; the two need to become lovers. In this segment we will build on commonalities between science and religion, understanding that science needs to harness the faith, passion, and commitment of religion and that religion must learn to embrace the contributions of science and consider Darwin's "idea" not so much a danger as a great gift. Evolution, according to this third approach, can awaken in theology a fresh way of thinking about the central claims of traditional theistic faith.

Methodological Parallels between Science and Religion

Recent philosophical discussions of the nature of science have called into question sharp contrasts between religion and science. Science, it appears, is not as pure and objective as we used to think, nor religion as subjective. Both science and theology generate imaginative metaphors and theories to interpret certain kinds of "data," but in neither case is it always clear just where metaphor or theory leaves off and "fact" begins. Indeed, the consensus of philosophers today is that there are no uninterpreted facts. And so we are now more aware than ever before that in both science and religion there is an aspect of human "construction" that we previously failed to notice.

Recent examinations of the culturally and historically conditioned nature of scientific understanding, for example, make us question whether we can simply assume science to be the pure model of objectivity that scientific textbooks make it. A sizeable literature exists on the scientific method, but there is little consensus among authors. This does not mean that scientists do not know what they are doing. Doing and explaining may be two different things. Scientists agree, however, that the following elements are involved in thinking scientifically:

Induction: Forming a hypothesis by drawing general conclusions from existing data.

Deduction: Making specific predictions based on the hypotheses.

Observation: Gathering data, driven by hypotheses that indicate what to look for.

Verification: Testing the predictions against further observations to confirm or falsify the initial hypotheses.

This process constitutes the core of what philosophers of science call *the hypothetico-deductive method*. It is not possible to say which came first, the observation or the hypothesis, since the two are inseparably interactive. The process is a constant interaction of making observations, drawing conclusions, making predictions, and checking them against evidence. And data-gathering is not made in a vacuum. The hypotheses shape what sorts of observations one makes of nature, and these hypotheses are themselves shaped by one's education, culture, and particular biases as an observer. According to the science historian Michael Shermer, "There is no question but that science is heavily influenced by the culture in which it is embedded."[11]

Scientific data are theory-laden, not theory-free. Theoretical assumptions enter the selection, reporting, and interpretation of what are taken to be data. Moreover, theories do not arise from logical analysis of data but from acts of creative imagination in which analogies and models often play roles. Conceptual models help scientists to imagine what is not directly observable. Many of these same characteristics are present in religion. If the data of religion include religious experience, rituals, and scriptural texts, such data are even more heavily laden with conceptual interpretations. In religious language, metaphors and models are also present. Clearly, religious beliefs are not amenable to strict empirical testing, but they can be approached with some of the same spirit of inquiry found in science.

Science does not lead to certainty, for its conclusions remain incomplete, tentative, and subject to revision. Theories change over time, and we should expect current theories to be modified or overturned, as previous ones have been. But science does offer reliable techniques for testing and evaluating theories. Ian Barbour mentions four such procedures:

---

11. Shermer, *Why People Believe Weird Things*, 41.

(1) *agreement with data*;

(2) *coherence* or consistency with other accepted theories;

(3) *comprehensiveness* of scope, applicable to wide ranges of relevant variables and supported by a variety of kinds of evidence; and

(4) *fertility* or future promise in providing the framework for ongoing research.[12]

Interestingly, the assessment of beliefs within a religious community can be undertaken using the same criteria listed for scientific theories, though the criteria are applied somewhat differently.

1. *Agreement with Data*: religious beliefs must provide a faithful rendition of the areas of experience that are taken by the community to be especially significant. The primary data are individual religious experience, communal story, and ritual.

2. *Coherence*: consistency with other accepted beliefs ensures the continuity of a tradition. The polity (standards) and religious beliefs (doctrinal statement) of the community provide protection against individualism and arbitrariness. However, due to reformulation and reinterpretation, the ideas of religious communities have undergone considerable change throughout history.

3. *Scope*: religious beliefs can be extended beyond the primary data to interpret other kinds of human experience, particularly other aspects of our personal and social lives. In a scientific age, these need to be consistent with proven scientific findings. Religious beliefs can contribute to a coherent worldview and a comprehensive metaphysics.

4. *Fertility*: In science, theories are judged partly by their promise for encouraging an ongoing research program. Because religion involves a greater diversity of activities and serves functions quite different from those of science, fertility here has many dimensions. At the personal level, religious beliefs can be judged by their power to effect personal transformation and the integration of personality. They should have the capacity to inspire and sustain compassion and create love. They should be relevant to urgent issues of our day, such as environmental degradation, and should promote social, gender, sexual, and racial equality.[13]

---

12. Barbour, *Religion and Science*, 109.
13. Ibid., 113.

Beyond Belief

Religious Experience

As previously noted, the basic structure of religion is similar to that of science in some respects, though it differs at several crucial points. Whereas scientific concepts and theories rely on corroboration from particular observations and experimental data, the data for a religious community consist of the distinctive experiences of individuals plus the stories and rituals of a religious tradition. In all authentic religions, religious experience is primary, but it is always interpreted by a set of concepts and beliefs. These concepts and beliefs are not the product of logical reasoning from the data; they result instead from acts of creative imagination in which, as in science, analogies and models are prominent. Models are also drawn from the stories of a tradition. Models, in turn, lead to abstract concepts and articulated beliefs systematically formalized as theological doctrines.

Barbour identifies six distinctive types of religious experience that recur in a variety of traditions around the world:

1. *Numinous Experience of the Holy*: persons in many cultures have described a sense of awe and reverence, mystery and wonder, holiness and sacredness. Here individuals typically express awareness of their dependence, finitude, limitation, and contingency. The experience is often interpreted in terms of a personal model of the divine.

2. *Mystical Experience of Unity*: mystics in many traditions have spoken of the experience of unity, found in the depth of the individual soul and in the world of nature. Achieved in the discipline of meditation, unity is characterized by joy, harmony, serenity, and peace. In its extreme form unity may be described as selfless loss of individuality and joy as bliss or rapture. The numinous and the mystical seem to be the most common types of religious experience around the world.

3. *Transformative Experience of Reorientation*: in the lives of some individuals, acknowledgement of guilt has been followed by the experience of forgiveness. Others have described a transition from brokenness and estrangement to wholeness and reconciliation. Such reorientation and renewal, whether sudden or gradual, may lead to self-acceptance, liberation from self-centeredness, openness to new possibilities in life, a greater sensitivity to other persons, or perhaps dedication to a style of life based on radical trust and love.

4. *Courage in Facing Suffering and Death*: suffering, death, and transiency are universal human experiences, responses to which are found in virtually every religious tradition. Meaninglessness is overcome when

people view human existence in a wider context, beyond the life of the individual. Attitudes toward suffering and death are affected when trust replaces anxiety (in the West), or when detachment replaces the attachment that gives suffering and death their power over us (in the East). Such experiences can be described psychologically, but in religious traditions they are understood in relation to a view of ultimate reality beyond the individual.

5. *Moral Experience of Obligation*: many people have felt moral demands overriding their own inclinations. Though the voice of conscience is in part the product of social conditioning, it may also lead persons to express judgment on their culture or moral outrage in the face of evil, even at the risk of death. Judgments of good and evil, right and wrong, are made in the light of one's view of the nature of ultimate reality.

6. *Awe in Response to Order and Creativity in the World*: at the intellectual level, the presence of order and creativity in nature has served as the basis for inferring a divine source of order, beauty, and novelty. At the experiential level, people have responded to the world with reverence, appreciation, gratitude for life, and with wonder that nature has a rational order intelligible to our minds.[14]

Although such experiences sometimes appear private and individual, traditionally they occur in the context of a community. If the task of the theologian is systematic reflection on the life and thought of the religious community, this will include critical assessment according to the fourfold set of criteria that religion shares with the scientific community.

Story in Christianity: The Necessity of Myth

In addition to experience, religious tradition includes additional data, namely a set of stories and rituals.[15] Traditions are transmitted primarily through stories and their reenactment in rituals, rather than through abstract concepts and doctrinal beliefs. Before they were recorded in scriptures, religious stories were products of experiences and events, interpreted imaginatively. Scholars of religion often use the term "myths" to refer to the central narratives of a religious tradition, insisting that the term does not imply any judgment either for or against the historicity or validity of the narratives.

14. Ibid., 111–12.
15. The material in this segment is adapted from Barbour, ibid., 114–15.

Beyond Belief

The central religious myths are understood to manifest the character of the cosmic order and our relationship to it. Significant in personal and communal life because they endorse particular ways of ordering experience, myths provide exemplary patterns for human actions. Such narratives inform us about ourselves; our self-identity as individuals and as communities is in part constituted by these narratives. They are recalled in liturgy and acted out in ritual. Past events become present (re-presented) in symbolic reenactment. For example, creation stories portray the essential structures of reality and the cosmic context for human existence; other stories exhibit a saving power in human life that can overcome some of its flaws or distortions. The power to transform life and restore relationships may be expressed in a personal redeemer or in a law or discipline to be followed.

Three central stories are re-presented in Christianity:

1. *The Creation of the World*: the opening chapters of Genesis set human life in a framework of significance and meaning. They portray a world that is good, orderly, and coherent. They picture a God who is free, transcendent, and purposeful. These theological affirmations are conveyed through a dramatic narrative, which assumes a prescientific cosmology. The creation account is the basis for gratitude for the created order, celebrated in the liturgy of ancient psalms and modern prayers and hymns. A view of creation also affects care toward nature and appropriate ways in which to treat the environment.

2. *The Covenant with Israel*: the Exodus stories of liberation from captivity and the giving of Torah at Sinai are central in Judaism but are also significant in Christian identity. Here the community's existence is understood as response to a God who is liberator and redeemer as well as creator. The biblical narratives are connected to historical events, but as they appear in scripture they involve centuries of elaboration and interpretation.

3. *The Life of Christ*: the most important stories for the Christian community recount the life, teachings, death, and resurrection of Christ. These narratives, historically based but inescapably involving interpretation, are central to individual and communal religious identity. The most prominent ritual (Eucharist) and festivals (Christmas and Easter) celebrate and re-present crucial portions of this story. Pentecost celebrates the continuing activity of God as Holy Spirit.

"The data of religion, then, are the characteristic experiences, stories, and rituals of particular religious communities. Often the early memories of formative experiences and events are recorded in scriptures, to which members of the community respond in later generations, adding new layers of experience and ritual. Systematic concepts, beliefs, and doctrines are elaborated and reformulated to interpret these primary religious phenomena."[16]

Science and the Cosmic Story

In 1930 the famous British physicist James Jeans wrote that modern science paints a distressing picture of a universe hostile to life and consciousness, one destined for death at the hands of entropy. Entropy, as he understood it, indicated that the universe was either indifferent or hostile to life, for all human aspirations were but doomed to final frustration. No question in science and religion is more to the point, or strikes more directly at the heart of human concerns, than that of cosmic purpose. And if the universe holds no purpose overall, what does this say about who we are and about what sort of individual destiny awaits us?

Once again we need to affirm that the particular discoveries of science cannot but have a bearing on the question of cosmic purpose.[17] In an age of evolutionary biology and Big Bang physics, science has helped people of faith to widen their teleological outlook. In moving us away from narrow concepts of the cosmos, scientific discoveries are causing us to change in significant ways our understanding of God as well as to abandon unduly narrow concepts of God's designs. As the understanding of science has expanded, theology has been challenged to move away from its formerly naïve, and generally anthropocentric, articulations of nature's possible purpose.

Scientific developments during the past century and a half—including the results of evolutionary biology, particle and relativity physics, astronomy and Big Bang physics, and chaos theory (the fact of a self-organizing universe)—now make it possible for us to think of the cosmos as an unfolding story. And since it is in the form of story that religions have always expressed meaning, it is not inconceivable that we can assimilate the scientific story of the universe to the narrative pattern that has always

---

16. Ibid., 115.

17. The material in this segment is adapted from Haught, *Science and Religion*, 172–80.

Beyond Belief

shaped our religious consciousness. In particular, the major ingredients of the new cosmology can be meaningfully contextualized by the story of promise and hope through which Abrahamic religious tradition has already shaped our way of looking at the world.

Until recently science has been somewhat abstract and law-oriented. It has not taken into account the story underlying the laws. And as long as the universe was seen as essentially storyless—as unoriginated, eternal, and necessary—it was not difficult for science to think of it as pointless. Nowadays, however, much of that thought has changed. The laws of nature are no longer viewed as the offspring of an underlying eternal necessity but as the contingent outcome of a definite story with a definite past. We do not yet know all there is to know about the origin of the cosmos, for example, but at least we can say that it is no longer completely lost in the fog of an eternally remote past. Although we cannot absolutely rule out the possibility that there could have been "many worlds" prior to this one, it is sufficient for our purposes to begin with the singularity of the Big Bang; this gives our universe a relatively clear point of origin.

If, then, the cosmos has a finite past, its evolutionary unfolding can be expressed in a narrative form. And if the cosmos is fundamentally a story, then it is inevitable that we think about the "point" of it all. As we humans question the purpose of our existence, it is proper to think of our purpose in the larger scheme of things. Although we do not expect our search to terminate in any clear conclusion about the larger "point" of the universe story, science has recently brought to our attention some surprising ways in which the cosmic story corresponds with the basic religious sense of reality as rooted in a promise that invites from us the response of hope.

Nature, it seems, can be viewed as having always been pregnant with promise. From the first moments of the cosmic dawn, for example, the physical organization of matter already fell within the almost unimaginably narrow range of numerical possibilities that would allow it to become hydrogen atoms, galactic clusters, supernovas, carbon, life, and eventually minds. The various episodes in this amazing story all developed in ways that could never have been anticipated. Science confesses that it could never have predicted such outcomes at the time of cosmic beginnings. And who knows what outcomes may yet be found within the billions of years of evolution that probably lie ahead.

Even entropy is now being given a new reading.

> Instead of signaling only the heat death of the universe, entropy is now positively embraced as an essential condition for matter

to realize new possibilities. For without an entropic cosmic tendency toward disassembling or fragmentation, the most primitive forms of order would have dominated indefinitely, keeping the world stuck in an inflexible sameness from age to age. There would have been no room for emergent complexity, since the cosmos would have permanently solidified into triviality. Without entropy . . . matter could not realize its promise. Entropy guarantees that the cosmic story will avoid repeating forever the same refrains, and permits it to wend its way toward an always open and often surprising experimentation with novelty. It is such openness to an indeterminate future that the new scientific accounts of the universe are now setting before us. A theology that makes contact with this cosmic openness will be immeasurably enriched.[18]

Material reductionism, on the other hand, still tries to suppress the obvious fact of nature's inherent openness. In its obsession to explain emergent new phenomena (such as living beings and thinking humans) only from the bottom up, or only in terms of already mastered principles of chemistry and physics, reductionism ignores any appreciation of the world's future indeterminacy. Rooted in this sterile reductionism, matter is forced to be eternal or necessary so that the cosmos cannot open itself up to a truly new and creative future.

The cosmic future seems more open today than it has at any time since the birth of modern science. A promissory universe, then, such as we have sketched, makes room once again in a scientific age for religious faith. The universe that science is now laying before us, with its openness to new forms of order—such as we see in atoms, cells, brains, and societies—seems truly open to teleological interpretation.[19]

---

18. Ibid., 178.
19. See chapter 14 for a more complete discussion of Darwinism and design.

11

Nonreductive Physicality: The Hierarchy of the Sciences

It has long been recognized that the sciences can be organized into a hierarchy, with physics at the bottom, then chemistry, then biology, psychology, and the social sciences.[1] Since physics studies the smallest, most basic constituents of reality, it appears at the base of the hierarchy.[2] Chemistry studies how these subatomic particles are arranged to form atoms and molecules. A tremendous number of chemical phenomena can be explained in terms of physics. Similarly, in biology much of what one learns about cell function, metabolism, and so forth, essentially involves complex chemical reactions. The rationale for adding psychology above biology is based on the notion that human behavior can be understood as an aspect of brain function and especially of brain chemistry. Because currently there is much interest in genetic explanations of human psychological differences, it seems reasonable to place psychology in the hierarchy above biology and chemistry. Many sociologists would place their discipline next in the hierarchy, claiming that social phenomena can be explained by laws of individual psychology.

Thus we have a hierarchical model for ordering the sciences. Higher sciences permit study of more complex organizations or systems of the entities at the next level down.

---

1. The material in this segment is adapted from Murphy, *Reconciling Theology and Science*, 12–17.

2. While this model may have merit, as noted below, its opponents urge caution in taking a "nothing buttery" approach, which, in the case of physics, might reduce its subject matter to "nothing but particles," for instance. I thank my colleague Joel Cannon of the Physics Department for raising this important point.

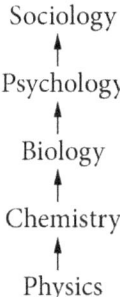

While the hierarchical model is well accepted among scientists and philosophers, there has been longstanding debate concerning the issue of reduction, an idea promoted by the logical positivists, whose views originated in the work of the Vienna Circle of the 1920s and 1930s. This group of philosophers, scientists, and others were united by their interest in unifying the sciences. Their goal was based on the hierarchy of the sciences just described. However, the positivists were interested in a more radical unification of the sciences than mere hierarchical ordering. They wanted to show that each science could be reduced to the one below. Ultimately, they hoped, everything would be understood as a consequence of the laws of physics.

While reduction was and remains an important research strategy, the success of this strategy became a justification for a metaphysics or theory about the nature of reality that creates more problems than it solves. The most obvious problem relates to human freedom. If human behavior is entirely reducible to chemistry and ultimately to the laws of physics, does this not render human free will an illusion?

As logical positivists were refining and promoting their reductionist program for the sciences, philosopher Roy Wood Sellars (1880–1973) was developing a nonreductionist view of the hierarchy of the sciences given such names as "emergent realism" and "evolutionary naturalism." A more common term today is "nonreductive physicalism." Sellars began in 1916 to elucidate a conception of the mental as an emergent property in the hierarchy of complex systems. He ultimately developed a conception of nature as forming a nonreducible hierarchy of levels, specifically the inorganic, organic, mental or conscious, social, ethical, and religious or spiritual.

Sellars expressly opposed reductive materialism. According to him, the natural world is one great system, displaying levels of complexity that have emerged over time. He criticized the reductionists for their overly mechanistic and atomistic view of nature, arguing that "organization and wholes are genuinely significant" and not mere aggregates of elementary particles. Reductive materialism overemphasizes "stuff" in contrast to organization. But matter, he claims, is only a part of nature. We all know that medium-sized material objects—a desk, for instance—are made up of atoms. One way to make Sellar's point is to raise the question of which is real, the desk or the swirling mass of atoms? The reductionist says only the atoms are real; Sellars says the desk is equally real and must be taken into account in giving an adequate description of the world.

Sellars claimed science and philosophy were in his own day (1930s) becoming aware of the principles involved in levels of organization to which the old materialism was blind. While the reductionistic position presently remains by far the predominant position in philosophy and science, the balance is shifting from reductive to nonreductive physicalism, as evidenced by developments in the philosophy of mind as well as in science. Many scientists working at a variety of levels are recognizing that analysis and reduction do not yield a complete or adequate account of the natural world. In simple terms, to understand an entity, one has to consider not only its parts but also its interactions with the environment. This means that both a "top-down" and a "bottom-up" analysis are needed.

Biochemists, for example, recognize that chemical reactions do not work the same in a flask as within a living organism. The science of ecology is also based on recognition that organisms function differently in different environments. This means that in general the higher-level system, which is constituted by the entity and its environment, needs to be considered in giving a complete causal account. Thus in any science there are questions that can be answered by reference to factors at the level in question, while other questions can be answered only by referring to factors at a lower level. In addition, there are questions that can be answered only by reference to factors described at higher levels of analysis, questions called "boundary questions."

In sum, there have always been objections to a reductionist view, especially in the human sciences. How else can we explain arguments over nature versus nurture, or biological versus social environment? Until recently, the reductionists seemed to have won the day in the natural sciences and were vocal in the human sciences as well. The tide may be turning, however, even in the natural sciences. "Many now accept that reductionism in science has its limits and that higher levels in the hierarchy have their own causal role to play in the total system of nature."[3]

Having arrived at this position, we are close to addressing the relations between theology and this nonreductive account of the sciences. However, before doing so, we need to add a refinement to the hierarchy of the sciences. So far, when referring to higher levels, it is not clear whether they pertain to more encompassing wholes (such as ecology, the study of organisms in relation to one another within their natural environment) or to more complex systems. If the hierarchy is taken to be based on more encompassing wholes, then cosmology is the highest science possible in the hierarchy, since it studies the universe as a whole. However, if the hierarchy of the sciences is based on increasing complexity of the systems studied, then the question arises whether a social system is or is not more complex than the abstract account of the cosmos provided by cosmologists.

Since there is no good way to answer this question, it is helpful to represent the relations among the sciences by means of a branching hierarchy, with the human sciences forming one branch and the natural sciences above biology forming the other. We need to think of the hierarchy of the sciences as rather like a tree, with physics, inorganic chemistry, biochemistry, and the various levels of biology forming the trunk. One branch completes the natural sciences with cosmology. Another branch contains the human sciences, including psychology and the social sciences.

We have reached a point where it is possible to consider a more radical addition to the hierarchy of the sciences, one made by Arthur Peacocke. His proposal is that theology should be placed at the top of the hierarchy, since it is the study of the most encompassing system possible—God in relation to everything else that is. Such a hierarchical arrangement can be diagrammed as follows:

---

3. Murphy, *Reconciling Theology and Science*, 15.

Beyond Belief

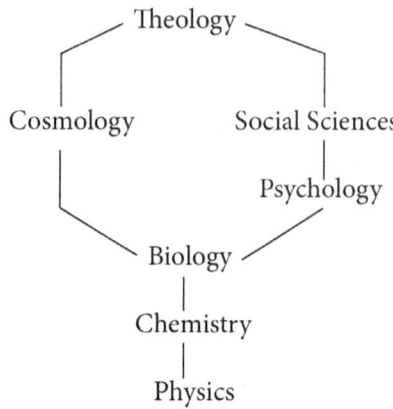

This depiction bears a superficial resemblance to the hierarchical image rejected in chapter 1. We must, however, keep in mind that nonreductive physicalism develops in a way far different from that earlier model, for it values both top-down and bottom-up relationships. Theology is at the top, not because of primacy of value or authority but because of its subject matter. This model honors the ideals of the Engagement approach to science and religion. It also reconciles the best insights of both the Conflict and the Contrast models. On the one hand, it recognizes with the dualists that theology and science are truly different. Just as psychology's concerns are different from those of biology, so theology has its own proper subject matter—mainly God. It also recognizes that theology and the sciences employ different languages. There is no equivalent in biology for psychological terms such as "neurosis" or "ego strength." Similarly there is no scientific equivalent for terms such as "salvation," "grace," and "sin." On the other hand, this model recognizes that one cannot isolate theology from the rest of knowledge. As we saw earlier, theology is enough like a science to warrant its being placed in relation to the other sciences. Theologians, like reasoning scientists, use hypothetico-deductive reasoning, while also paying attention to data at their disposal, including experience, community practices, and historical events. While each science has its own kinds of data, those used in biology are not the same as in physics. And sociologists and psychologists use different kinds of data than cosmologists. While data of this type differs from the sorts physicists and biologists use, each of the sciences uses data specific to its own discipline.

Nonreductive Physicality: The Hierarchy of the Sciences

God's "Two Books"

We return to a topic introduced earlier—the role of scripture in Christianity—examining that topic in light of the engagement model. Building on the conviction that science and religion are fundamentally irreconcilable, many conservative Christians believe that the only choices a person can make about the Bible are that it is either the infallible, inerrant word of God or it is a collection of fairy tales with little or no value for modern people. Since the latter is what unbelievers think, evangelical conservatives believe they must view the Bible as God's very word of truth, defending it in all respects, even on such matters as science. For many, the Bible's reliability in matters of science is so critical that they will argue, "If I can't believe the Bible when it speaks about science (or creation), then how can I believe it about Jesus Christ and salvation?" To frame the question of the inspiration and authority of the Bible in this manner, however, is to do an injustice to the traditional doctrines of the inspiration and authority of scripture.

From the early years of the Christian church until the beginning of the seventeenth century, the theologians most respected concerning the nature of biblical authority and also the doctrine of creation held a common position on the relationship between the Bible and science. In the early seventeenth century Cardinal Baronius expressed this principle succinctly: "The intention of the Holy Spirit is to teach us how to go to heaven, not how the heavens go."[4] In uttering this statement, Baronius had Copernicus in mind, who challenged the theory of geocentrism and therefore was condemned for disbelieving the biblical teaching that the sun moves, not the earth (Joshua 10:13, Psalm 19:6; 96:10). Baronius's statement was fully in accord with the perspective of Augustine, Thomas Aquinas, and John Calvin, who developed the classic Christian theology of creation and who were united in their conviction that Christ is the center of scripture and not science, meaning that what the scripture teaches is the message of salvation through Christ.

In the centuries following the Reformation, as the conflicts intensified between Catholics and Protestants, persons on both sides began to emphasize the literal sense of the Bible. Some argued that the Bible is without error not only in what it teaches about God, Christ, salvation, and the Christian life, but that it is also infallible in whatever statements it makes about any area of human knowledge, including science. This

---

4. The material in this segment is adapted from Schneider, *Science and Faith*, Essay III: "Does the Bible Teach Science?" The quotation is cited by Schneider.

position gathered strength during the nineteenth century, when scientific discoveries and theories about the age of the earth and evolution as well as the development of modern biblical criticism seemed to call the authority and trustworthiness of the Bible into question. While influential conservative scholars such as T. M. Lindsay and James Orr rejected inerrancy as a necessary defense of the Bible's inspiration and trustworthiness, conservative theologians such as Charles Hodge and Benjamin B. Warfield argued with great force that the Bible is free from error in every respect. Thus, conservative Christians were themselves divided over the extent to which they ascribe inerrancy to scripture, disagreeing over the extent to which the Bible should be considered authoritative in matters of science, history, economics, and other areas of human knowledge and practice.

Any discussion of the Bible requires an additional important qualification: the distinction between revelation and interpretation. Whereas revelation pertains to the communication of divine truth, interpretation is the human effort to understand it. Since there is no such thing as an objective reading of scripture—for interpretation involves meaning, which is clearly subjective—one cannot say: "I believe exactly what Genesis 1 says and I don't need any theory of reconciliation with science." Such an assertion confuses revelation with interpretation. Simply accepting the truth of the biblical writings does not specify their meaning. The problem still remains: what does Genesis 1 mean for twenty-first-century Christians? Just as our observations of the natural world must be interpreted within some explanatory framework, scripture also must be interpreted. The question for the Christian becomes: what interpretive framework can offer the most fruitful way to understand the meaning of biblical cosmology in the light of modern scientific knowledge?

One such framework is provided by the concept of the Two Books, the Book of Nature and the Book of Scripture. This influential notion was articulated by Tertullian (c. 160–c. 230), an early Christian theologian, whom Galileo cited approvingly in his 1615 treatise on the use of biblical quotations in matters of science. Galileo agreed with Tertullian that both nature and scripture proceed alike from the creative Word of God. Therefore, when properly read and interpreted, the truths revealed at each level cannot contradict one another. Sir Francis Bacon (1561–1626), who promoted the scientific method of induction, agreed with Galileo that if one establishes by assured empirical and logical processes the truth of something in nature that appears to be in conflict with a biblical passage, then the problem is not with what the biblical text *says* but with the *interpretation* placed upon its words.[5]

The notion of God's "Two Books" became a commonplace in Christian thought and is still cited by those writing about the relationship between religion and science. Even the great nineteenth-century champion of inerrancy, Charles Hodge, agreed with Galileo and Bacon, but he put the matter even more bluntly. He insisted "in common with the whole Church, that this infallible Bible must be interpreted by science," a proposition he considered "all but self-evident." Hodge used the Copernican revolution as the classic example of this view: "For five thousand years [sic] the Church understood the Bible to teach that the earth stood still in space, and that the sun and stars revolved around it. Science has demonstrated that this is not true. Shall we go on to interpret the Bible so as to make it teach the falsehood that the sun moves round the earth, or shall we interpret it by science and make the two harmonize?"[6]

Throughout history, those who promoted the "Two Books" concept were concerned to defend the integrity of both the study of nature and the study of scripture, but when the language of the latter seems to contradict the former, as in the classic example Hodge used, they encouraged readers of scripture to invoke another important element in their interpretive framework, the principle of accommodation. Accommodation is the notion that the biblical writers describe phenomena of nature in a way that was understandable and accessible to ordinary and unlearned people.

Augustine utilized the principle of accommodation in his interpretation of the "six days" of Genesis; Thomas Aquinas likewise used it when he interpreted Genesis 1 in light of Aristotelian science. John Calvin, in his commentaries on Genesis and Psalms, was quite clear in stating that the sacred writers described nature simply as it appeared to their senses: "The Holy Spirit," he wrote, "had no intention to teach astronomy; and in proposing instruction meant to be common to the simplest and most uneducated person he made use by Moses and other prophets of the popular language."[7] Noting that the author of Genesis 1 "did not treat scientifically of the stars" but referred to them "in a popular manner," he invited readers interested in learning science to come not to Genesis 1, but "to go elsewhere." Galileo was thoroughly orthodox when he wrote: "These propositions [regarding the phenomena of the heavens] uttered by the Holy Ghost were set down in that manner by the sacred scribes in order

---

5. Ibid.
6. Cited by Schneider, ibid.
7. Cited by Schneider, ibid.

to accommodate them to the capacities of the common people."[8] Thanks to this widely accepted principle, theologians could hold that the biblical writers accurately and truthfully described the creation as they perceived and understood it. But they were describing natural phenomena within their ordinary human understanding, using the common language of everyday speech; they were not being guided to make revelatory statements about the nature of the universe. The "Two Books" concept remains for many theologians and scientists a fruitful metaphor for understanding the relationship between biblical and scientific knowledge.

One insight that historians and philosophers of science have given to our generation is that the theories and models that scientists construct to make sense of natural phenomena are always provisional. Such are true so long as scholars continue to offer the best account of the operations of nature; their superior explanatory power and the fruitful results of scientific research make them convincing. Yet, even though these theories may be so compelling as to be accepted as true for hundreds of years, they may still be replaced or modified whenever new knowledge provides the impetus and necessity to construct new theories to explain nature and its operations. Our knowledge of the universe remains incomplete, for the sum of human knowledge about the natural world is always increasing. The final description of the universe has yet to be devised, the full potential of science yet to be realized.

Thus, as meaningful a model as the ancient Near Eastern peoples had constructed to account for the phenomena they observed in the heavens and upon the earth, it was bound to be superseded, just as every subsequent model of the universe has been replaced or significantly modified to the present day. It is here that our contemporary understanding of scientific truth joins hands with the principle of accommodation. Ancient biblical cosmology needs to be understood as a time-bound conception of human knowledge and understanding that provided a context for the biblical writers' revelations about God, rather than as a timeless statement about the nature of the universe.

This brings us back to that earlier question: "If I can't believe the Bible when it talks about science (or creation), then how can I believe it when it talks about Jesus Christ and my salvation?" This question, however, and the "all or nothing" thinking that lies behind it, is simply wrong-headed. First of all, this line of thinking confuses priorities. If the purpose of the Bible is to point to Jesus Christ, as theologians have taught for centuries,

---

8. Cited by Schneider, ibid.

then one's belief in the Bible needs to be based on the message proclaimed about Christ and the effect those words have on one's life. All else is secondary, and no interpretations regarding other topics, including those having to do with nature, should be held up as criteria for believing in its inspiration and authority. Furthermore, this way of thinking confuses the Bible's theological proclamations about creation with the cosmological model of the creation that forms the backdrop to these teachings. It assumes wrongly that what biblical texts state about the nature of the heavens and the earth are timeless scientific descriptions, implicitly confusing interpretation with revelation.

This mindset has done a great disservice to believers and to the Bible itself because of the false dilemma it creates. Having been taught that what the Bible teaches about creation is valid scientific truth today and is opposed to certain theories of modern science, and having become convinced that the latter are true, many go where intellectual integrity leads, even if this means abandoning the biblical message altogether. The other unfortunate outcome is that some believers feel forced to reject modern scientific theories or models such as Big Bang cosmology or human evolution, which conflict, "not with what the Bible says about God, but with a human interpretation that is confused with revelation. The operations of nature as modern science depicts them, then, are perceived as threats to belief, and science is treated as an enemy of faith."[9]

Both of these outcomes can be tragic. They set up an unnecessary conflict between science on the one hand and the Bible and Christian faith on the other, perpetuating a dissonance between the kinds of knowledge revealed in each of "God's Two Books." In the United States, they have produced a cultural conflict harmful to both the work of science and the cause of Christianity.

While science and religion both presuppose the reality of depth in the universe, they do not read it in the same way. Science does not—indeed should not—formally address the dimension of depth. In fact, science employs methods that seemingly push aside, at least currently, religion's tacit awareness of the inexhaustibility of the world. Each science abstracts in its own unique way from the rich dimensionality of the universe, contemplating from its vantage point what it considers its subject matter. However, as we noted in the discussion concerning the hierarchical model, explanation is an abstraction begging to be complemented by yet other kinds of explanation. No given scientific field can legitimately claim to have swallowed

---

9. Schneider, ibid.

reality whole. No allegedly "scientific" readings of nature, having mastered the alphabet and grammar of a particular level, can claim to have read the entire text of nature. It is reductionism that brings scientists into conflict with religion, just as biblical literalism inevitably leads religious people to reject aspects of science.

Whenever it takes its founding metaphors and symbols too literally, religion also loses its own depth. For example, Judaism, Christianity, and Islam represent the depth of nature in personal or anthropomorphic terms. They do so in order to render vivid their intuition that the universe is grounded in an all-encompassing love and promise. However, the sense of nature's infinite depth can sometimes be pushed aside by religious fixation on certain images of a personal God. The danger here is that the deity may then come to seem smaller than the universe itself. Such a "God" becomes too small to command the response of genuine worship. And when our sacred traditions become too literalist in their understanding of a personal God, the universe of science may seem to open up a deeper and more enticing context for spiritual adventure than that provided by religion.

Sharing the Toolkit

In 1998, in an article in *The American Scholar*, William Cronon listed ten qualities he most admired in people he knew who seemed to embody the values of a liberal education.[10] The first nine—listening, reading, talking, writing, problem solving, truth seeking, tolerance, leadership, collegiality—lead to the tenth: the ability to connect with others in authentic community. A liberal education is about gaining the power, the wisdom, the generosity, and the freedom to connect.

Inspired by the unfathomable nature of reality and the plurality of ways by which it can be experienced and expressed, I have identified seven qualities that religiously minded and scientifically guided individuals might share in their common quest for truth. Some were suggested by the late Carl Sagan in his moving personal work, *The Demon-Haunted World: Science as a Candle in the Dark*. In chapter two he writes of his lifelong love affair with science. Science, he affirms, is more than a body of knowledge; it is a way of thinking and, we might add, a way of connecting. Religion is also a way of thinking and of connecting. Religion and science are less than perfect instruments of knowing, but they are the best we have, and it's

---

10. Cronon, "Only Connect."

important that they find ways to complement one another. My list of personal qualities for liberally educated scientists and people of faith include the following aptitudes:

1. *Intuition.* The role of intuition in scientific discovery is virtually universally acknowledged. Intuition and imagination are rarely part of a scientist's education, but they have been essential to some of science's greatest achievements. They are regarded as a gift of birth endowing some more than others with superior intuition. Furthermore, intuitive insight comes at unexpected moments—in the bath for the physicist Archimedes, when getting onto a tram car in Paris for the mathematician/physicist Poincare, or while looking into the fire after an excessive amount of drink one evening for the chemist Kekule. The history of science is filled with these anecdotes, which are qualities of experience that regularly accompany scientific insight.

Scientists are often confronted with problems not solvable by logical deduction from basic principles. For instance, how is it possible to reconcile the observations that electrons or photons can behave as particles and as waves? How are we to understand the loss of weight of a body immersed in a liquid? Again, how can the strange properties of a molecule such as benzene be reconciled with its chemical formula? Solutions to such problems are arrived at by the creative human process that involves intuition. Models may be guided by observation and by logical constraint, but the underlying principle is often an insight, a hunch, or simply by thinking "outside the box." While science is committed to facts, it remains open to new ideas, even when they don't conform to preconceptions. Science counsels adherents to entertain alternative hypotheses and see which best fit the facts.

Likewise, liberally educated religious practitioners, while committed to scriptures, traditions, theological principles, and other tenets of their faith tradition, remain open to new understandings and interpretations, even when they don't conform to presuppositions.

2. *Self-criticism.* The scientific way of thinking, like the liberally religious way, is at once imaginative and modest. It urges on us a delicate balance between no-hold-barred openness to new ideas, however heretical, and the most rigorous skeptical scrutiny of everything—new ideas and established wisdom. This kind of thinking is also an essential tool for a democracy in an age of change. One of the reasons for the success of science is that it has built-in, error-correcting machinery at its very heart. There are no forbidden questions in science, no matters too sensitive or delicate

to be probed, and no sacred truths. That openness to new ideas, combined with the most rigorous, skeptical scrutiny of all ideas, sifts the wheat from the chaff. It makes no difference how smart, sincere, or beloved you are. In the realm of science, one must prove one's case in the face of determined, expert criticism. Valid criticism is expected, and debate is valued. Opinions are encouraged to contend, but they must be substantiated.

Though this may be an overly broad characterization for science, as certainly for religion at its best, every time we exercise self-criticism, every time we test our ideas against the outside world, we are doing science. When we are self-indulgent and uncritical, when we confuse hopes and facts, we slide into pseudoscience and superstition. Humans may crave absolute certainty; they may aspire to it or pretend, as partisans of certain religions do, to have attained it. But the history of science teaches that the most we can hope for is successive improvement in our understanding, learning from our mistakes, but always with the proviso that absolute certainty is elusive. One of the great commandments of science is, "Mistrust arguments from authority." Too many such arguments, in science and religion, have proved painfully wrong. Authorities, like everybody else, must support their contentions. This independence of science, its occasional unwillingness to accept conventional wisdom, makes it dangerous to doctrines less self-critical, or with pretensions to certitude.

3. *Reverence and awe.* In its encounter with nature, science and religion invariably elicit a sense of awe. The very act of understanding is a celebration of joining, merging, even if on a very modest scale, with the magnificence of the cosmos. Recognizing our place in the immensity of space and in the passage of time; grasping the intricacy, beauty, and subtlety of life—that soaring feeling, that sense of elation and humility combined—these are surely spiritual. So are our emotions in the presence of great art, music, literature, or acts of exemplary selfless courage such as those of Mohandas Gandhi or Martin Luther King Jr. "Spirit" comes from the Latin word "to breathe." What we breathe is air, which is certainly matter, however thin. Science is not only compatible with spirituality; it is also a profound source of spirituality. The notion that science and spirituality are somehow mutually exclusive does a disservice to both.

4. *Humility.* Science understands human imperfection. All humans, including revered scientists and theologians, have been wrong. Some people consider religion arrogant, especially when it resists change or forbids questioning self-imposed ecclesiastical authority. Science, too, appears

arrogant, especially when it purports to contradict beliefs of long standing or when it introduces bizarre concepts that seem contradictory to common sense. While this can be profoundly disturbing, like an earthquake that rattles our faith in the very ground upon which we stand, science is displaying humility. Scientists do not seek to impose their needs and wants on nature, but instead humbly interrogate nature and take seriously what they find.

Like scientists, religionists should value independent verification of proposed tenets of belief. Science is constantly prodding, challenging, seeking contradictions or persistent residual errors, proposing alternative explanations, encouraging heresy. Science gives its highest rewards to those who convincingly disprove established beliefs. Whenever possible, religion should follow suit. In religion there should be something comparable to scientific humility.

5. *Experimentation.* Science may be hard to understand. It may challenge cherished beliefs. And when its products are placed at the disposal of politicians or industrialists, they may lead to weapons of mass destruction and grave threats to the environment. But one thing can be said about science: it delivers the goods. Not every branch of science can foretell the future, but many can do so with stunning accuracy. To know when the next eclipse of the sun will be, one might try magic or mysticism, but will do much better with science, which can routinely predict a solar eclipse, to the minute, a millennium in advance. If interested in the sex of your unborn child, you can consult a medium, who may be right, on average, only one time in two, or you can try amniocentesis and sonograms. Every religion on the planet yearns for a comparable ability—precise and repeatedly demonstrated before committed skeptics—to foretell future events. No other human institution, not even religious prophecy, comes close. Whenever possible, scientists experiment. Which experiments they conduct often depend on which theories currently prevail. Scientists are intent on testing theories to the breaking point, not trusting what is intuitively obvious. That the earth is flat was once obvious. That heavy bodies fall faster than light ones was once obvious. That some people are naturally and by divine decree slaves was once obvious. That there is such a place as the center of the universe, and that the earth sits in that exalted spot, was once obvious. The truth may be puzzling or counterintuitive. It may contradict deeply held beliefs. Experimentation is how one gets a handle on it.

While religion and science differ in subject matter, lack of experimentation is one of the reasons that the organized religions fail to inspire confidence. Which leaders of the major faiths acknowledge that their beliefs might be incomplete or erroneous and establish institutes to uncover possible doctrinal deficiencies? Beyond the test of everyday living, who is systematically testing the circumstances in which traditional religious teachings may no longer apply? Scripture is said to be divinely inspired—a phrase with many possible meanings. But what if it's simply made up by fallible humans? Miracles are attested, but what if they're a mix of charlatanry, unfamiliar states of consciousness, misapprehensions of natural phenomena, and mental illness?

At dinner some years ago the physicist Robert W. Wood was asked to respond to the toast, "To physics and metaphysics" (by "metaphysics" people then meant something like philosophy or truths one could recognize intuitively). Wood answered along these lines: The physicist has an idea. The more he thinks it through, the more sense it seems to make. He consults the scientific literature. The more he reads, the more promising the idea becomes. Thus prepared, he goes to the laboratory and devises an experiment to test it. The experiment is painstaking. Many possibilities are checked. The accuracy of measurement is refined, the error bars reduced. The physicist is devoted only to what the experiment teaches. At the end of careful experimentation, the idea is found to be worthless. So the physicist discards it, frees his mind from the clutter of error, and moves on to something else. The difference between physics and metaphysics, Wood concluded, is not that the practitioners of one are smarter than the practitioners of the other. The difference is that the metaphysicist has no laboratory.

6. *Democracy*. The values of science and the values of democracy are concordant, in many cases indistinguishable. Science thrives on, indeed requires, the free exchange of ideas, its values being antithetical to secrecy. Individual insights are never simply accepted, the status of the insight as objective truth depending upon intersubjective consensus between practicing scientists. If there is no consensus, there is no truth. This is the democratic aspect of scientific discovery, which depends upon a community of individuals who practice a shared methodology of investigation. Science holds to no special vantage points or privileged positions. Both science and democracy encourage unconventional opinions and vigorous debate. Both demand adequate reason, coherent argument, rigorous standards of evidence and honesty. Science is a way to call the bluff of those who

only pretend to knowledge. It is a bulwark against superstition and against religion misapplied. If we are true to its values, it can tell us when we are being deceived. It provides a mid-course correction to our mistakes. If we don't practice these tough habits of thought, we cannot hope to solve truly serious problems—and we risk becoming a nation of pushovers, up for grabs by the next charlatan who comes along.

7. *Elegance*. Because science carries us toward an understanding of the actual world, rather than as we would wish it to be, its findings may not in all cases be immediately comprehensible or satisfying. A little work may be needed to restructure our mindsets. Some of science is very simple. When it becomes complicated, that's usually because the world is complicated—or because we're complicated. Here the concept of "elegance" comes into play, elegance being essential to scientists working in all fields. While we usually associate a sense of elegance with art or fashion design, poetry or dance, the idea of elegance is surprisingly important in science as well.[11] The initial insight that leads a scientist to a consistent description of a set of observations, gathering them into a coherent whole, involves both subjective experience and qualitative evaluation: elegance, simplicity, beauty, truth, are the most common descriptors. The resulting theory is often parsimonious, suggesting that the simpler the theory, the closer to the truth the assumption. The implication is that truth, like nature, should be parsimonious.

In his famous book, *The Structure of Scientific Revolutions*, Thomas Kuhn argued that when scientists decide which of several alternative paradigms should be adopted, their selection would be based on, among other things, arbitrary considerations, some of which are aesthetic. The most frequently cited aesthetic qualities on the basis of which some ideas in science may be accepted are simplicity, symmetry, and elegance. Scientists often share a sense of admiration and excitement on hearing of an elegant solution to a problem, a theory, or an experiment. For scientists, as for artists and theologians, elegance implies beauty, simplicity, clarity, and proportion; the elegant solution has a kind of stunning and unalterable rightness that inspires wonder and awe. The idea of elegance may seem strange in a discipline that prides itself on objectivity, but only so if science

---

11. As the scientist and philosopher Stephen Hawking stated in *The Grand Design*, 5, a scientific model is a good model if it: (1) is elegant; (2) contains few arbitrary or adjustable elements; (3) agrees with and explains all existing observations; (4) and makes detailed predictions about future observations that could disprove or falsify the model if they are not borne out.

is regarded as a dull activity of counting and measuring. It is, of course, far more than that, making elegance a fundamental aspect of the beauty and imagination involved in religious and scientific activity.

12

The Theory of Evolution: A Brief Overview

TESTS, POLLS, AND OTHER informational resources demonstrate that Americans on the whole lack scientific knowledge and awareness. While select American students win international competitions in science and mathematics, dismal trends plague average students in the United States. In tests of average seventeen-year-olds in many regions of the world, the U.S. ranks last in algebra. On identical tests, American students averaged 43 percent and their Japanese counterparts 78 percent. In a chemistry test, students in only two of thirteen nations did worse than the United States. Britain was so high it was almost off-scale, and 25 percent of Canadian eighteen-year-olds knew as much chemistry as a select 1 percent of American high school seniors. The best of twenty fifth-grade classrooms in Minneapolis was outpaced by all twenty classrooms in Sendai, Japan, and nineteen out of twenty in Taipei, Taiwan.[1]

Americans should be concerned not only with producing the next generation of first-rate scientists and mathematicians, but also with cultivating a scientifically literate public. For example, 63 percent of American adults are unaware that the last dinosaur died before the origin of the first human; 75 percent do not know that antibiotics kill bacteria but not viruses; 57 percent do not know that electrons are smaller than atoms. Polls show that nearly half of American adults do not know that the earth goes around the sun and takes a year to do so. It seems amazing that more than four and a half centuries after Copernicus, most people on earth still think that our planet sits immobile at the center of the universe, making humans profoundly special.

Is it possible that in America, religion contributes to this high level of ignorance? I believe it is certainly a contributing factor. If one accepts the literal truth of every word of the Bible, as 30 percent of Americans claim,

---

1. Sagan, *Demon-Haunted World*, 323–24.

then one might conclude that the earth is flat. Coincidentally, the same is true for the Qur'an. In some Muslim communities, pronouncing the earth round makes one an atheist. In 1993 the supreme religious authority of Saudi Arabia, Sheik Abdel-Aziz Ibn Baaz, issued an edict declaring that the world is flat. Anyone affirming a round globe demonstrated disbelief in God and should be punished.[2]

Many Christians in America disbelieve in biological evolution and take offence at the concept. Polls reveal that only 9 percent of Americans accept the central finding of modern biology that human beings, together with all other species, have slowly evolved by natural processes from a succession of more ancient beings with no divine intervention needed along the way. When asked merely if they accept evolution, 45 percent of Americans say they do. By contrast, 53 percent of Americans consider themselves creationists, meaning that they disavow evolution altogether. Evidence seemingly has little influence, for most Americans know very little about the scientific details of evolution, either about the enormous amount of evidence already gathered in its support or the dominant theory of natural selection that explains how it happens. Part of the problem explaining this widespread ignorance lies with the politics of local education in many parts of the country. Teachers in public schools often skip the topic because it is controversial. Many youngsters are exposed in their churches to a negative view of evolution. They are taught that evolution is contrary to the Bible, that they cannot believe in both God and evolution, that evolution is an atheistic philosophy, and, sometimes, that evolution is an invention of the devil. Any information they receive about evolution in sermons or Sunday school usually comes from Young Earth Creationists and not from evolutionary scientists. This ignorance is true both of Christians who accept evolution and support teaching it in the public schools of the United States and of those who reject it and oppose its teaching, even though this concept is at the core of every life science from genetics to biochemistry to ecology. This ignorance is even more appalling when we take into consideration that the term "evolution" is used to describe not only the emergence of new species on this planet but also the emergence of the cosmos from the Big Bang. We live in an evolving creation, in which we really cannot understand scientific reading and finding in the Book of Nature unless we understand evolution.

A significant number of scientists from many religious faiths, including Christian traditions, are among those who promote the research that every year more firmly points to evolution as a valid scientific way of

2. Ibid., 325.

The Theory of Evolution: A Brief Overview

understanding the history of life. They earnestly desire that all Christians understand what evolution actually is and why one can accept it without giving up belief in God, the doctrine of creation, and other wonders of the Bible. To those who approach this assertion with skepticism, I ask that they try to set aside their negative views or feelings and listen to the voices of scientists, including their fellow Christians, as they explain evolution.

First we need to revisit a serious misunderstanding about evolution. "Evolution" is commonly presented as a materialistic philosophy by both Young Earth and Intelligent Design opponents as well as by those at the opposite end of the spectrum of opinion who claim that the material world is all there is. Whether one reads the works of anti-evolutionists like Young Earth Creationist Ken Ham and Intelligent Design advocate Phillip Johnson, or evolutionary materialists like scientist Richard Dawkins and philosopher Daniel Dennett, one discovers that these strange bedfellows agree on one thing: if evolution explains everything and if you accept evolution, then you can dispense with religion and belief in God. Those who accept evolutionary science and believe that God's creation is an evolving one reject this mistaken notion. The materialists argue that their philosophy necessarily follows from the science, and therefore evolution removes any need for God. The creationists, strangely, accept this faulty argument, and agreeing that one cannot separate the science from the philosophy, reject both. So the Young Earth Creationists offer their "creation science" and the Intelligent Design proponents their "theistic science." Both sides tend to make their voices heard in the public arena through speeches, debates, books, articles, on-line sites, and cable news channels. But they are the extremes that exclude the middle, which is: "evolution as science is not a materialistic philosophy; it makes no assertions about any realm of reality outside of nature; it makes no claims for or against the existence of God or the notion that we live in a created universe."[3]

While materialists claim support from the science of evolution for their belief system, the belief system and the science are not identical. The scientific concept of evolution simply accounts for the world as nature presents it. Evolution needs to be understood and evaluated as science, not as philosophy. I want to make this point clearly because what I present below is science.

---

3. Schneider, *Science and Faith*, Essay IV: "Big Bang and the Universe Story."

Cosmic Evolution and the Universe Story

When scientists describe the universe today, sooner or later they tell a story because they understand the universe far differently than did Sir Isaac Newton and his eighteenth-century successors.[4] Newton understood the universe to be static: space is infinite, time marches onward, and in the three dimensions of space, the solid matter making up the stars and planets of our galaxy ceaselessly follows the law of universal gravitation. Newton and his contemporaries believed that their universe was created, and that God was responsible for setting it in motion.

How differently scientists understand the universe today! Scientists now know that we live in an *unfinished* universe, with a beginning and probably an end, though that end is not yet in sight. It is a fact that we live in an expanding universe, that space is filled with a background radiation left over from the Big Bang, and that galaxies and stars are still coming into existence and passing away. Some 13.7 billion years ago, all the matter and energy that we now discern or confidently theorize was compressed into a "singularity" of zero size and infinite density, governed by laws of physics not yet understood. From this singularity, space-time erupted into existence in a cosmic fireball. An infinitesimal moment later, still within the first second of its existence, the universe underwent a period of inflation, which lasted less than the blinking of an eye. Fluctuations in the density of matter and energy occurred; the temperature of the universe dropped considerably, and vast bubbles of matter and energy were formed throughout. The emerging universe, now dominated by radiation, entered a new phase, as certain elementary particles, including protons and neutrons, were formed. Shortly thereafter, when the temperature of the universe had fallen yet again, the process of nucleosynthesis began. Protons, the nuclei of ordinary or "light" hydrogen, and neutrons combined in a process called fusion to form heavy hydrogen nuclei. The nuclei (not yet atoms) of the two most abundant elements in the universe throughout its history—hydrogen and helium—were formed in the very first minutes of its existence.

Expansion continued uneventfully for the next three hundred thousand years, a period that scientists call the Radiation Era. By the end of that phase, the temperature dropped significantly once again. Radiation now moved independently of matter. And matter, no longer affected as it had been by radiation, undertook another critical and sudden step in the formation of the cosmos. Electrons and protons combined to form hydrogen atoms in a process so efficient that it was completed by the end

---

4. The material in this segment is adapted from Schneider, ibid.

of the first million years. During that time, as more and more hydrogen atoms were formed, the universe, now rid of the fog of blackbody radiation coupled with elementary particles, became transparent.

Something else not transparent, cold dark matter, began to add its gravitational force to visible matter. Smaller clouds of hydrogen and helium gas coalesced into larger clouds, and around two hundred million years after the Big Bang, the first stars ignited, thus beginning galaxies of one hundred billion stars or more. Most stars in the galaxies were formed during the first five billion years of the universe's history, though these stellar and galactic processes continue today. Many of the first stars were massive, consuming their fuel rapidly and within a few million years exploding as giant supernovae. These explosions created the heavier elements, from carbon on up, and from the enormous dust clouds created by these explosions, aided by gravity, successive generations of stars appeared. Eventually, thanks to these stellar explosions, all of the elements in our universe were created. Planetary systems began to form around stars; our own sun, a third-generation star, formed about 5 billion years ago, and our earth became a planet by about 4.6 billion years ago. Upon it began another universe story, the story of life.

All during the billions of years of our universe's existence, the galaxies and their clusters continued to be carried by the expanding space, and at this time, no end of the process is in sight. Looking out into space, we see a visible universe that presently is about 28 billion light-years across; looking back in time, we see the remnants of its earliest moments 13.7 billion years ago. Far from static, our universe is characterized on the cosmic level by the emergence of new stars and galaxies with their own life cycles. And on our planet, over its immense age, new forms of living things have continually emerged into existence and lived out their own life cycles. There is no sign that these evolutionary processes are reaching a conclusion. Hence, paleontologist Pierre Teilhard de Chardin (1881–1955) could often say that the "cosmos is not a fixed body of things, but a *genesis*—a still unfolding drama . . . The world is still coming into being."[5]

Because the universe has a history, the metaphor of the Book of Nature is still relevant. But nature's book and the story of nature it tells are unfinished; the story is still being written. When they tell the story, scientists can take it only to the present moment. People might speculate about its future on the basis of what science has learned about its past, with some confidence that the processes by which nature has unfolded over time are likely to continue. Nevertheless, the future remains open, whatever one might speculate.

---

5. Haught, *Deeper Than Darwin*, 162.

Biological Evolution and the Human Story

Today's naturalists view with astonishment the extent and range of life in all of its incredible diversity. As evolutionary biologists point out, more than two million existing species of plants and animals have been named and described: many more remain to be discovered, at least ten million according to most estimates. The 2 million include approximately 250,000 species of living plants, 100,000 species of fungi, and 1.5 million species of animals and microorganisms, each occupying its own peculiar ecological setting or niche. The fossil evidence from earth's long history indicates that many more, perhaps 90 percent of all species ever alive are now extinct. No less astonishing is the incredible variety of species and their habitats. Living species range in size from the giant sequoias of California to bacteria less than one-thousandth of a millimeter in length. The range of life's habitats is equally staggering, for species are found in every nook and cranny on earth, from the peaks of the Himalayas to the deepest ocean vents, in the coldest ice masses in Antarctica and the hottest springs in Yellowstone Park. While thousands of species of microbial life do good or ill in your intestines, mites too small for the naked eye clean our eyelashes.[6] There is hardly a niche on earth where life does not dwell.[7]

How does one account for all of this incredible diversity? Scientists claim it is the outcome of evolutionary processes. All living things are interrelated, all descending over time from one or a few common ancestors. Charles Darwin called this process descent with modification, a phrase still accurately describing what scientists today technically call macroevolution.

A great deal of unnecessary confusion exists over the meaning of the word "evolution." When a state school board such as Alabama's directs that all science textbooks carry a "warning label" stating that "evolution is a theory, not a fact," the board members have misunderstood both "fact" and "theory" and quite likely have misunderstood "evolution." Let us address the confusion. Biological evolution is a broad unifying scientific concept. It consists of a large array of proposed mechanisms that draw on a wide range of observational data from geology, paleontology, ecology, population biology, genetics, developmental biology, and other

---

6. The Human Microbiome Project, a recent effort involving hundreds of scientists and dozens of universities, has counted over 10,000 microbial species in humans, weighing a total of 6 or more pounds in a 150-pound person.

7. The material in this segment is adapted from Schneider, *Science and Faith*, Essay V: "Evolution for Christians."

The Theory of Evolution: A Brief Overview

related fields of science. As a unifying scientific concept, it provides a core of solidly established fact and theory combined with a number of related theories and hypotheses.

As an overarching scientific concept, evolution is considered factual. It is important to understand that a scientific *fact* does not mean an absolute proven unquestionable truth. Rather, such a fact refers to a truth generally accepted to a degree of precision as to have predictive value in subsequent experiments and in the accumulation of data, or, as paleontologist Stephen Jay Gould put it, "confirmed to such a degree that it would be perverse to withhold provisional assent."[8] Newtonian mechanics are factual in that no one expects an apple to move upward from the ground to a tree, contrary to gravity, or that the earth will suddenly fly out of its orbit and depart from its pathway round the sun. In the same way, evolutionary scientists assert that the cumulative evidence for descent with modification is so extensive and so strong that it is appropriate to say that evolution in this respect is a *scientific fact*.

Likewise, the word *theory* needs to be clarified. In popular speech we often use theory to mean "a guess." But scientists never use the word in this way. Rather, by theory scientists generally denote "an explanation supported by repeated observation and confirmed repeatedly by further experimentation and data."[9] Under theory are classified the various explanations put forth to account for the descent of life, such as Darwin's theory of natural selection or its revised version known as the Modern Synthesis.

The evolutionary sciences constitute a web or constellation of facts, theories, and speculative hypotheses established by the ongoing scientific work of gathering data and making predictions on the basis of testing hypotheses. Their practitioners are like all scientists, confident that the basic concepts are unlikely to be altered, yet incomplete in that there is more to be discovered about the evolution of life. Many hypotheses will be confirmed or abandoned as new facts of nature are brought to light. Like the story of the cosmic universe, the narrative of the history of life will continue to be revised, its portrait redrawn.

One often hears critics of evolution say that they accept *microevolution*, that is, the variants within species due to genetic modification and environmental pressures (the widely varying breeds of dogs exemplify microevolution), but not macroevolution, the process of change or diversification over time, or descent with modification. In public debates over

---

8. Gould, "Evolution as Fact and Theory," 255.
9. Cited in Schneider, *Science and Faith*, Essay V: "Evolution for Christians."

evolution, this claim has been expressed so often that it seems a plausible alternative, but such an option is simply untenable. The genetic mutations that lead to the varieties within species are the same kinds of changes in hereditary material that eventually lead to macroevolution, or the emergence of new species. The distinction often made between micro- and macroevolution may serve some analytical functions but does not indicate that these are essentially different evolutionary processes. In reality, they are not.

An enormous amount of empirical evidence makes such a compelling case for macroevolution that, with few exceptions, it is accepted by the world-wide community of biological scientists. This evidence has not been uncritically accepted, however, for the community of scientists is most critical. They, not their opponents, continually gather new information from nature, testing and arguing over their own hypotheses and theories about the mechanisms of evolution and the historical reconstruction of life's descent. They do not doubt that evolution has occurred; rather, they are debating how it happened and what pathways it has taken.

In the speech he sought to read into the court record following the verdict in the Scopes "Monkey" Trial of 1925, creationist champion and trial prosecutor William Jennings Bryan challenged Charles Darwin's arguments for human evolution set out in the 1874 edition of *The Descent of Man*. There, Darwin had argued that human beings were the distant descendants of an arboreal Old World primate. Bryan noted, with some scorn, that Darwin also gave "some fanciful reasons for believing that man is more likely to have descended from the chimpanzee rather than the gorilla."[10] He went on to condemn Darwin's argument. And he was not alone. So many people said then, and still say, that they cannot accept the notion that they are descended from apes or monkeys.

Of course, neither Darwin nor any other scientist studying human evolution has ever asserted that humans are descended from apes. What all have said is that the hominids, which include our species *Homo sapiens*, and the other primates, to which the family of the great apes belong, diverged from a common ancestor millions of years ago. That part Bryan and a lot of other people have gotten wrong. Furthermore, it turns out that Darwin's hypothesis was right on the issue of relationship. The great apes are, biologically speaking, distant cousins; we humans are closer

---

10. The material in this segment is adapted from Schneider, *Science and Faith*, Essay VI: "Human Evolution and the Image of God." The quote is cited by Schneider.

The Theory of Evolution: A Brief Overview

genetically to the African chimpanzees. Nevertheless, these distinctions do little to dispel the feelings evoked by the thought of human descent from primates. The sight of monkeys in a zoo or trained chimpanzees performing silly tricks evokes an amused contempt. Surely we humans, who are made in the image of God, cannot be the descendants of, or related to, these disgusting creatures.

Many Christians reject the notion of human evolution on purely biblical and theological grounds. They assert that the Bible's creation accounts in Genesis 1 and 2 are historical fact, which they interpret to mean that God separately created each species, culminating in the first couple, Adam and Eve, superior to all other forms of life in that they bear the divine "image and likeness." Understood in that way, human evolution raises serious issues of faith for many Christians about the historicity of Adam and the claim that humans bear the image of God. To address these issues, I divide the topic into two parts. In the remainder of this chapter, I examine the empirical evidence for human evolution from the primate lineage. In the following chapter, I reflect upon the implications of these scientific discoveries for theology and biblical interpretation, examining how an evolving humanity can be said to bear the image of God.

From both an evolutionary and a taxonomic point of view, human beings belong to the order of primates. This order includes, among others, old world monkeys, chimpanzees, gorillas, orangutans, gibbons, and new world monkeys. Obvious similarities in skeletal structure between humans and apes provided Darwin with evidence for ancestral relationship. Humans and other primates also share such traits as nails instead of claws, prehensile hands, opposable thumbs, erect postures, increased reliance on vision, identical number of teeth (in apes and humans), relatively large and complex brains, lengthened periods of maturation, and habitation in year-round social groups containing members of both sexes.

In the late twentieth century, advances in genetic research have provided direct evidence for genealogical relationships and have bolstered the evidence based on anatomical similarities. While varying models of the primate family tree exist,

> there is a pretty firm consensus now that human beings are genetically most closely related to chimpanzees, then to gorillas, then to other primates. This hypothesis has been strengthened by comparative studies of such common proteins as hemoglobins, cytochromes, and serum albumins. For example, the *cytochrome-c* molecule in humans and chimpanzees contains the same 104 amino acids in exactly the same sequence. Using

a technique that compares primate serum albumin, researchers established that chimpanzees are least dissimilar in albumin structure from humans, followed by gorillas. In fact, the analyses of many of these proteins yield the same results: human and chimpanzee proteins are 99 percent identical in structure.[11]

These and many other kinds of comparisons at the molecular level are so conclusive "as to justify, on the basis of molecular structure alone, status as sibling species."[12]

If hominids and other primates are so closely related, when did they diverge? Using DNA analysis scientists have provided varying results. One study estimates that human and chimpanzee lines diverged between 7.7 and 6.3 million years ago (MYA), and that gorillas split off earlier, approximately 8 to 10 MYA. As its own lineage developed, the family of *Hominidae*, to which the genus *Homo* and our species *Homo sapiens* belong, developed traits that have set its members apart from other primates. These include adaptations of the skeleto-muscular system to allow straight-knee bipedalism, loss of opposability in the big toe, increased cranial height and capacity, and dental changes leading to reduced projection of the face. And humans have developed, alone among primates, the abilities of language, abstract and symbolic thought, culture and technology, the ability to think about the past and plan for the future, to think about the differences between what is and what ought to be, and to communicate experiences of transcendence.[13]

As the twenty-first century begins, the study of hominid evolution is in a state of flux. Many more skeletal remains of the genus *Homo* have been found than have those of earlier pithecines, including sites with remains of campfires, meals, and burials. Anthropologists have not yet reached a consensus regarding the classification of certain specimens, nor of their relationships, although the notion of a linear descent has been largely abandoned, and there is general agreement that the biological lineage leading to modern humans has been marked, like those of other animal species, by diversity. Modern humans are but one of several twigs on the hominid branch, and there appears to have been a long period during which several species were contemporaries, perhaps living in proximity

---

11. Ibid.

12. Price, *Biological Evolution*, 269.

13. Schneider, *Science and Faith,* Essay VI: "Human Evolution and the Image of God."

and competing with one another. This is most evidently the case with *Homo sapiens* and *Homo neanderthalensis*.

While clear links have not been established, fossil remains argue for the emergence of new hominids in a strong unbroken sequence from *Australopithecus* to *Homo erectus* to *Homo sapiens*. Critical changes have been noted, occurring in gradual stages over several million years, in "(1) reduction in the size of canine teeth, (2) development of a larger braincase and a more complexly organized brain, (3) reduction in the maxilla (facial area), (4) increase in body size, and (5) decrease in size difference between males and females . . . Although it cannot be proven, the simplest conclusion is that the latter forms were descended from the earlier ones."[14]

There is also general agreement that the first members of our genus were living in Africa about 2.5 MYA. Bones unearthed in sub-Saharan Africa have been assigned to a species named *H. habilis*. Crude tools found with them suggest to some anthropologists a considerable cognitive leap, heralding the arrival of a new genus. A contemporary eastern African *H. ergaster* made an appearance probably around 1.5 MYA and may have been responsible for another technological innovation, the hand axe.

Some of the first specimens of a new arrival, *Homo erectus*, were first found in Asia, and were originally referred to as "Peking man" and "Java man." Their body size approaches that of modern humans, although their average cranial capacity of about 1000 cc is smaller than the 1400 cc average of the modern human. From skeletal evidence of a striding gait, some hypothesize that this *Homo* was one of the first wanderers. *H. erectus* appears in the fossil record from about 1.8 to about 0.2 MYA. Anthropologists disagree whether the species arose in Africa and migrated to Europe and the Far East, or whether their homeland was located somewhere in the latter regions.

A hominid species named *H. heidelbergensis*, found in Africa but named from later European specimens, appeared about six hundred thousand years ago. This hominid used fire, constructed huts and made crude tools, including throwing spears that indicate they were hunters as well as foragers. Several anthropologists speculate that *H. heidelbergensis* was the common ancestor of *H. neanderthalensis* and *H. sapiens*.

None of our now-extinct ancestors have engendered so much fascination as have the Neanderthals, thanks to the many remains which allow a more detailed reconstruction of their history. The earliest fossils, found mostly in Europe but a few also in Africa and Asia, indicate that the

---

14. Hurd, "Hominids in the Garden?," 220, 230.

Neanderthals appeared about two hundred thousand years ago. The last Neanderthal disappeared from the earth only recently, around twenty-five thousand years ago. Their skeletal remains show many similarities with modern humans, but there are enough differences in the forms of the skull and other features to argue for a separate species. Their cultural remains, including the finest flint tools yet crafted, certainly show an advance over previous species.

Yet anatomically modern humans, *H. sapiens*, who appear on the scene around 130,000 to 120,000 years ago (though some anthropologist argue for an even older date 180,000 years ago), show cultural differences revealing superiority in thinking and the making of artifacts, as well as many anatomical features that differ from their Neanderthal contemporaries. Among the latter are a smaller face, a higher forehead, and a less-robust postcranial skeleton. There is also evidence that these humans possessed language and a much greater capacity for symbolic representation. Artifacts dating back forty thousand years show far more variety and sophistication in materials and workmanship. Our early *H. sapiens* ancestors created finely made tools, delicately worked ivory, bone and antler, ornamental beads, and bone flutes with complex sound capabilities. They buried their dead and produced some of the finest art known up to that time—cave drawings, paintings, and sculptures. The human family had arrived.

Another question engages anthropologists: has *H. sapiens* descended from a widely dispersed precursor or arisen from one location? The majority of anthropologists favor the "Out of Africa" theory, arguing that modern humans began in Africa and, from there, spread into the Near East, Asia, and Europe. These wandering populations replaced Neanderthal and remaining *H. erectus* populations. An opposing view, dubbed by its advocates the Multiregional Hypothesis, maintains that modern humans descended from already widespread *H. erectus* populations. Interbreeding among various populations led to exchanges of varying genetic traits (gene flow), out of which emerged anatomically modern humans. Physical differences resulted from isolated developments in different regional populations. A third group of anthropologists argues for a compromise between these two theses, suggesting that the "Out of Africa" theory best explains developments in Africa and Western Eurasia while "Multiregional" developments account for Eastern Asia phenomena. Whatever the truth, all evidence from fossil and DNA studies indicates a strong biological unity among modern humans. We humans truly are all related.

13

Evolution and Human Nature

How do Christians, in particular conservative Christians, react to the scientific evidence that a continuum exists between pre-human and human creatures? If one believes that the creation is a kind of "Book of Nature," a metaphor used by theologians for centuries, then all of the data from fossil, genetic, and radioactive dating studies that support the conclusion that humans have evolved from an earlier hominid species cannot simply be dismissed out of hand. But if Christians takes this evidence seriously, then what are they to make of the biblical stories and references that appear to depict a separate creation by God of a first man and woman? And how is one to understand that human beings are created "in the image and likeness of God," in the light of human evolution? Is there a way to harmonize the evidences from the "Two Books"? Is there a way to reconcile the place of Adam in scripture and theology with the fossil and DNA evidence that our biologically united modern human species emerged between one hundred thousand and two hundred thousand years ago? Christians have responded in various ways. Here I examine two positions—conflict and concordance—before I reflect on the meaning of *imago dei* ("the image of God") in humanity.[1]

Conflict

Young Earth Creationists—those who interpret Genesis to mean that Adam was literally the first human being and that he was created directly by God some six thousand or so years ago—believe that the Bible is infallible and inerrant in all areas of knowledge and that the creation stories in

---

1. The discussion on conflict and concordance is adapted from Schneider, *Science and Faith*, Essay VI: "Human Evolution and the Image of God," particularly "Part II: Theological Implications of Human Evolution."

Genesis 1–3 present scientific and historical truth about origins, including human origins. Since the Bible is "the word of God," its statements, they assert, must be superior to any conclusions of science. Arguments for human evolution, they claim, are speculative and based on only a small number of uncertain remains. Creationist John Woodmorappe (pen name of Jan Peczkis), after criticizing evolutionary interpretations of hominid fossil evidence, states that *H. ergaster, erectus, heidelbergensis* and *neanderthalensis* are all racial variants of modern man, descended from Adam and Eve and representing the separations that took place after the Tower of Babel incident.

However, anyone who has carefully examined the skeletal remains of these species will recognize that this assertion lacks scientific merit. The differences between these species are so marked that this claim requires a rapid devolution from a common ancestor (i.e., "Adam") into hominid forms that then disappeared unremembered during historical times. This argument, contradicted by reason and common sense, exemplifies the Conflict approach to science and faith, for Young Earth Creationists absolutely reject any evolutionary interpretation of empirical data that contradicts their literalistic interpretation of the Bible.

Concordance

Many Christians accept the evidence for an ancient earth and for hominid precursors to *H. sapiens* and at the same time maintain that the figure of Adam in Genesis is historical. These concordists, using anthropological evidence, recognize that the writer of Genesis 2–4 has described the family of Adam as cultivators of domesticated plants and herders of animals, as well as metalworkers who made utensils and musical instruments. The biblical record, they say, describes human cultural developments in the ancient Near East that do not go back more than ten thousand years ago, the beginning of the Neolithic Age. Dick Fischer, for example, argues that Adam lived between four thousand and five thousand years before Christ, at the point when the Neolithic Age was merging into the Bronze Age, around 3500 BC.[2] Others disagree with this chronology, since cities (see Genesis 4) first appear circa 9000 BC.

If Genesis 2–4 is based on historical anthropology, then one has to account for the evidence from physical anthropology and archeology that *H. sapiens* appeared prior to one hundred thousand years ago. The

2. Fischer, "In Search of the Historical Adam: Part I," 242.

concordists attempt to do so. Fischer, for example, asserts that one can hold to the view that God separately created Adam and Eve, but that their descendants intermarried with an indigenous population of "pre-Adamites" (e.g., Cain's wife), thus merging with the long line of *H. sapiens* and its hominid ancestors. Adam and Eve, while historical persons, are not to be literally understood as the first humans, but rather as the first individuals God created to function as God's representatives. They were the first to bear the "image of God."

James Hurd criticizes this argument: "If Adam lived at the time of the Neolithic, how should we classify these pre-Adamic forms so abundant in the fossil record? If they walked like humans, worked like humans, and worshipped like humans, were they not human? Did they not have 'godness' [i.e., the 'image of God']?"[3] Furthermore, what sense does it make for God to separately create two humans who have the same DNA and basic protein molecules, and are similar in every other way to all humans who descended from those who appeared more than one hundred thousand years ago?

Other scenarios have Adam and Eve appearing as early as forty thousand years ago, a time during which archeologists note a cultural explosion, as verified by the presence of more sophisticated stone tools, cave art, and ritual burials. Pushing the chronology back, however, does not eliminate the objections stated above, and such an "Adam" would not fit the description of the Neolithic farmer and his family depicted in Genesis 2–4.

There are other and better ways to understand the figures of Adam and Eve. One is to apply the principle of accommodation: the writer of Genesis 2–4 was depicting the origin of humankind in a way that was comprehensible to the people of his time. Many Christians understand the figures of Adam and Eve as representative theological symbols of humanity in its origins and not as the literal, historical first man and woman.

Viewed in this way, Adam and Eve in Genesis 2–4 are identified with the unnamed figures of man and woman referred to in the separate account of creation given in Genesis 1—the male and female who bear the image of God. This interpretation allows one to frame a different and more fundamental question: how does one understand *theologically* the meaning of *imago dei* in an evolving humanity? Historically, Christian theology has provided a number of interpretations.

---

3. Hurd, "Hominids in the Garden?," 224–25.

Image of God in Humanity

The expression "image of God" refers to the divine gifts of love and compassion, or intellectual and moral reasoning and imagination, or creativity, or free choice. Obviously, the expression does not mean to suggest that we are made in God's physical image, but rather in God's mental or intellectual image. For this reason, although animals are living, they are not made in God's image as we are. Bound up with thought and reason is the capacity to act freely. We, like God, have choice. Thus we are spiritual and moral beings.

In Genesis, the "image of God" is connected with two fundamental notions, relationship and stewardship.[4] The first refers to the relationship or communion between man and woman (and by extension within the whole human family) and the relationship between humanity and God. To display the divine image is to be in the kind of loving and harmonious relationship depicted in chapters 1 and 2 of Genesis between God, the man and the woman, and between God and the whole creation.

Stewardship extends the notion of relationship for human beings to the rest of creation: humans are given dominion and entrusted to care for the earth. Human beings are to image God by treating one another and the rest of creation in the way God intends the creation to be treated—with love and care. The implications of this teaching for ecology and care for the earth are plain. The meaning of "the image of God" is also to be found in the human vocation, whereby humans partner with God in ways that reflect the covenant love of God. Love and compassion, the very traits that can be said to be literally true of God, are the very traits that humanity is to mirror in its relationship to the creation.

The New Testament extends the notion of *imago dei* in its declarations that Jesus Christ is the image of the invisible God (2 Corinthians 4:4; Colossians 1:15; Hebrews 1:3). Through the saving work of Christ, humanity is offered the gift of grace that enables the believer to be "conformed to Christ," as St. Paul claims (Romans 8:29; 2 Corinthians 3:18). The divine image given in creation and disfigured through sin can be realized to its fullest by living into the image of Christ, for Christ became human in order to display in its wholeness the image of God and restore it to all of humanity. Through Christ Jesus, in whom the fullness of God dwells, the believer may finally realize the fullness of communion with God, with

---

4. The material in this segment is adapted from Robert J. Schneider, *Science and Faith*, Essay VI: "Human Evolution and the Image of God," particularly "Part II: Theological Implications of Human Evolution."

one another in the Body of Christ, and with all of creation. In this sense, the image of God emerges when we imitate the life of Jesus, who did not aspire to status or privilege but rather humbled himself, becoming a servant of all (Philippians 2:6–8).

If this is the biblical understanding of what it means to be created in "the image of God," then does it require a separate creation for human beings—for H. sapiens—to be made in this image? Many Christian scholars think that it does not. As evangelical Graeme Finlay wrote, "That God created human beings (Genesis 1:27; Psalm 100:3) does not imply instantaneous action. God's creation of humanity encompasses past primate history, the present, and whatever is to come. The sweep of human evolution illustrates how God's work of creation is a continuing relationship of dependence between the world and God, a continuing act of God's will, an eternal covenant relationship."[5] And accepting the notion of an evolving human species can still leave a place for the figure of Adam as a historical reference, as Robin Collins argues. He suggests that "Adam" can be seen as representing in a symbolic way the "father" of the "first group of evolving hominids who gained moral and spiritual awareness."[6]

The book of Genesis implies that humanity and all the other living beings are made of the same stuff and given the same breath of life (Genesis 2:7, 9, 19; cf. Ecclesiastes 3:19–21), and modern science has shown that we share the same DNA and other molecules with virtually all living things. If the divine image has emerged in humanity through an evolutionary process, it can be understood to have done so also through God's providence. It does not denigrate either God or humanity to hold that God's creative evolutionary processes brought humanity to a point where it would be capable of expressing those qualities that both scripture and theology have associated with the "image of God."

The Soul

What are humans made of? Are they solely the atoms and molecules of physics, biology, and chemistry? Many Christians believe humans have another part, a "spiritual" part, which they generally call the soul. An essential part of Christian theology is belief that our rational soul makes us distinctively human (*imago dei*). This second part has been considered essential, for the soul is often thought of as saved for eternal life or

---

5. Finlay, "*Homo divinus*," 16–17.
6. Collins, "Evolution and Original Sin," 486.

damnation. It is also thought to account for our capacity to be in relationship with God in this life. Not that the body is to be considered bad or irrelevant. In fact, Jewish thought always gave the body a significant role. From this influence it is part of Christian belief that, in some sense, after death body and soul will be one. The soul will be, as it is now, "embodied"—although the apostle Paul makes it clear that while we now have a physical body, then we will have a spiritual body: "It is sown a physical body, it is raised a spiritual body" (1 Corinthians 15:44).

Increasingly our culture is developing an understanding of the human person as purely physical. Much of this view comes from sciences such as biology as well as by philosophical arguments. Evolutionary biologists find it inconceivable that a soul could be evolved by natural selection. Most recently neuroscience (study of the brain and nervous system), has made it appear that the brain does most or perhaps all of the things people once attributed to the soul. We seem to have reached an impasse. Reductionism is the philosophy or methodology that aims to explain away everything in terms of molecules and the like, denying reality to all higher-level entities like minds and souls. Virtually by definition a religion making souls central is bound to clash with a theory like Darwinism, which is bound to be thoroughly reductionistic. Christianity is nonreductionistic, for it affirms the existence of minds and/or souls.

Does this mean that the Christian community is headed for another conflict with science? Not unless one resorts to either/or thinking on this issue. There is another option. First we need to gain some historical perspective; the word "soul" has had different meanings at various points in church history.

Let's begin with the Bible and with what it says about the soul. It is widely agreed that the Hebrew word *nephesh*, translated "soul" in the Hebrew scriptures, didn't mean what later Christians have meant by soul. In most cases, "soul" is simply a way of referring to the whole living person. So *nephesh* should be translated as "person" or even "life." It is also used of animals, so in such cases it is best translated as "living being." Those who detect a body-soul dualism in the Old Testament, including many of the earlier translators, have been reading it into the text rather than finding it there.

When one examines the New Testament, the results agree on the whole with the Old Testament, although the agreement is more complicated because various authors used different words and ideas concerning the makeup of the person. Any attempt to harmonize the New Testament authors on this subject will only leave us frustrated and confused. Does that mean Christians can believe anything they want about the makeup of persons? Not at all! Some views are compatible with Christian teaching, while others are not. I will list four current theories.[7] The first two are extreme positions that are not compatible with Christian teaching, while the latter two are compatible.

1. *Dualism*: This view understands humans to be composed of two parts, an eternal soul and a perishable body. The person is identified with the soul. The goal of life is to escape from the body. This view is inconsistent with Christian theology because it implies that the material world is evil. This contradicts the doctrine of creation and the Christian understanding of incarnation.

2. *Reductive materialism*: This view reduces humans to physical bodies. Everything about us can be explained. Moral behavior is something programmed by our genes, while religious experience is explained as abnormal neurological events, similar to hallucinations. The very existence of religion can be explained sociologically—humans create religion to foster social cohesion. Humans are just intelligent animals who deceive themselves when they think they have moral obligations or can have a relationship with God.

3. *Holistic dualism*: This view considers humans as composed of two parts. We can use the terms "body" and "soul," but both parts are essential. Humans are only truly themselves when the two parts are united and functioning harmoniously together. Thus it may be possible for the two aspects to come apart temporarily at death, but the Christian position is that persons are not really themselves again until the body is restored at the resurrection. This holistic dualism has been the most common position through church history. But developments in science are calling this view into question. It is not that neuroscience can prove there is no soul, but rather that the functions of the soul are explainable with certain brain functions, so the concept of the soul seems more and more an unnecessary complication.

4. *Nonreductive physicalism:* While this view may seem the same as reductive materialism, in that there is only one entity—a physical, biological organism—it acknowledges that our brain and neurological system give us the capacities to think about right and wrong and sometimes to choose the good. Our brain, with its large neocortex, is what enables us to recognize transcendence.

---

7. Murphy, *Reconciling Theology and Science*, 58–59.

Nonreductive physicalism is certainly close to the ancient Hebrew conception of the person. It maintains the holistic view of the person found in both the Old and the New Testaments. Ancient philosophers believed that to produce living things, a non-material soul had to be added to matter. Aristotle called it "entelechy." Medieval and modern Christian scientists called it "a vital force" or simply "vitalism," a view that biologists now find inadmissible. What is needed is not a different kind of part, a non-material one—but a special *organization* of the parts. The argument here is that at the level of psychology we do not need to add a non-material part, such as "mind" or "human soul," to get a human being. Consciousness and all of our human traits depend instead on a special organization of the brain. A nonreductive physicalist account of the person fits nicely into this scientific model.

Top-down causation is crucial for this view. Just as humans can act in a top-down manner in lower levels of the hierarchy, so God can act in a top-down manner to influence us. So we should not confuse this model with a reductionist account, in which only bottom-up causation is recognized.

Nonreductive physicalism is highly sensitive to order. The whole point about the DNA molecule is that one gets every different kind of gene, all the information possible, not from different subunits, but from the same subunits ordered in the chain in different ways. That is what the genetic "code" is all about. The same is true of the brain. Order the molecules in one way and you get junk. Order the molecules in another way and you get Albert Einstein. The important notion in physicalism is denial that the order represents a new kind of thing or substance. The order exists, but it is not a thing in the way that a molecule is a thing. To think otherwise is to enter a way of thinking that gives existence to such nonuseful entities as those already mentioned "life forces" popular in philosophical circles in the early twentieth century. The assembled and functioning DNA molecule is not a new substance, but is instead smaller substances ordered. The very crux of Darwinian explanation of the distinctiveness of humanity is that we are ordered, and thus can function in ways that are not possible for other animals. It is not that we have something different at the substance level, but rather that we are different because of the way that we are put together: by natural selection for adaptive ends.

If one thinks of the soul as did Thomas Aquinas, as something that animates the body, and that the distinctive human aspect of this is intelligence linked with freedom of moral choice, then this is very much in

Evolution and Human Nature

line with what the Darwinian sees as our having evolved through natural selection. Although there is work yet to be done, one can see ways of exploring how the soul as now conceived might survive death—God is not preserving a substance but rather *information* that, at some point, can be reactivated—but in other respects there are still potential tensions between Darwinism and Christianity. If the soul is conceived as empirical—empirical, but not simply material—one can dispense with its miraculous origins, as demanded by Roman Catholicism. In this sense, the soul has evolved from lower organisms, and the transition has been made from animal to human souls. And who is to say that this evolution of the human soul, viewed not as some one-of-a-kind event but as part of everyday life, cannot be a God-backed process?[8]

There is a fear on the part of many Christians that the concept of evolution lowers human dignity by blurring the distinctions among matter, life, and human personhood. While it may seem so at first, careful reflection suggests that no such danger exists. Yet there is a reason why evolution gives this impression. Examining traditional Western theology, Catholic theologian John Haught notes that Western thinking, together with much of the rest of the world, has clung to a hierarchical cosmology. By "hierarchical" he means that the universe was understood to be organized *vertically* into a "Great Chain of Being," running from lifeless matter at the lowest level, through plants, animals, and humans to God at the highest level.

The evolutionary perspective, viewing life and mind as emerging gradually in a *horizontally* framed cosmic drama, apparently by accident and out of a universe that is fundamentally lifeless and mindless, considers humans as emerging only recently in time, as brains grew in size and cognitive capacity. At some point life became human, and humans in turn produced ideas about the good and about God. Evolution views things chronologically or historically; classical religion and hierarchical cosmologists (sometimes called the "perennial philosophy") view things vertically. If we take an either/or approach, and decide that the evolutionary approach is correct, no sharp lines separate matter from life, or life from mind. The question than arises whether there exists any basis for the timeless assumption by religions and cultures that life is "higher" than matter, or that mind, spirit or soul even exist at all.

Haught believes that a revised version of the hierarchical view—one that understands that nature can be *both evolutionary and hierarchical* at

8. Ruse, *Can a Darwinian Be a Christian?*, 79–82.

the same time—can be shown to be consistent with evolutionary data.[9] In evolution, nature's hierarchy is an *emergent* one (gradually arising over time), and so it cannot be understood in purely vertical and static terms. Thus even after Darwin, we can still clearly distinguish among various levels and values of being. We can preserve both evolutionary continuities and hierarchical discontinuities by recognizing the role of *information* in living beings.

For some time now scientists have noted that nature is not just a continuum of matter and energy. Rather, nature is composed of matter plus energy plus information. Hierarchy entails discontinuity between one level and the next. And it is informational (organizational) patterning that introduces the discontinuity. The presence of distinct informational patterns can organize the world into discontinuous hierarchical "levels" without causing any suspension of the physical and chemical processes in which the information is encoded. The information resident in DNA, for example, can shape life without violating any laws of chemistry.

"The quiet presence of information," Haught concludes, "can bring about hierarchical discontinuity in evolution without in any way disturbing the continuity at the levels of biological or chemical processes. So it is simply illogical to conclude that evolutionary science reduces life and mind to lifeless physical stuff. Information makes all the difference in the world, though it does so in a very quiet, unobtrusive way."[10]

While it is no longer acceptable, on a scientific level, to argue that evolution involves invoking special directing forces of a divine nature, from the earliest days of evolution there have been many, beginning with Darwin himself, who have affirmed nonguided direction. Our understanding of the mind/brain is proceeding at such a speed that it would be foolish to make any definitive and final judgments, scientific or theological, on these questions.

Evolution of the Brain and Mind

Before we resume our science/religion comparison, we need to address the evolution of the brain. "No evolutionist questions that the explosion of brain size was essentially adaptive, for it is clear that hominids with bigger brains had an adaptive edge over those with smaller brains. Precisely how the brain works has always been a matter of some debate, but

9. Haught, *Responses to 101 Questions*, 24–26.
10. Ibid., 26.

now, in the computer age, there are many fruitful hypotheses showing how the brain can operate as a calculator to process and use information. One particularly popular thesis invokes the idea of the brain being built on the modular pattern. Thus there is not one central unit in the brain doing everything at once, in an all-purpose fashion, but rather there are units performing different tasks connected up in various ways."[11]

This brings us to the issue of consciousness. Darwinians take consciousness very seriously. Consciousness seems so essential to what it is to be a human that it would be very improbable that natural selection had no role in its production and maintenance. Since it seems obvious that consciousness is in some sense connected to or emergent from the brain, consciousness must have some biological function in its own right. In particular, one would expect that primitive consciousness emerged as animals developed bigger and better brains, and then was included by selection in its own right, developed and refined, perhaps pulling brains along in its wake to provide the material underpinning.

But what is consciousness, and what function does it serve? Why should not an unconscious machine do everything that we humans can do? Is consciousness merely an add-on tangentially related to the brain's electronics? Almost certainly not! One major function is that of serving as a filter, guide, and coordinator to all the information presented by the brain. Because information needs to be routed, consciousness provides this service, seeing that the brain does not get overloaded with unusable material. Consciousness is surely an important factor in such essential human functions and abilities as moral and social interaction and in making choices among alternative possibilities (free will or choice). Consciousness gives humans a power and flexibility not possessed by those who do not have it.

None of this, of course, fully explains consciousness. No one, certainly not the Darwinian, seems to have any answer as to why a bunch of atoms should have thinking ability. This ignorance in no way denies that consciousness is sentient. We humans seem to be as certain of our sentience as we are of anything else about us. The point is not whether or not we are sentient, but that there is no scientific answer.

Philosophers have provided answers. Some, like Plato and Descartes, have argued that consciousness is a substance, but different from physical things: thinking substance (*res cogitans*) rather than material or extended substance (*res extensa*), to use the Cartesian dichotomy. However,

---

11. Ruse, *Can a Darwinian Be a Christian?*, 72.

although examples of such "dualism" continue, most notably with Karl Popper, most people (including most Darwinians) feel uncomfortable with this philosophy. It is difficult to understand how separate substances, mind and body, can interact. Most prefer to think of mind and body as manifestations of the same substance; such thinkers are "monists," subscribing to the "identity theory." Here they follow Dutch philosopher Baruch Spinoza (1622–1677), who argued that consciousness is in some way a manifestation of material substance. This is not to say that it is just material substance as traditionally conceived—thinking is not red or hard or round—but that it is part and parcel of material substance, with nothing more added.

Where one goes from here is difficult to say. The point is that consciousness is real, whether or not it is separate, and it is something that seems open to the forces of evolution. More we cannot and need not say.[12]

Going back to Christianity and to a Christian understanding of the soul, we find two options as well.[13] One is a kind of Augustinian position, in turn Platonic, which sees the soul as something more or less distinct, in a substance sense, from the body. Plato taught that the person is composed of two parts: a mortal body and an immortal soul. He believed the soul to be eternal; it pre-exists the body and is only temporarily imprisoned in the body during earthly life. The soul's true home is an ideal world, a transcendental realm of "Ideas." Augustine's views are similar. Augustine, probably the most influential theologian since the apostle Paul, taught that the person is composed of soul and body. The soul is immortal, but not eternal, since it has a created beginning. He described the soul as using a mortal body—using rather than being imprisoned in it, since the doctrine of creation forbids considering the body evil.

Plato's student, Aristotle, developed strikingly different views on many subjects. During the first millennium of Western Christianity, Plato and his followers were seen as the most useful resource for theologians, but during the Middle Ages Aristotle finally had his turn. Thomas Aquinas, influenced by Aristotle, became famous for resolving conflicts between Christian theology and the science and philosophy of Aristotle. Aquinas developed a more sophisticated account of the soul than had any of his predecessors (and perhaps anyone since).

---

12. Ibid., 72–73.

13. The following is adapted from Murphy, *Reconciling Theology and Science*, 48–50.

Evolution and Human Nature

We must begin with the account of matter that both Aquinas and Aristotle were using. For them, matter is passive. It has the potential to become all sorts of things, but only if some active principle affects it. The active part of any entity, in this view, is the Form. So every existing thing is composed of matter and form.

Living things have abilities or capacities that go far beyond those of non-living things. Rocks, for instance, cannot grow or reproduce. This means living things must have more potent and interesting forms than do rocks. These more interesting forms are souls. Plants have economy-model souls—forms that give them capacities to take in nutrients, grow, and reproduce. These are nutritive or vegetative souls. Animals have nutritive powers but also the capacity to perceive things and to move around. Human souls possess all these capacities and more; the rational soul is the deluxe model.

The soul is thought of as having three major levels of functioning. The lowest powers of the human soul, shared with both plants and animals, are the *vegetative faculties* of nutrition, growth, and reproduction. Next higher are the sensory faculties, shared only with animals. The sensitive or animal level of the soul also provides for the power of locomotion and for lower aspects of appetite—the ability to be attracted to sensible objects such as food or a mate. This *appetitive faculty* is further subdivided between a simple tendency toward or away from what is sensed as good or evil and a more complex inclination to meet bodily needs or threats with appropriate responses.

The *rational faculties* are distinctively human. They include passive and active intellect and will. The two intellectual faculties together enable abstraction, grasping or comprehending concepts, judging, and remembering. The will is a higher appetitive faculty whose object goes beyond things we can perceive with the senses. Remember, we share with animals the ability to be attracted to physical things such as food. So Aquinas is saying we humans have an additional capacity to be attracted to good things of a different sort. In fact, he says, the object of this faculty is the good itself, which is God. Here we have our commonsense notion that the soul is what enables us to relate to God. Morality is a function of attraction to the good combined with rational judgment as to the identity of the good.

For Aquinas (following Aristotle), the human soul—identified with the intellectual faculty, which makes a human a living human being—is not a thing, in the sense of a material substance. It is rather more a principle of ordering or what, in Aristotelian terms, is called the Form. Although it is something real that can act as a kind of cause, it is not a substance. Therefore the soul is not a body but that which actuates a body. All organisms have souls as such: this is what makes them living. Only humans have "intellectual souls." This, Aquinas argued, is the "image of God."

Brain Localization Studies

There is a growing body of data on regions of the brain responsible for various mental and emotional capacities.[14] This research began with the study of patients incapacitated by tumors or strokes. Careful note was taken of their symptoms. After autopsy these symptoms could be correlated with the regions of brain damage. More recently, various sorts of brain scans have made it possible to study these correlations in living subjects.

These varied techniques have allowed for localization of a vast array of cognitive functions. For example, certain areas in the left frontal region and in the temporal lobe are involved in speech. Other areas affect the person's command of color vocabulary, nouns, verbs, proper names, and so forth. There are also apparently social regions of the brain, such as those allowing for facial recognition and perception of emotion. The parietal lobes are involved in memory of faces.

Victims of localized damage may show the inability to recognize emotions. While there does not seem to be a single location responsible for this capacity, there are patients whose brain damage has resulted in its loss. Studies of causes of mental illnesses involving troubling emotions, such as depression, have shown a significant role for neurotransmitters such as serotonin. Neurotransmitters are chemicals involved in conveying signals from one neuron to another.

The higher mental faculties attributed by Aquinas to the rational soul are less understood. However, all involve language. Thus even if we do not understand how they depend on brain functioning, we know that they do so because of the close association of linguistic abilities with specific areas of the brain.

The appetitive function attributed to the rational soul was, for Aquinas, the ground of moral behavior. Antonio Damasio's fascinating book, *Descartes' Error*, tells the story of Phineas Gage, a twenty-five-year-old construction foreman for a railroad who in 1848 was the victim of an

---

14. The material in this segment is adapted from Murphy, *Reconciling Theology and Science*, 50–55.

accident that sent an iron bar through the front of his brain. He survived the explosion and was able to recover almost entirely in less than two months. He was able to touch, hear, and see. Although he lost vision in his left eye, his vision remained perfect in the right. He walked firmly, used his hands with dexterity, and had no noticeable difficulty with speech or language.

Yet this astonishing outcome pales in comparison with an extraordinary change in Gage's personality. Gage's body remained alive and well, but a new spirit animated him. Whereas he had been an honorable individual, possessing a well-balanced mind and temperate habits, the changes became apparent as soon as the acute phase of brain injury subsided. He was now fitful, irreverent, impatient, capricious, and vacillating. The change was so radical that friends and acquaintances hardly recognized the man. His intellectual capacities were undamaged, but he lost the appetite for good, which in Thomistic language meant he lost his appetite for God. So changed was he in character that his employers had to let him go shortly after he returned to work.

The foregoing is a brief sketch of points at which biology and neuroscience have provided accounts of the dependence on physical processes of specific faculties once attributed to the soul. It is interesting to note in addition the rough analogy between Aquinas's (and Aristotle's) three levels in the soul's hierarchy of faculties (nutritive, animal, and rational) and the gross anatomy of the human brain. We share with the lower animals the reptilian complex at the base of our brains, which is responsible for territoriality, sex drive, and aggression. With the higher animals we share the limbic system, responsible for emotion. We alone have a large and highly developed neocortex, responsible for theoretical reasoning.

What does all this mean? It is important to remember that the specific concepts of the soul used by Western Christians were developed by philosophers to account for capacities that seemed not attributable to the body alone. But developments in science certainly call this view into question. While developments in neuroscience can never prove there is no soul, one can always look at the localization studies and say that functions of the soul are surprisingly well-correlated with certain brain functions. But the concept of the soul seems more and more an unnecessary complication. It appears that Plato and Augustine and Aristotle and Aquinas may simply have been wrong.

Original Sin

In addition to the doctrine of the soul and the uniqueness of rationality and consciousness associated with human life, another theme central to creationist theology helps to explain their rejection of an ancient earth and its long history of life. This is the doctrine that there was no death before the fall of Adam and Eve, which some creationists consider an essential, core doctrine of Christian faith. According to their interpretation of Romans 5:12, death itself first came into the world as a result of Adam's sin; further, if there had been no Fall, there would have been no need for Christ's redemptive work. This doctrine has had a long history in Christian thought, but it has not been universally held. In fact, the idea that we inherit from Adam some kind of original sin is based more on a shallow biblical literalism than upon general Christian teaching regarding sin and redemption.

Some theologians have interpreted the curse in Genesis 3 as referring to the spiritual death of Adam and his descendants, not physical death for all living things. This interpretation fits well with the evident scientific fact that living creatures have died long before the advent of humankind. The Young Earth Creationist interpretation is based on questionable exegeses of Genesis 3:3, 19 and Romans 5:12, and ignores the fact that these passages do not refer to the death of animals.[15]

Privileging Genesis, or rather, their interpretation of Genesis, over the New Testament, is an error many creationists commit. "If we can't believe Genesis," Ken Ham insists, "then how can we believe in Christ? How can we believe the rest of the Bible?"[16] But this argument turns Christian faith on its head. Jesus Christ is the foundation of Christianity, not someone's interpretation of Genesis. Faith in Christ is the "good news" of the gospel, not faith in a six-day creation, never a core doctrine of historic Christianity. What Ham, Henry Morris, and others are saying in effect is that their interpretation of Genesis is essential to Christian faith and that if one abandons it, one must abandon Christianity. The tragedy is that some have followed this logic and given up their religious faith altogether.

Thankfully, there are a number of Christians in the sciences who once accepted strict creationism but years later abandoned it without losing their faith, for what the creationists are defending is a particular interpretation of scripture, not scripture itself. An awareness of the scientific

---

15. Robert J. Schneider, *Science and Faith*, Essay VIII: "Young Earth Creationism."
16. Ham, *The Lie: Evolution*.

notion of evolution can help us arrive at a deeper and more meaningful understanding of original sin than previously held.

The classic doctrine of original sin has two separable parts. One is the historical claim that the first human beings, Adam and Eve, sinned by eating fruit God forbidden them by God. The second is the psychological claim that human nature was once virtuous, but was corrupted by the first sin. Both claims, however, can be disputed, for both can be shown to be false. As Patricia Williams demonstrates in her groundbreaking book *Doing without Adam and Eve*, the alleged corruption of human nature is found neither in Genesis 3 nor anywhere else in the Hebrew scriptures. Genesis 3 explicitly states that Adam and Eve became more like gods after they ate the fruit of the tree of knowledge (Genesis 3:22). The idea of a fall—a corruption in human nature—is not prominent in the New Testament; the event of Genesis 3 is only mentioned in passages associated with the apostle Paul (Romans 5, 1 Corinthians 15, and 1 Timothy). Only later, in the writings of Saint Augustine, does the doctrine of original sin become formulated in any significant way.

In a chapter titled "The Demise of Adam and Eve," Williams asserts that it took the birth of modern science to challenge the predominant model of the universe and of human nature that had survived for over a thousand years. The scientific theory of biological evolution made clear that successful species like humans do not pass through single-pair bottlenecks; there is certainly no evidence that this was true of *Homo sapiens*, a species that seems to have been widely spread around the earth. Genetic evidence indicates that human populations never consisted of fewer than several thousand individuals.

Scientifically speaking, Adam and Eve can no longer be viewed as the progenitors of all humanity, for they were not historical figures. If not historical figures, they could not have disobeyed God. If they did not disobey God, then we have no basis for original sin and therefore no fall and no corruption of human nature.[17] Thus, the narrative about them cannot be used to explain the human inclination to sin or the origin of evil. That said, there is no need for despair. If one is prepared to accept a metaphorical interpretation of the Adam and Eve story, while insisting on the relevance of evolution, a ready understanding of original sin emerges.

As Darwinians have demonstrated, the struggle for existence and the consequent selection of variations leading to adaptations designed for success in this struggle often involve self-interest, if not outright selfishness,

---

17. Williams, *Doing without Adam and Eve*, xiv, 79–80.

with the host of features, attitudes, and characteristics that most humans find offensive and that Christians judge as sinful. Of course, to be self-interested is not necessarily to be immoral. No one judges ill the person who eats a meal because he or she is hungry, or who falls in love with a pretty girl or a handsome young man and wants to have that person as a mate. But, all too quickly, self-interest degenerates into qualities like greed, lust, and boastfulness. There are good biological reasons for this. The man who feeds himself or his family is better off than the man who has no food or just some leftover scraps. The man who impregnates a hundred women is ahead (in the Darwinian game of survival) of a man who impregnates just one. The person who lies and cheats his way to the top of the corporate ladder is more successful than he who loses.

Original sin as part of the biological package comes with being human. We inherit it from our parents and they from their parents. Moreover, overlapping our selfishness is a genuine altruism, a very necessary adaptation given the human path of sociality. We are loving, kind, and generous because that is just as much a part of our nature as is our selfishness. Acknowledging that sin remains central to the human condition, Williams supplies insights from the field of sociobiology, such as the influence of genes, the environment, and the misuse of human freedom, to account for the origin of sin and to deal with the problem of evil. With respect to original sin, sociobiological *Homo sapiens* are practically identical to Christian *Homo sapiens*. Both camps see humans as deeply self-centered, selfish even, but with a genuine moral overlay, guiding (at least, instructing) our actions in social situations and interactions. The surface stories are very different, but the underlying concerns are the same: humans are truly sinful, with goodness fighting for control.[18]

As understood by Augustine, who coined the term, original sin is a biologically transmitted tendency to evil desires (*libido*) that arose with Adam and has contaminated all of humanity. However, most theologians today would consider such an interpretation extremely shallow. According to contemporary theological interpretation, original sin refers not to a specific act committed by a parental couple in the remote past, but to the general state of our present human estrangement from God, from each other, and from the natural world. Seeking new ways to account for the ambiguities of life and the presence of evil, Teilhard de Chardin spoke of original sin as "the reverse side of all creation."[19] We are all born into a

---

18. Ruse, *Can a Darwinian Be a Christian?*, 209–10.
19. Teilhard de Chardin, *Christianity and Evolution*, 40.

world that is already deeply flawed, in great measure by human greed and violence. The notion of original sin, in this sense, also reminds us of our human incapacity to save ourselves from this state of affairs. As Haught makes clear, "the need for a savior is in no way diminished by our recent evolutionary knowledge. There is no contradiction between evolution and a realistic notion of original sin . . . It appears that we do inherit instincts that run counter to our social, ethical, and religious values. We have to keep these in check in order to live ethical or virtuous lives. But do we need to see them as a consequence of original sin? Certainly they mark us as ambiguous and unfinished beings. But I believe it wiser to understand original sin not in terms of the genetic continuity we have with the rest of life, but primarily in terms of the complex of social and cultural pressures that channel our native impulses in destructive directions."[20]

In an evolving cosmos, life has not yet achieved a state of finality. This incompleteness of the cosmic project is nobody's fault, including the Creator's. The only universe a loving and caring God could create, after all, is an unfinished one. For God's love of creation to be actualized, the beloved world must be "other" than God. An instantly created ("finished") universe would in principle have been only an emanation or appendage of deity and not something truly other than God.

The assumption of an original perfection of creation, as envisioned by creationists, has in fact led religious speculation to imagine that the source of the enormous evil and suffering in the world must be either an original principle of evil—an idea unacceptable to biblical theism, which views the creation as inherently good—or else some intraworldly being or event. The latter supposition has led to the demonizing of various events, persons, animals, genders, and races. By contrast, it is enough for us simply to wonder what a salutary thing it would be if religious thought were now to take the reality of evolution with complete seriousness. Understanding evil as the result of an initial transgression has made reparation and expiation a priority for all who follow biblical religion. The vital problem, both for Christ and for us, is to find a culprit and remove its influence. The assumption of original sin opened up the possibility of interpreting suffering essentially as punishment, necessitating an ethic of retribution.

Evolution, to repeat our theme, means that the world is unfinished. And if unfinished, then we cannot justifiably expect perfection. There is inevitably a dark side. The notion that present evil can be attributed to a culprit that somehow spoiled the primordial creation has led to a

20. Haught, *Responses to 101 Questions*, 80–82.

misunderstanding of the "history of salvation" as a drama of "restoring" the original state of affairs. This emphasis has caused theologians to subordinate the expectation of the far more accurate and fulfilling understanding of the history of salvation as *transformation*—the novelty and surprise at the fulfillment of God's promises—to that of *restoration*—the recovery of a primal perfection of being. This is why evolution is potentially such good news for theology. Evolutionary cosmology invites us to complete the biblical vision of a life based on openness to the future and hope for surprise rather than allowing us to wax nostalgic for what we mistakenly imagine once was.

In an unfinished universe, we humans remain accomplices of evil, of course. But our complicity in evil may now be interpreted less in terms of a hypothesized break from primordial innocence than as our systematic refusal to participate in the ongoing creation of the world. According to this new way of thinking theologically, sin and evil now include our resistance to the call of "being more," our deliberate turning away from participation in what is still coming into being. In an evolutionary context, we might wish to go beyond Teilhard and suggest that "original" sin is not simply the reverse side of an unfinished universe in process of being created. It is also the aggregation in human history and culture of all effects of our habitual refusal to take our appropriate place in the ongoing creation of the universe. It is this kind of corruption—and not the defilement of an allegedly original cosmic perfection—by which each of us is "stained."

14

Darwinism and Design

CHARLES DARWIN PUBLISHED *THE Origin of Species* in 1859. More than 150 years later Christians are still divided over interpreting it. It seems that the media and society in general display a predilection for stories about conflict. As a result, it is easy to overlook the fact that many Christians have no objections to evolutionary theory. So even as I mention below some historical and current reasons for conflict between Christianity and evolutionary theory, I must emphasize that many have found it not only possible but helpful to their Christian understanding to conceive of biological life in evolutionary terms.

In 1832 the young Charles Darwin was naturalist on the *HMS Beagle* starting a five-year voyage around the world. His critical experience on the trip was his study of slight variations among species, especially variations found among those living on the islands in the remote Galapagos chain off the western coast of South America. On each island a species lived in isolation from neighboring islands with similar environmental conditions. Six years later, reading Thomas Malthus on the effects of human population pressure and competition, Darwin found the clue for a theory by which to interpret the data collected on the voyage. As he later recorded, observing the struggle for existence that occurs repeatedly, "it at once struck me that under these circumstances favorable variations would tend to be preserved and unfavorable ones to be destroyed. The result of this would be the formation of new species. Here, then, I had at last got a theory by which to work."[1]

His theory of natural selection combined several ideas: (a) random variations; (b) the struggle for survival; and (c) the survival of the fittest. Over a long period of time this process would result in the natural selection of favorable variations and the corresponding reduction of other less favorable variations, so that gradual transformation of the species would

---

1. Darwin, *Life and Letters*, 1:68.

occur. Darwin held that natural selection is the main factor determining the direction of evolutionary change. Before finally publishing *On the Origin of Species*, he spent twenty-seven years amassing an amazing array of facts on the variation of species. He studied in detail the breeding of domesticated animals, the hybridization of plants, comparative structures of embryos, and the geographical distribution of animal and plant forms, both living and extinct. The sheer range and magnitude of the data he brought into correlation with his theory is staggering.

In *Origin* Darwin avoided mention of humanity, but a dozen years later he gave a thoroughgoing discussion of human origins in *The Descent of Man* (1871). In this work he tried to demonstrate how all human characteristics might be accounted for in terms of the gradual modification of anthropoid ancestors by the process of natural selection. The close resemblance of humans and gorillas in anatomical structure had already been widely noted; Darwin indicated how upright posture, larger brain size, and other distinctive changes might have been produced. He insisted that human moral and mental faculties, including forms of feeling and communication, differ in degree rather than in kind from the capacities of animals. Human existence, previously considered sacrosanct, was thus brought within the sphere of natural law and was analyzed in the same categories applied to other life forms.

Four topics were central in the theological debate that followed the publication of Darwin's *Origin*: (1) the challenge to scripture; (2) the challenge to design; (3) the challenge to the status of humanity; and (4) evolutionary ethics and social Darwinism. In this chapter, I focus on the question of design.

Arguments against Darwinian Evolution (Arguments Supporting Design)

In 1802 British theologian William Paley provided the best-known treatment of the teleological argument for the existence of God. His argument, based on natural theology, introduced one of the most famous metaphors in the philosophy of science, the image of the watchmaker. He argued that if he found a stone on the heath and were asked how it came to be there, he might answer that it could well have been there forever. If, however, he were to find a watch on the ground, the answer could not be that it had always been there, for the watch is a purposeful instrument, made by an intelligent designer. The universe, Paley claimed, is like a watch.

Beginning with the premise that the world exhibits intelligent purpose, order, and other marks of design, he inferred the existence of an intelligent grand designer to account for the purpose-revealing world.

Since Darwin, versions of the argument from design like that of Paley have been viewed as particularly vulnerable, since they started from the observed adaptation of organic structures to useful functions. Such adaptation could now be accounted for by the impersonal process of natural selection without the need for any preconceived plan. The species now living are here because they have survived while thousands of others lost out in the competitive struggle. Moreover, some of the facts that had always proved difficult for the advocates of design, such as useless rudimentary organs and traces of limbs, could now be readily explained. In the years between the return of the *Beagle* and the publication of *Origin*, Darwin moved from the traditional religious beliefs in which he had been brought up to a tentative deism. He rejected miracles, revelation, and special creation, and objected on moral grounds to the idea of hell. He said that the suffering in nature, which he had observed so frequently, was inconsistent with the notion of a beneficent God. He argued that detailed providential design would have resulted in perfect adaptation, but he saw evidence only of differential adaptation, which was all that was required for natural selection to be effective.

Over time, Christians objected to Darwinian evolution on numerous grounds. The following represent some of the more persistent objections.[2]

1. One reason is that it spoils the popular argument for the existence of God based on the fitness of organisms to their environments and the apparent design of their organs to serve specific purposes. In effect, Darwin proposed a competing hypothesis to explain biological adaptation. He argued that a combination of random variation and natural selection was sufficient to account both for the development of effective organs and appendages and for the remarkable adaptation of organisms to their environments.

Ironically, shortly before Paley published his book, the philosopher David Hume had pointed out the vulnerability of arguments like Paley's—there are alternative hypotheses.[3] First, the universe shows a great deal of order, but there is disorder and evil as well. Furthermore, the universe is not sufficiently like the productions of human design to support the

---

2. This argumentation is adapted from Murphy, *Reconciling Theology and Science*, 63–67.

3. Hume's *Dialogues Concerning Natural Religion* was published posthumously in 1779. It appears that Paley was unaware of Hume's classic critique of the teleological argument.

argument. Lastly, the analogy from artifact to divine designer fails because one has no other universe with which to compare this one. We would need to make such a comparison in order to decide if it were a designed universe or simply one that developed on its own.

As important as Darwin's contribution is in offering an alternative model of biological development, it doesn't altogether destroy the argument from design. The theist has at least two ways of reviving the argument. First, one can argue that the process of natural selection is the way in which a divine designer might work out his purpose for the world, and the inference to the existence of a designer can then still be construed as the best explanation. Alternatively, one can turn one's attention away from biological structures and look for marks of design elsewhere in the universe—as, for example, in the apparent "fine tuning" of the natural laws and physical constants. Hence, regardless of whether a design inference is warranted as an explanation for biological purpose, such an inference might be warranted as an explanation for those other features of the universe.

2. A second source of controversy involves human conceptions of their place in the universe. Many Christians feel insulted by the claim that humans are closely related to animals. Such a reaction, however, is biblically unjustified. While true that the creation stories in Genesis underscore the special role of humans in the created order and in relation to God—we are made in the "image of God"—these stories nevertheless testify equally to our continuity with the rest of nature: we are made "of the dust of the earth." So Christian objections to kinship with animals come not so much from the Bible as from Greek philosophy, where all of reality was conceived of in terms of a hierarchy of value. Humans were thought to occupy a distinct rung on this metaphysical ladder, above the animals but just below divine beings.[4]

3. Christians in Darwin's day objected to evolutionary theory because of its association with ethical and social applications now referred to as "social Darwinism." The argument here is that competition for survival results in evolutionary biological progress. Therefore this competition should be allowed and even encouraged in the human world as well, and no provision should be made to encourage the survival and propagation of the weaker members of society. However, it is not clear whether Darwinian theory was the source of such conclusions or whether Darwin's

---

4. A similar emphasis is found in the Bible in Psalm 8:5–8.

concept of the survival of the fittest was influenced by economic and social theories already then existing in Britain.

4. Much of the resistance to evolutionary biology can be traced to limited views of divine action. The problem is to suppose that an event must be either an act of God or a natural event. Historically, however, Christian theologians have denied such a strict opposition. For instance, medieval theologians described God as the primary cause of all events and natural causes as secondary or instrumental.

In the early modern period, however, the concept of a law of nature developed. This was originally a theological metaphor to express God's governance of the natural world: just as God governs humans by means of law, so too God governs the motions of the planets by law. Gradually, however, the metaphorical and theological nuances were lost. God was still seen by many to be the source of the laws of nature, but these were granted a force and status of their own. So Christians had become used to the idea that one could distinguish between acts of God and the regular processes of the natural world. Darwin's achievement can be described as bringing the phenomena of life under the rule of natural laws. The claim that the origin of life could be explained in terms of natural laws seemed to some a denial of divine action.

A common strategy for reconciling evolutionary theory with Christian theology has been to claim that God has created living things by working through the evolutionary process. Recall the description of the hierarchy of the sciences mentioned in chapter 11. Using the model of nonreductive physicalism (emergent realism), it becomes evident that the same event can be described at a number of levels. For example, we can describe a long and complex molecule in chemical terms as DNA, or we can describe it in biological terms as the gene for green eyes.

The benefit of recognizing theology as one of the levels in this hierarchy of description is to make clear that a theological account and a biological account can both be true and valuable descriptions of the same set of processes. The biologist looks for the natural antecedents of a biological event and seeks patterns among these chains of events. The theologian can describe the same series of events in terms of God's purposes and achievements.

5. Many evangelical Christians mention conflict with Genesis as a major historical reason for rejection of Darwin's theories. While there was some of this, it needs to be emphasized that the issue as often understood today, in terms of literal reading of an inerrant text, has only become central in recent years. Reading the first chapters of Genesis as though they

are historical or scientific accounts of the origin of the universe and of life has not been customary. From earliest days Christians have recognized that there are various kinds of literature in the Bible, each deserving to be read accordingly. The notions of literal reading and inerrancy arose in the late nineteenth and early twentieth century as a reaction against the historical-critical study of the Bible and as part of the modernist-fundamentalist controversy within mainline Protestantism.

The problem described above concerning divine action is one of the most significant theological issues of our day. I believe it underlies much of the disagreement among contemporary Christians about how to read the Bible. The question of divine action is thus more fundamental than the controversy over biblical literalism. If divine acts and natural events are thought to be mutually exclusive, then the process of revelation is likely to be understood as a direct intervention into human history, and it will not be possible to give adequate attention to the human character of the biblical texts. However, if God's action is understood to take place ordinarily in and through natural and historical processes, then one can recognize both the human and divine authorship of scripture. A natural consequence of this recognition takes into account the contexts and purposes of the human authors.

6. Another reason for negative assessments of evolutionary theory by Christians is also related to the exclusive approach taken by some scientists and philosophers, as well as some Christians, who assume that if scientific explanations can be given of natural processes, then this rules out theological accounts. This approach, taken by biologist Richard Dawkins, cosmologist Carl Sagan, and philosopher Daniel Dennett, promotes evolutionary biology as evidence that religious claims are false.

Carl Sagan, one of the best known of these proponents, develops what might be called a "naturalistic religion." Beginning with biology and cosmology, he then uses concepts drawn from science to fill in what are essentially religious categories. These categories fall into a pattern surprisingly parallel to the Christian conceptual scheme. Sagan has (a) *a concept of ultimate reality*: "The Universe is all that is or ever was or ever will be"; (b) *an account of ultimate origins*: Evolution with a capital "E"; (c) *an account of the origin of sin*: the primitive reptilian structure in the brain, which is responsible for territoriality, sex drive, and aggression; and (d) *an account of salvation* that is gnostic in character—that is, it assumes that salvation comes from knowledge. For Sagan this knowledge is scientific but could be advanced by contact with extra-terrestrial life forms more advanced than we. While the entire scheme sounds religious, the appeal to alien life could be construed as mystical.

The model of the hierarchy of the sciences is helpful in explaining this pseudo-religious phenomenon in science. In chapter 11, I argued that the sciences raise boundary questions they alone are not competent to answer. Thus for an intellectually satisfying account of reality, one needs some account of ultimate reality at the top of the hierarchy. Christians, of course, can turn to theology. But without some recognizable theological system at the top of the hierarchy, there is an emptiness that cries out to be filled. Sagan, Dawkins, Dennett and others oblige by creating new scientific religions.

Biology in particular raises boundary questions concerning the meaning of human life. While atheistic worldviews do need to be addressed by Christians, the goal should not be to discredit evolutionary theory but to show where legitimate claims of evolutionary biology end.

Arguments Disputing Design

There are numerous reasons why people in the modern era dismiss the biblical notion of creation, together with the corollary view that purpose and design were built into the fabric of nature from the start. I will focus on two: the antiquated perspective of the biblical period and biological evidence of human adaptation.

Limitations of the Biblical Perspective

The first reason for dismissing the biblical doctrine of creation comes from the Bible itself, particularly from an examination of the beliefs of people in biblical times. Biblical authors and their audiences lived in highly superstitious times, when it was highly likely that biblical audiences were superstitious as well. Their universe was three-tiered, with heaven above and hell below, and earth—believed to be flat—at the center of the cosmos. Early Christians believed human behavior to be regularly influenced by angels, spirits, and demons. Though most believers were monotheists, they were surrounded by polytheistic beliefs, which included the plausibility of divine incarnations and interventions. When polytheists looked to the skies and saw the sun, they envisioned a deity named Helios taking his daily chariot ride across the sky. Visions and dreams were viewed as means of divine communication. Droughts, storms, tornadoes, and earthquakes were manifestations of divine displeasure. And worship, particularly sacrificial worship, was considered the primary means to placate a deity. Because there was no knowledge of evolution, all species were considered to be fixed and unchanging; no one imagined that one species might give rise to another, by adaptation, natural selection, or any other means.

While Enlightenment thinkers followed a different mindset, one guided by science and reason, the majority of Christians rode out the Age of Reason seemingly content to live in two worlds simultaneously, one modern, progressive, and anti-superstitious, the other premodern, traditional, and superstitious.

A great watershed occurred in 1859, when Charles Darwin published his brilliant discovery concerning natural selection in his *Origin of Species*. From that point on, it seems, two divergent paths emerged. The first, based on science and evidence, led progressively away from the world of the Bible and toward an uncertain but progressive future. The other, reactionary and conservative, held tightly to traditional teachings and to an ever-increasingly inerrant scripture. Predictably, a middle way emerged, enabling its travelers to embrace the best of both worlds, enjoying the benefits of science and technology while clinging to traditional religious beliefs.

Over time, however, this *via media* compromise seemed increasingly unsatisfying. Its adherents, rightly viewed with suspicion by both sides, were considered "liberal" by their more conservative religious counterparts and "inconsistent," "close-minded," or "illogical" by their progressive scientific counterparts.

The field of biblical studies, meanwhile, supplemented by emerging disciplines of archaeology, literature, history, psychology, and sociology, became increasingly specialized, using historical critical methodology to gather evidence that questioned traditional understandings of biblical authorship. Utilizing modern scholarship, scholars found evidence that the Pentateuch, the first five books of the Bible, could no longer be attributed to Moses, but were the product of multiple authors over the span of some six hundred years. Additional changes in dating and authorship affected the meaning of other books and passages. The book of Isaiah, for example, came to be seen as the work of at least three different authors, spanning a period of some three hundred years; the book of Daniel could no longer be dated to the sixth century BC but was produced during the second century BC, four hundred years after the presumed author lived; few if any of the Psalms could be attributed with certainty to King David; the patriarchal narratives came to be viewed as historically unreliable; and the stories in Genesis 1–11 came to be read as etiologies, as mythical accounts written to answer sociological questions about the causes of cultural effects.

Eventually the same methodology was applied to the field of New Testament studies, though it took a bit longer to unfold. As literary parallels to the biblical gospels were found, their authors came to be viewed as theologians in their own right, with specific biases and distinctive points of view reflecting the views of specific communities of faith rather than of individual authors bent on historical accuracy. In addition to the reliability of the gospels, other concerns arose, such as the authenticity of the letters attributed to Paul, six of which are now disputed, including three letters known as the Pastoral Epistles (1 and 2 Timothy and Titus), which scholars increasingly attribute to a later reactionary figure who attempted to deradicalize or domesticate Paul in such a way that views of Christianity and of the official Roman state could be made more compatible. The discovery of the Dead Sea Scrolls, written by a dissident group of sectarian Jews (generally acknowledged to be Essenes) shortly before the birth of Christianity, revealed numerous parallels in belief and practice with primitive Christianity, raising questions about its uniqueness and leading to speculation that Christianity may have been an offshoot of the Essene branch of Judaism.

Additionally, the presence of Jewish parallels to the book of Revelation, including the apocryphal 2 Esdras, written by a Palestinian Jew around the same time as the biblical book of Revelation (near the end of the first century AD), made scholars question the uniqueness of the closing book of the Bible. 2 Esdras, like Revelation, is an apocalypse revealing a mindset similar to that of early Christianity; its central section (chapters 3–14) consists of seven revelations that underscore the justice of God in dealing with evil, including the wickedness of Rome (called "Babylon" here as in the book of Revelation).

Finally, I mention the issue of the rhetorical nature of the New Testament, which indicates that this material was written not so much to provide a foundational historical narrative but rather to persuade and instruct believers and potential converts. Rhetoric, apparently, was woven into every aspect of Roman civic, religious, social, and political life. The early Christians, evangelizing this world, followed suit. Knowing that Christians wrote rhetorically challenges popular understanding of the nature of scripture and can result in new perspectives regarding the purpose and nature of scripture, leading to a reexamination of cherished Christian phenomena such as miracles and even the doctrine of the resurrection.

Many Christians today continue to read this Bible as though it contains timeless teachings divinely revealed. Viewed in this manner, it provides security for individuals caught in a matrix of rapid change. However, the preceding discussion should cause us to question such understandings of the Bible. The Bible, apparently, was a product of its own era, and reading it with that understanding actually enhances its value for the present.

On the whole, the gulf between organized religion and the educated populace is widening at an alarming rate. Modern ecclesiastical religion, unfortunately, is becoming increasingly fundamentalistic in its stance toward traditional doctrine and scripture. While fundamentalism encourages its constituency to perpetuate the status quo, to recite the creeds, and not to change its mind, the Postcritical Paradigm, like modern science, is more hopeful, for it remains open to change. Such approaches to reality embrace new possibilities and are committed to revising cherished hypotheses.

Current accumulated knowledge is said to be doubling every six years, causing college texts to be re-edited and rewritten regularly to accommodate new ideas and changes in perspective. When science books contain errors, they are corrected in subsequent editions. Books about evolution are believed not because they are holy but because of the evidence they contain. While many books of the Bible were revised in ancient times, they now have canonical status, meaning they can no longer be edited, only interpreted. For most Christians, the process of inscripturation brought divine revelation to a close.

But as Jewish audiences discovered long ago and as Protestant Christians learned only recently, the Bible is the product of its religious community. The Hebrew scriptures did not create Judaism; rather, Judaism created the Hebrew canon. Likewise, the gospels, as the rest of the New Testament, are the creation of the church. As Roman Catholics maintain, the Bible is the product of the church.[5] This means that the church is not based on the Bible; rather the Bible is based on the church. Many Protestants, following the arguments of the Reformers, maintain the reverse. And this view is no longer intellectually tenable. Modern Muslims need to come to a similar understanding with regard to their Qur'an. Their scripture, while attributable to the genius of Muhammad, must also be acknowledged as

---

5. I am grateful to Walt Weaver, summer instructor of Religious Studies at Washington & Jefferson College, for bringing this point to my attention.

the product of tradition. These scriptures, like the American Constitution, need to be subject to ongoing revision, amendment, and progressive interpretation. The church, like science, must remain open to the future, adhering to a progressive understanding of its scriptures even as it embraces the contributions of science. "Truth," as understood by biblical people and by their spiritual heirs, is dynamic, not static. When humans relate to truth as though it were static, they become spiritually stagnant and stifle their potential. Truth, like Torah, is far more than law, and when reduced to that level it loses its status as gift.

Modern Christians entrenched in the Conflict or Opposition camp (those who affirm that science and religion are fundamentally irreconcilable) find two models for truth competing for their allegiance, one closed and unchanging (scripture) and the other open and changing (science). Viewed in that fashion, the two appear incompatible and force believers to choose between them. And this is what most traditionalists have done, accepting scripture as their primary authority for belief and practice. Secular persons, facing that either/or dilemma, generally move in a contrary direction, limiting the Bible's value to the category of ancient literature. A third group, called Separatists or Contrasters, responds to the dilemma by adopting a fence-sitting position. Acknowledging both models as authoritative, they compartmentalize reality into two realms, science and religion.

Over time, belief in God has helped explain the mysterious and unknowable areas of reality. For many people, the existence of God served to answer the ultimate questions and to explain life's gaps. Today millions of people across the planet continue to place their trust in supernatural theism, believing unreservedly in the God of the Bible. And if college educated, many do so primarily on the basis of "the God of the Gaps," continuing to believe in the existence of a God who fills gaps in present-day knowledge or understanding. This strategy, however, has been strongly condemned by theologians such as Dietrich Bonhoeffer, who recognized that gaps shrink as science advances, meaning that God is destined to have little to do and nowhere to hide.

One of today's prominent gaps, used by creationists and advocates of Intelligent Design such as cell biologist Michael Behe, is the notion of irreducible complexity in nature. The key to demonstrating irreducible complexity is to show that none of the parts could have been useful on their own. As a physical example of an irreducibly complex system, Behe cites a mousetrap: something with five parts (base, spring, hammer, and so forth), any one of which is individually necessary for the mousetrap's functioning. The trap could not have originated naturally in one step, and could not have done so gradually. Any part would not function properly alone, and any part missing would mean failure of the whole. It had to be designed and made by a conscious being—a fact true also of organisms.

Behe believes that an irreducibly complex biological system must be a major challenge to a Darwinian mode of explanation, for Darwinism insists on gradualism: "Since natural selection can only choose systems that are already working, then if a biological system cannot be produced gradually it would have to arise as an integrated unit, in one fell swoop, for natural selection to have anything to act on," which essentially means that natural selection is redundant.[6]

As it turns out, Behe's choice of a mousetrap as an exemplar of intelligent design is unfortunate. All sorts of parts can be eliminated or twisted and adapted to other ends. There is no need to use a base, for example. You can just attach the units directly to the floor, a move that reduces the trap's components from five to four. But even if the mousetrap were an accurate example, it would hardly make Behe's point. No evolutionist ever claimed that all of the parts of a functioning organic feature had to be in place at once, nor did any evolutionist ever claim that a part used now for one end must always have had that function. Ends get changed, and something introduced for one purpose might well take on another purpose. It might be only later that the new purpose is incorporated in such a way that it becomes essential.[7]

One of Behe's favorite examples of "irreducible complexity" is the immune system, for which he claimed that science would never find an evolutionary explanation. His position was shown to be in error when, under legal cross-examination, he was presented with fifty-eight peer-reviewed publications, nine books, and several immunology textbook chapters about the evolution of the immune system. Since this was one gap he was unwilling to relinquish, he simply insisted that evidence was still insufficient. Eric Rothschild, chief counsel for the plaintiffs in the trial, chided Behe in his summation by pointing out that "Professor Behe and the entire intelligent design movement are doing nothing to advance scientific or medical knowledge and are telling future generations of scientists, don't bother."[8]

6. Behe, *Darwin's Black Box*, 39.
7. Ruse, *Can a Darwinian Be a Christian?*, 117.
8. Dawkins, *The God Delusion*, 133.

Darwinism and Design

Nowadays the gaps have narrowed significantly, to the point where belief in supernatural theism is not only increasingly less plausible but appears contradictory. Whereas belief in God once served to answer our problems, today belief itself has become problematic. As traditional arguments for the existence of God have been shown to be circular, only belief in God remains to support belief in God. Logically one cannot support faith with faith, and yet that's essentially all believers in God have left.

Of the arguments against the existence of God, two are considered persuasive by critics of supernatural theism:

1. The biblical God is inactive today. This God neither intervenes in nature to prevent good people from suffering equally with bad people nor answers prayer in any verifiable way (the faithful, of course, declare all results to be God's will).

The results of scientific investigation into cosmology and biology have forced theologians to reconsider their understanding of God, relegating God to a distant deistic Creator whose omnipotence is no longer relevant to the cosmos or to the perspective of process theology, where divine influence in the cosmos is limited to persuasion. In either case, God's omnipotence is redefined.[9]

2. The biblical God is immoral. In *The God Delusion*, Richard Dawkins examines the Old Testament's portrayal of God and concludes that this figure is "arguably the most unpleasant character in all fiction: jealous and proud of it; a petty, unjust, unforgiving control-freak; a vindictive, bloodthirsty ethnic cleanser; a misogynistic, homophobic, racist, infanticidal, genocidal, filicidal, pestilential, megalomaniacal, sadomasochistic, capriciously malevolent bully."[10]

This verdict is hardly balanced. The God most of us grew up trusting and worshipping is a benevolent Creator, who is both Lord of the universe and friend to sinners, a God who loves the world and who sent the very best when he sent Jesus to be our savior.[11] This message, however,

---

9. My own response to this argument against supernatural theism is found in chapter 5, particularly in the discussion concerning the possibilities inherent in panentheistic views of God.

10. Dawkins, *The God Delusion*, 31.

11. The Bible, as most acknowledge, is a complex book, with paradoxical and even conflicting views on many topics, including the nature of God. Just as one can find verses that present God as vengeful and violent, there are many that present God as kind, reconciling, and compassionate, and against favoritism and violence. For Christians, the tension between these paradoxical views can be resolved not by turning a blind eye to difficult passages but by turning to Jesus, the "canon within the canon." If the Bible is intended to bear witness to Christ, then consulting Jesus seems like

somehow gets lost when we recite the creeds constructed by institutional Christianity, for in these creeds God appears as one who is all-knowing, all-seeing, and all-powerful. Of course throughout history this God was also portrayed as masculine, pro-Semitic, pro-slavery, totalitarian, vindictive, misogynistic, and homophobic.

In Genesis God sends a flood to destroy humanity. This is the first of many stories depicting a God who sends natural disasters upon human beings because of their sins, which is a dominant explanation for such things as droughts and plagues, and one reason why natural scientific explanations for these phenomena were not pursued. In the Bible God not only punishes sinners with natural disasters, God also declares all humans to be guilty and judges them with death. Yes, the Bible teaches that natural death is not natural but rather the result of sin, individual and cosmic (Genesis 2:17; Ezekiel 18:4; Romans 5:12).

The Old Testament mandates capital punishment for people having extramarital sex (Deuteronomy 22:13–30), for homosexual behavior (Leviticus 20:13), for breaking the Sabbath law (Numbers 15:32–36), even for children who are deemed incorrigible (Deuteronomy 21:18–21). In the New Testament there are texts that speak of cutting off body parts if they cause someone to sin (Matthew 5:29–30; 18:8–9). The second-century church father, Origen of Alexandria, took this literally and castrated himself so he could tutor women without suspicion. There are also sayings about hating one's parents that cultists have used in brainwashing young converts (Luke 14:26); guilt-producing texts like the unforgivable sin of blasphemy (Matthew 12:31–32); and even anti-Semitic passages (1 Thessalonians 2:14–16), which were used by some in Germany to justify the Holocaust. Then there's the ultimate threat of hell in the lake of fire (Revelation 20:11–15), the most terrifying threat of all.

While humans have always longed for immortality, the doctrine of the afterlife has been shown to have originated rather late in biblical times,

---

the best approach on this and other controversial matters. And the resulting reality that emerges is that in Jesus we find a stunning portrait of God: Jesus never killed anyone, nor did he hate anyone. He practiced what he preached: reconciliation, not retaliation; kindness, not cruelty. His weapons were love, not hatred; courageous and compassionate resistance, not violence; outstretched arms on a cross, not stockpiles of arms, nuclear or otherwise. On Good Friday God was located first and foremost with the crucified one, identifying with humanity. In the Bible, God is with the slaves, not with the slave-drivers; God is found among the displaced refugees, not those stealing their lands. And God is found in the one being spat upon, not in the one spitting. That God—the God displayed through the life and death of Jesus—is the God Christians worship. That is the God Richard Dawkins is unwilling—or unable—to encounter.

under the influence of Persian belief. Modern scholars and theologians alike are increasingly debunking beliefs in heaven and hell as products of wishful thinking about rewards and punishments. Since we have no evidence concerning the existence of the afterlife, this concept continues as one of the "gaps" in our knowledge. Belief in heaven and hell has profoundly affected the course of Western morality, serving either as a deterrent for wrongdoing or as a motivation for well-doing. Both factors are poor incentives for morality. We humans must become responsible for our own moral behavior.

The classic arguments for the existence of God, such as the argument from motion, from cause, from degree, from contingency, or from design, all seem to involve an infinite regress; in other words, the answer to one question raises a prior question, and so on. All the arguments take the idea of a regress and make two common assumptions: God terminates the regress, and God is immune to the regress. If we examine the argument from design, which is the only one in regular use today, we find that a designer God cannot be used to explain organized complexity because "any God capable of designing anything would have to be complex enough to demand the same kind of explanation in his own right. God presents an infinite regress from which he cannot help us to escape."[12] All such argumentation turns on the familiar question: "If God exists, who created God?" If the answer be, "God has always existed," the answer is ultimately no more satisfying than to argue that "matter has always existed" or that at some point "something came from nothing." Both answers, incidentally, are scientifically plausible.[13]

Biological Evidence against Design

In addition to disagreement with biblically based reasoning, supported doctrinally by the classic creeds of Christendom, a second source of argumentation for dismissing the biblical doctrine of creation comes from

12. Dawkins, *The God Delusion*, 109.

13. Modern theists support their notion that God has always existed by insisting that God's reality cannot be explained by the workings of the natural world, since God is not a member of the universe. If God is not subject to the rules and procedures of science, the grounds for belief in God are therefore quite different from those found in science. On the basis of this line of thinking, Christian philosopher Diogenes Allen concludes that "any attempt to have God involved within the processes that science studies is theologically utterly unacceptable," *Troubled Believer*, 40. Such logic, based on fideistic (and presumably biblical) assumptions, is unassailable, but such a God would be unapproachable, unrelatable, and unlovable.

evolutionary biology. In a chapter titled "History Written All Over Us,"[14] Richard Dawkins notes that vestiges of our evolutionary history are written in the bodies of all living creatures. Classic examples of vestiges are the rudimentary wings of the ostrich and the blind eyes of cavefish. While vestigial structures may have ongoing functions of some sort, as creationists are prone to argue, what matters is that rudimentary ostrich wings are useless as normal flying wings, and that rudimentary cavefish eyes are useless as normal sighted eyes. Vestiges may be functional, but speculative arguments against vestiges based upon their possible functions completely miss the point.

Dawkins illustrates his discussion with a human vestige known as "goosebumps."[15] Why is it, he asks, that humans get goosebumps when they are cold, elated, or are badly frightened? The answer is that our ancestors were mammals with hair all over, and these were raised or lowered due to sensitive bodily thermostats. When cold, hairs were raised to enhance the layers of insulating trapped air. When warm, the coat was flattened to allow body heat to escape more easily. In later evolution, the hair-erection system was adapted to allow for the expression of emotions. When animals are made angry or when they become alarmed, hairs stand on end to increase the body's apparent size and to scare off dangerous rivals or predators. We humans still have the machinery to raise barely existent or non-existent hairs, and we call it goosebumps. The hair-erection machinery, like nipples on a male chest, is a vestige, a non-functional relic that performed a useful job in our long-dead ancestors. Nipples on males and goosebumps are among the many instances of history written all over us. They constitute persuasive evidence for the occurrence of evolution.

According to Dawkins and other antisupernaturalistic biologists, organisms created by an intelligent designer, even one using evolution as a means, would surely be near perfect, demonstrating evidence of purposeful design. Living organisms, however, ourselves included, are loaded with what Stephen Jay Gould once called "the senseless signs of history."[16] Our bodies no not display design so much as they reveal the evidence of evolutionary ancestry. Human embryos, for example, form a yolk during the early stages of development. In birds and reptiles, the very same yolk sac surrounds a nutrient-rich yolk, from which it draws nourishment to support the growth of the embryo. Human egg cells have no comparable

---

14. Dawkins, *The Greatest Show on Earth*, 339–71.
15. Ibid., 339.
16. Cited in Miller, *Finding Darwin's God*, 100.

stores of yolk. Being placental mammals, we draw nourishment from the bodies of our mothers, but we form a yolk sac anyway, a completely empty one. This empty sac is simply one more sign that our ancestry can be found in egg-laying reptile-like animals.

These signs of history are the telltale marks of evolution in all organisms. Because evolution can work only on existent organisms, structures, and genes, it seldom finds the perfect solution for any problem. Instead, evolution tinkers, improvises, and cobbles together new organs out of old parts. A true designer would face no such problems, and could produce genuinely new structures, molecules, and organs whenever needed. Unfortunately, it doesn't work that way. The many imperfections of the human backbone, for example, which become increasingly apparent as we age, can hardly be attributed to intelligent design. They are easy to understand, however, if we appreciate the fact that our upright posture is a recent evolutionary development. To adopt the explanation of design, we are forced to attribute a host of flaws and imperfections to the designer. Our appendix seems to serve only to make us sick; our feet are poorly constructed to take the full force of walking and running; and even our eyes are prone to optical errors and to lose their ability for close focus as we age.

Speaking of eyes, we would have to wonder why an intelligent designer placed the neural wiring of the retina on the side facing incoming light. This back to front arrangement scatters the light, making our vision less detailed than it might be, and even produces a blind spot at the point that the wiring is pulled through the retina to produce the optic nerve that carries visual messages to the brain.[17] One reason that the eye sees better than it should is that the brain does an amazing job of cleaning the images it receives. When the great nineteenth-century German scientist Hermann von Helmholtz examined the eye, he said: "If an optician wanted to sell me an instrument which had all these defects, I should think myself quite justified in blaming his carelessness in the strongest terms, and giving him back his instrument." Dawkins's assessment is far blunter: "send it back. It's not just bad design; it's the design of a complete idiot."[18]

The same can be said for the laryngeal nerve, a branch of one of the cranial nerves that lead directly from the brain rather than from the spinal cord. On one side of the neck, one of the laryngeal nerves goes straight to the larynx (voice box), following a direct route that a designer might have chosen. The laryngeal nerve on the other side of the neck, however,

---

17. Ibid., 101.
18. Dawkins, *Greatest Show on Earth*, 354–55.

follows an astonishing detour, diving into the chest, looping around one of the main arteries leaving the heart, before heading back up the neck to its destination. In humans, the detour represents several inches. But in a giraffe, the detour can be up to fifteen feet.[19]

Another consequence of our ancestral past concerns the sinuses, which give many of us such grief because their drainage hole is in the very last place a sensible designer would have chosen. In humans the drainage hole is at the top, where gravity cannot drain them. In a quadruped, however, from which bipeds evolved, the "top" of the sinuses is not the top but the front, and the position of the drainage hole makes much more sense.[20]

As Dawkins notes, "This pattern of major design flaws, compensated for by subsequent tinkering, is exactly what we should *not* expect if there really were a designer at work. We might expect unfortunate mistakes . . . but we do not expect obvious stupidity, as in the retina being installed back to front. Blunders of this kind come not from poor design but from *history*."[21] If one were to posit a designer's motivation from this data, there is only one conclusion possible: such a designer was incompetent.[22]

Eyes, nerves, sinuses, and backs are poorly designed from the point of view of individual welfare, but the imperfections make perfect sense in the light of evolution. The same applies to the larger economy of nature, including the suffering caused by plagues, pestilence, and parasites. A beneficent designer might seek to minimize suffering in nature, but that is certainly not what happens. The suffering among wild animals is so appalling that sensitive individuals would best not investigate it. Darwin wrote of this in a letter to his friend Joseph Hooker: "What a book a devil's chaplain might write on the clumsy, wasteful, blundering low and horridly cruel works of nature."[23] The total amount of suffering per year in the natural world is unimaginable. Every minute, thousands of animals are being eaten alive, others are running for their lives, others are being slowly devoured from within by parasites, while thousands are dying of starvation, thirst, and disease.

Take for example the ichneumon wasp, with its habit of paralyzing but not killing its victim before implanting an egg so that the larva can

---

19. Ibid., 356.
20. Ibid., 370.
21. Ibid., 356.
22. Miller, *Finding Darwin's God*, 102.
23. Cited by Dawkins, *The Greatest Show on Earth*, 390.

feed from within. The female wasp stings its prey to keep it alive so that it might provide fresh meat for the growing larva feeding within. The larva, for its part, eats the internal organs in an orderly manner, beginning with the fat bodies and digestive organs, leaving the vital heart and nervous system till last.

Such events in nature make sense from the perspective of natural selection and survival of the fittest, but make no sense in a world designed and maintained by a beneficent creator. As Darwin remarked, "I cannot persuade myself that a beneficent and omnipotent God would have designedly created the ichneumonidae with the express intention of their feeding within the living bodies of caterpillars." Australian science broadcaster Robyn William declares such a designer, if there were one, "a sadistic bastard."[24]

One final issue can be mentioned, that of speciation. Careful studies of the mammalian fossil record show that the average length of time a species survives after its first appearance is around two million years. Two million years of existence, and then extinction. The story is similar for insects and for marine invertebrates. In simple terms, no creation of this designer is able to make it over the long term. What do we make of this? Quite simply, the advocates of design seem to be faced with a logical contradiction. They would like to claim that the perfection of design seen in living organisms cannot possibly have been achieved by a random, undirected process like evolution, and that an intelligent agent is required to account for such perfection. But when one looks at the record, the products of this intelligent design consistently fail to survive. For the record, ninety-nine percent of all species that ever lived have become extinct.

To explain this inconsistency, biologist Kenneth Miller tells the story of a visitor at a zoo who walked past one of the cages, marveling at the sight of a lion and a lamb sleeping peacefully next to each other. Amazed, he sought out the zookeeper. "That's incredible!" the visitor said. "How do you make them get along so well?" The zookeeper smiled. "It's easy. All we have to do is to put in a new lamb every day."[25] Such a zookeeper, of course, should be fired and replaced immediately. Miller concludes that no hypothetical intelligent designer should be given an award for design perfection, certainly "not for designing new life forms that consistently look like jerry-rigged modifications of his last creations. You might think

---

24. Cited ibid., 370.
25. Miller, *Finding Darwin's God*, 102.

the guy had no sense of originality. Worse yet, you might even think that evolution was going on."[26]

Cosmic Promise Rather Than Cosmic Design

Before Darwin, many religious thinkers had argued that laws and patterns in nature could not have come about by chance, but only by intelligent design. And, of course, the intelligent designer had to be "God." Darwin, however, gave us a drastically different explanation of the design in living beings. He did not deny that nature is intricately ordered, but his theory implied that the complex patterning in living beings is the natural product of an enormously lengthy process of trial, error, and adaptation. During the course of evolution, because most organisms had been too crudely "designed" to survive in their habitats, they died out, leaving no offspring. Only relatively few, the best adapted, were able to survive and reproduce. However, if we look closely even at the survivors we can see that none of them, including ourselves, can be said to be "perfectly" designed either. Evolutionary biology calls our attention to the ample evidence of imperfect adaptation, and to the clumsy and even "wasteful" history of experiments that lies buried beneath the surface of extant life forms.[27]

At its own level of understanding—one that refuses to engage in any theological inquiry—science has a very good explanation of design, as we have seen. However, evolutionary biology, like any other branch of science, is compelled to look for a purely natural explanation of design. I believe we must allow science to go as far as possible in explaining adaptive design in a "naturalistic" way. But I also affirm that evolutionary biology is only one level of a whole hierarchy of explanations needed to understand in depth the story of life. Theology can be part of such a hierarchy of explanations. Indeed I think we must at some point appeal to theology to explain ultimately why there is any order or design in nature at all—as well as why there is also instability and process. We can explain life and its complex designs on many levels without opposing one level to the other. Physics can explain order and design quite adequately from a thermodynamic point of view without interfering with biological accounts. Chemistry too can explain life at its own level. And so can theology. Problems arise only when experts on one level claim that theirs is the sole adequate explanation of life.

26. Ibid., 103.
27. Haught, *Responses to 101 Questions*, 85.

Darwin, along with many of his followers, concluded that the theory of evolution undermines the time-honored belief that the order or "design" in living organisms requires a divine designer. And so, if God is thought of primarily as an intelligent designer, evolution does appear to challenge religious belief. However, if God is thought of not simply as the ultimate source of order (or design), but also as the source of novelty (as the biblical God "who makes all things new"), then evolution is consonant with biblical faith in the God of new creation.

If we are going to speak honestly and intelligently about God after Darwin we must do much better than simply polishing up old design arguments. There must be a better way to account for living complexity than either a pure naturalism that rejects the notion of God altogether, or a supernaturalism that must occasionally and arbitrarily appeal to the miraculous.

John Haught offers a wonderful solution.[28] He starts with the Augustinian suggestion that a creator has richly endowed the universe, from its opening moments, with the potential for evolving toward the kind of complexity we see in the cell and genetic DNA. Having done so, there is no need for God to tinker with the cosmic process. The universe is given an internal capacity for self-organization that removes the need for special divine manipulation. The sprouting of life and mind in the universe is analogous to the blossoming of an oak tree from the inauspicious beginnings of a simple acorn.

From that starting premise, Haught moves to a second possibility, that God "seeds" the universe not with design but with the promise of novelty and a complexity that eventually becomes alive and conscious, at least here on earth, but quite possibly elsewhere in the universe as well. The "word of God," which according to Genesis hovers over creation in the beginning, is a word of promise. The self-organizing universe, inseparable from God's promise of a future, may be seen as continuously moving through a "field of promise," consisting of all the possibilities offered at the start. For Haught, in some sense God (or "the Spirit of God") is this field of promise. "Ultimately it is the world's moving more fully into God, and God's quietly coming into the world in the mode of promise, that allows nature to evolve and self-organize in the direction of life and mind. Such intimate involvement with the world on God's part remains, however, completely outside of the range of scientific detection."[29]

---

28. Ibid., 92–93.
29. Ibid., 93.

Haught's thesis is that cosmic purpose lies deeper than either Darwin or design. The idea of "design" is too brittle to represent the richness, subtlety, and depth of the life-process and its raw openness to the future. Life is more than "order." Life requires the continual admittance of disruptive "novelty," and so the idea of "promise" serves more suitably than "design" to indicate life's and the universe's inherent meaning. This way of "reading" evolution seems consistent both with science but also with religious hope.

The key point is that evolutionary biology, now supported and widened by cosmology, has made us realize that we live in an unfinished universe. Scientific and religious systems, together with living species and all of the cosmos, are part of a process still coming into being. The history of religion, like that of science, is a long series of partially successful but mostly inadequate human attempts to adapt to the inexhaustible depths of the cosmos (which, in part, we label "God"). Religion tries to adapt humans to the world's depth through various symbols, myths, and creeds. But the infinite elusiveness of this depth forever evades exhaustive depiction. And so, the religious quest, like that of science, is always frustratingly incomplete. Thus we humans, much more than animals and plants, often feel a sharp sense of dislocation and lack of correspondence to our world because we are made to adapt not just to actuality, but even more to possibility (what we are calling "promise"). We are, in other words, "genetically wired for a world forever open to the future."[30] The fact that the universe is even now perhaps in the early phases of its full emergence helps us understand why, religiously speaking, we remain always somewhat in the dark, why our answers to the biggest of our questions will always be frustratingly opaque, why we must walk by faith as well as by sight, and also why it makes more sense to hope than to yield to despair. The physical universe is a work in progress, and religions, firmly embedded within nature itself, are continuous with this evolutionary responsiveness. This process of adaptation can by definition never reach a static point of completion. Hence the enormous amount of time involved in cosmic, biological, cultural, and religious evolution should come as no surprise, theologically speaking. Theology after Darwin can now suggest that the universe, understood as an adaptive process, evolves at all only because in the remote reaches of its endless depth there beckons something like a promise (this is akin to what theologians call "providence"). Promise (providence) is not manipulation of nature, but is instead a reservoir of possibilities offered to the world throughout its creative spread.

30. Haught, *Deeper Than Darwin*, 145.

Conclusion

IN THE PUBLIC MIND the label "creationism," a view generally associated with Christian fundamentalism and biblical literalism, is usually seen as opposed to "evolutionism," whether on a cosmic or a more narrowly human scale. In the preceding pages I have presented a variety of views about God and creation, ranging from theism—a traditional theology of divine sovereignty over nature's operations—to those that acknowledge in the creation a considerable degree of freedom.

In discussing questions related to the so-called "problem" of science and religion—questions about the existence of God, the human soul, the possibility of direction or purpose to the universe, and the place of theology in the hierarchy of the sciences—we examined three distinct positions on the relationship between science and religion: Conflict (opposition), Contrast (separation), and Contact (engagement).

At times in our lives we may have found ourselves straddling their somewhat artificial fences. The conflict approach may once have seemed the most compelling, though at other times we may have been attracted to the lucidity of Contrast, or to the cloudier possibilities of the Contact approach. The reason is that as we gain perspective, the various approaches seem to resemble less a fixed typology than differentiated phases of a single complex process.

The process of which I speak begins with conflation, the often naïve or undifferentiated merging of aspects of religion with a few casually understood scientific ideas. Were it not for an original confusion of religion with themes that eventually became the exclusive domain of science, the red flag of conflict would possibly never have been waved in the first place. Thus, even though we may consider the Conflict approach to be misguided, we may nonetheless appreciate it as an important, perhaps even inevitable, stage in the larger journey toward richer understanding.

However, as the process unfolds further, the Conflict approach appears too extreme, and so it often evokes the more temperate response of Contrast. Contrast allows us to separate science from religion without having to envisage them as enemies. It compartmentalizes them to the

Conclusion

extent that there is no longer any possibility of either conflation or conflict. Indeed, for some of us the journey from conflation, through conflict, to conversation may have to pass through the logically precise compartments established by Contrast.

But many are not content to remain in the safety of Contrast. The original dream of a unity of knowledge—the irresistible human longing for coherence—does not easily go away. First naïvely affirmed by conflation, the passion for synthesis arises once again in our third approach, beckoning us back from the brink of dualism. Contact (engagement), therefore, seeks relationship, but only opposite to the distinctions initiated by Conflict and refined by Contrast.

The fundamental unity of science and religion is most explicitly anticipated in Engagement. This way suggests that science and religion, different though they may be, share a common origin in the remote and mysterious fountainhead of a simple human desire to know. Both science and religion ultimately flow out of the same desire for truth lying at the heart of our existence. And so, it is because of their shared origin in this fundamental concern for truth that we may never allow them simply to go their separate ways.[1]

Living in a post-Darwinian universe, where evolution is a fact of life, does not demand that we give up the idea of God. Rather it asks that we think about God in a fresh way. Evolutionary knowledge, accepted and rightly viewed, can help blunt centuries of world-fleeing mystical spirituality and align our religious existence with the natural zest for life that links us biologically to our evolutionary past. The inherent adventurousness of religion may then receive a new birth. For a growing number of Christians today, evolution is a helpful and even a necessary ingredient in our thinking about God today. As the Roman Catholic theologian Hans Küng put it, evolutionary theory makes possible (1) a deeper understanding of God—not above or outside the world but in the midst of evolution; (2) a deeper understanding of creation—not as contrary to but as making evolution possible; and (3) a deeper understanding of humans as organically related to the entire cosmos.[2]

Skeptics, of course, will immediately ask how we can reconcile our ideas about a providential God with the role that chance plays in life's evolution.[3] This is a crucial question, which the Contrast camp cannot

---

1. Haught, *Science and Religion*, 202–3.
2. Küng, *Does God Exist?*, 347.
3. The material in the remainder of this segment is adapted from Haught, *Science*

Conclusion

address with finality, since it questions the reality of chance, attributing it to human ignorance of some larger divine plan. The Contact model, however, acknowledges chance to be quite real, but does not find that it contradicts the idea of God. On the contrary, if there exists a loving God who is intimately related to the world, we should expect an aspect of indeterminacy or randomness in nature. The reason is simple: love typically operates not in a coercive but in a persuasive manner. It refuses to force itself upon the beloved, but instead allows the beloved—in this case the entire created cosmos—to remain itself, though in such a way as to imply intimacy rather than abandonment.

If, as our religious traditions have always insisted, God truly cares for the well-being of the world, then the world must be permitted to be something other than God. Even if its being is fundamentally derived from God, it must have a certain amount of "freedom" or autonomy. If the world did not somehow exist on its own, it would be nothing more than an extension of God's own being, and hence not be a world unto itself. When viewed in a panentheistic perspective, then, there must be room for uncertainty in the universe. The fact of randomness in evolution thus becomes an instance of the absence of direct divine determinism required by a world related to a God who cares for its well-being. In other words, if the world is to be anything distinct from God, it has to have room for experimenting with different ways of existing. Leaving room for such latitude does not mean that there is no divine vigilance, but only that out of respect for the otherness of creation, divine love does not crudely intrude. God risks allowing the cosmos to exist in relative liberty, and in the story of life, the world's inherent "freedom" manifests itself through the random variations or genetic mutations that comprise the raw material of evolution. A certain amount of chance is quite consonant with a panentheistic understanding of God.

If God were a magician or a dictator, then we might expect the universe to be finished all at once and to remain eternally unchanged. But what an impoverished world that would be; it would lack all the drama, diversity, adventure, and intense beauty that evolution has in fact produced. A world of human design might have a listless harmony to it, and it might be a world devoid of pain and struggle, but it would have none of the novelty, contrast, danger, upheaval, and grandeur provided by evolution over billions of years.

---

and Religion, 61–63.

Conclusion

Fortunately, the God of our perspective is not a magician but a creator. And this God is much more interested in promoting freedom and the adventure of evolution than in preserving the status quo. The long creative struggle of the universe to arrive at life, consciousness, and culture is consonant with the conviction that real love never forces a particular outcome but always allows for freedom, risk, adventure—and also suffering—on the part of the beloved.

Viewed in this light, the evolution of the cosmos is more than just compatible with faith in a God of self-giving love; it actually anticipates an evolving universe. It would be very difficult for us to reconcile the religious teaching about God's infinite self-giving love with any other kind of cosmos.

The Issue of Purpose

A central issue keeps reoccurring whenever the topic of evolution arises. If, as we have noted, evolution is characterized by the elements of chance, natural selection, and long periods of time, these qualities have led many scientists to conclude that nature is largely unplanned and undirected.[4] In the light of the randomness, impersonality, and cruelty of natural selection, and the fact that life seems to have appeared only gradually over a period that science now estimates to be 3.8 billion years, can we speak meaningfully of purpose in the universe and of a place or role of humans in the cosmos? Fortunately, a group of philosophers and theologians, influenced by a version of Christian thought called "process theology," is addressing this issue.

Process theology reflects on God and nature in the light of ideas developed especially by the philosopher Alfred North Whitehead. This great thinker noted that all of nature, and not just life, is in process of becoming. To account for nature's restlessness, he insisted, we must postulate a principle that explains not only the order we observe in nature but also the novelty that emerges each fresh moment of the world's becoming. The ultimate source of both the order and the novelty in evolution is "God." God, according to process theology, is not interested simply in maintaining the status quo but desires a universe always open to new creation. God, therefore, influences the cosmos by holding out before it, at every instant, new ways of becoming itself. God does not force the world into any rigid design, for such coercion would be incompatible with genuine love.

---

4. This segment is adapted from Haught, *Responses to 101 Questions*, 135–43.

Conclusion

Rather, God's power is persuasive. As the source of novelty, therefore, God is also the reason for the breakdown of present order—in the physical, biological, social, religious, and political realms. Chaos, Whitehead says, is the "halfway house" between trivial and more interesting forms of order.

Evolution occurs because God is more interested in adventure than in preserving the status quo. By "adventure" process theology means the cosmic aim toward more intense versions of beauty, where "beauty" means the harmony of contrasts. In other words, God's will for the world is the maximization of beauty. God stimulates the world toward evolution so that deeper modes of beauty, along with beings capable of enjoying it, will come into existence.

To summarize, process theology argues that the God of biblical religion is a God of persuasive love, the source of novelty, and the stimulus to adventure. Unfortunately, Western theology has regularly domesticated this adventurous deity into the orderly, decent, gentlemanly God of the status quo. Evolution is important, then, for helping us recover a richer and more biblical sense of God.

Reflecting on this new understanding of the universe, process theology can see a new meaning in the random occurrences that might otherwise seem utterly absurd. What evolutionary scientists vaguely refer to as random mutations and unpredictable events in natural history are characteristics we should expect in a universe that is unfinished and open to new creation. Order is important to have an interesting universe, but there must also be room for random events.

For a process to be called purposeful it must be oriented toward the realization of a value. And so, in its aiming toward beauty, traditionally seen as a "transcendental" value, the universe shows itself to be purposeful. Certainly there is more than this to cosmic purpose. But our universe can justifiably be called purposeful if it is oriented, at least in a general way, toward actualizing instances of beauty. And that is precisely the scientific report: ours is a universe of emergent beauty. The renowned physicist Freeman Dyson writes that the universe follows a "principle of maximum diversity," by which he means that the laws and initial conditions of nature "are such as to make the universe as interesting as possible."[5] On the basis of Whitehead's metaphysics we might broaden Dyson's viewpoint, arguing that the point of this evolving universe is to maximize beauty and, along with beauty, the possibility of subjective enjoyment. This is a world that can glorify and give joy to the Creator as well as to its many creatures.

5. Cited in Haught, ibid., 140.

Conclusion

In an evolutionary cosmos, what do the notions of "evil" and "sin" mean in process theology? In a static, preevolutionary conception of the universe, evil might understandably have been defined as disorder. But in the world-in-the-making, evil also means anything that interferes with the world's ongoing evolution, including, interestingly enough, our human obsession with order and design. In an evolving universe, Haught suggests, there are two forms of evil: (1) the evil of disorder, examples of which are suffering, war, famine, and death, and (2) the evil of monotony. This evil involves "clinging to trivial forms of order" or "refusing to open up to what is fresh and renewing." One form of such evil, he declares, is the human predilection to "break our connections with the diversity that surrounds us as well as with the process that has produced us. Thinking of ourselves as the final end of cosmic creation, we may no longer feel the need to participate as one species among others in a complex earth-community. Or we may shape our civilized and religious lives in such a way as to exclude relevant social and economic diversity and novelty. In other words, we are tempted to the evil of monotony,"[6] which is known by another name: injustice. Whatever else we may understand by "sin," in an evolving universe it includes our refusal to participate in the ongoing creation and renewal of the cosmos.

6. Ibid., 141.

Epilogue

> The heart has reasons that reason cannot know.
>
> —Blaise Pascal

Søren Kierkegaard, the Danish existentialist philosopher, stressed decision as the foundation of ethics and religion. While he affirmed that one becomes a Christian by means of a leap of faith, for him this leap represented the commitment of one's entire being. Though doubt can never be completely overcome, the leap is not irrational, if it is impelled by one's heart, nurtured by one's will, and fueled by one's faith. Faith involves the will, but not a will uninformed by reasoning nor a will devoid of the concerns of the heart. We leap, not because there is a shortage of evidence, but because we recognize the reality of the domain of the heart.

The role of reason in Christian faith is informed by Pascal's famous distinction of three orders within human nature: body, mind, and heart. Since, according to this conception, faith and reason belong to different orders, they need not be opposed to one another. In this view, Christian faith is not a leap *within* the order of the intellect—a leap which violates the essence of that order—but a leap *from* the order of the intellect to the order of the heart.[1]

The key point for this understanding of religious faith is to acknowledge that belief in doctrines is not central, since they are themselves unprovable. While Christians honor physical, emotional, and intellectual knowledge, they place particular value on faith, both as source and end of knowledge, for faith involves heart-knowledge in addition to head-knowledge, the giving and committing of one's life to whatever we consider ultimate.

Whereas liberals and conservatives of his day focused on the content of religious faith, Kierkegaard opposed both by seeking not intellectual

---

1. Allen, *Christian Belief*, 145.

Epilogue

certainty but existential authenticity, focusing not on the content of Christianity but rather on what it means to be a Christian. For Kierkegaard, one does not become Christian by coming to know something one did not previously know. Rather, one becomes a Christian as one becomes a human, by embarking on a path. It would be quite normal to start on the path without ever reaching the goal, since one never actually becomes a Christian; one simply strives to become one.

In the Introduction we examined life's perennial question, as recorded in the celebrated Westminster Shorter Catechism: "what is the chief end of man?" We return now to that discussion. What then might be the purpose of our lives in an evolving universe? Our purpose, when situated in the context of cosmic evolution, is to carry forward in whatever way possible the general creative aim of the universe toward deeper and wider beauty. Once we have become aware, with the help of evolutionary science, that our own lives and labors can add something new to the ongoing cosmic creation of beauty, our efforts can gain a meaning only vaguely apprehended by the pre-Darwinian pictures of a static universe. A lively awareness of the general cosmic aim toward beauty gives us a rich context in which to cultivate the life of virtue.

Because Christians affirm that all knowledge remains "in part" (1 Corinthians 13:9), theology and science endure as unfinished tasks. Faith and service, however, need not await perfection of knowledge. The virtues we idealize are still the traditional ones—humility, compassion, justice, gratitude, hope, and so on—the same ones that our great religious traditions have always taught. But now, in the context of evolution, we can see more clearly than ever that the good life is one that contributes meaningfully not only to the spiritual growth of the individual person, but also to the ongoing creation of an entire universe.

I noted earlier that questioning supernatural theism revitalized my faith. Is belief ever sufficient? My experience indicates that to encounter God one must go beyond belief. I accept the struggle of faith as the sort of experience that triggers spiritual awakening. So, whether we go to scripture, to reason, to nature, or to experience for revelation, I embrace the uncertainty, despair, and joy of unknowing. All things come as gifts from our Maker, including opportunities to doubt and question.

Faith, however, is not a makeshift to overcome gaps in our knowing. Rather, faith is necessary because we recognize in this way of knowing—what we have called "unknowing"—a different order than that of the naked intellect. In this respect, it would be *irrational* to limit ourselves to the order of the intellect, since our human concerns push us beyond to the order of the heart, which complements the order of the intellect. Faith does not replace critical thinking, but mature faith seeks understanding. While faith cannot overcome intellectual doubt, it can overcome doubt about the significance and worth of our lives. Doubt that arises within faith, however, is part of our movement toward an authentic faith. This kind of doubt finds its resolution in faith, hope, and love, as noted in the timeless words of scripture: "For now we see in a mirror, dimly, but then we shall see face to face. Now I know only in part; then I will know fully, even as I have been fully known. And now faith, hope, and love abide, these three; and the greatest of these is love" (1 Corinthians 13:12–13). If the chief end of man is to experience fully this unfolding cosmic adventure called Love, let us revel forever in its emerging splendor. Knowing without certainty, hoping without assurance, loving without guarantee; such living is beyond belief.

Appendix A

Key Tenets of Process Theology[1]

(1) *Panentheism*. "Panentheism" is an appropriate term for the view that deity is in some real aspect distinguishable from and independent of any and all relative items, and yet, taken as an actual whole, includes all relative items.

(2) *Relatedness*. Panentheism is the result of conceiving "being" in terms of relationship or relatedness. This is why process theism is a type of panentheism, for "process" asserts that "entities" are inseparably interrelated, and thus that relationship, rather than substance, is "of the essence."

(3) Process theism is *located between traditional theism and pantheism*. Panentheism combines features of both pantheism, which regards God "as essentially immanent and in no way transcendent," and traditional theism, which regards God "as essentially transcendent and only accidentally immanent."

(4) *A reciprocal relationship between God and world*. Process thinkers disagree on the nature of that relationship. While some advocate a complete symmetry (God is internal to the world, as traditional theism said, yet the world is internal to God), other process thinkers pull back from full symmetry, arguing that the infinite divine Creator can be involved in deep reciprocal relations with finite agents without being the same as them.

(5) *The integrity of the natural order*. For genuinely autonomous agents to arise in evolutionary history, it is necessary that the natural order be regular, lawlike, and comprehensible to creatures. While most process theologians reject creation from nothing as well as the possibility of supernatural interruptions of the world's most normal causal processes (thereby overcoming arguments against the existence of a Divine Power such as the

---

1. These points are adapted from Clayton, "Beyond Orthodoxy."

problem of evil and the evolutionary nature of our universe), all process thinkers resist claims to the unlimited omnipotence of God. For the same reason, most are hesitant about ascribing physical miracles to God. Only in this way, they believe, is it possible to avoid making God responsible for the evil and suffering that occurs in the world.

(6) *The mind-body analogy.* Many process theologians appeal to some form of the mind-body analogy as a model for the God-world relation. This position can be expressed by saying, as does Charles Hartshorne, that God is essentially "the soul of the universe," being related to the universe somewhat in the way in which the human soul is related to its body. Credit goes to the feminist theologians Sallie McFague and Grace Jantzen, who have championed mind-body analogies to help conceive the God-world relation. Hartshorne made equally strong claims when he wrote that the mind-body analogy "is in fact the only way to achieve a just synthesis of immanence and transcendence, the only way to avoid the twin errors of mere naturalism and mere supernaturalism . . ."[2]

(7) *God as supreme example.* It is false to claim that process theologians equate God and finite beings. Whitehead called God the "chief exemplification" of his metaphysical principles. For Hartshorne God is not just another example of unity or totality but the supreme and most excellent example of goodness and other values. Marjorie Suchocki synthesizes the relational side of process theology with the idea of God as ethical standard. Her book *God, Christ, Church* does not focus on God as the most powerful or the most knowledgeable being. Instead, it is God as "the supremely related one" who becomes the chief exemplification of value.

(8) *Ethical implications.* Hartshorne's combination of panentheism with the autonomy of finite beings allows him to stress the wholeness and integrity of each individual. As he writes, "God is the wholeness of the world, correlative to the wholeness of every sound individual dealing with the world."[3] Process conceptions of the love of God start at this point. As Michael Brierley notes, "Panentheism is the result of process, mutuality, reciprocity or love, being made foundational to 'being.' This is why 'love,' as a term expressing relation, is such an important concept for process theologians, and why attention to love has been the cause of much doctrinal revisionism."[4]

---

2. Hartshorne, *Vision of God*, 208.
3. Hartshorne, *Natural Theology*, 6.
4. Brierley, "Quiet Revolution," 14.

Appendix A

(9) *Christology*. To be a Christian theologian is to relate one's beliefs about God in some important way to the life and teachings of Jesus. Process theologians have sought to understand the ministry and teachings of Jesus in light of the preceding principles. Thus Hartshorne writes, "The devotion of Jesus to his fellows was not mere benevolence, a wishing them well, or an eagerness to do things for them. It was a feeling of sympathetic identity with them in their troubles and sufferings, as well as in their joys, so that their cause and their tragedy became his . . . To say that Jesus was God, then, ought to mean that God himself is one with us in our suffering, that divine love is not essentially benevolence—external well-wishing—but sympathy, taking into itself our every grief."[5] Whitehead puts it even more simply: "The life of Christ is not an exhibition of over-ruling power. Its glory is for those who can discern it, and not for the world. Its power lies in its absence of force. It has the decisiveness of a supreme ideal, and that is why the history of the world divides at this point of time."[6] In what is his most famous and possibly also his most beautiful statement as a process thinker about the kingdom of God that Jesus proclaimed and lived, Whitehead notes: "There is, however, in the Galilean origin of Christianity yet another suggestion which does not fit very well with any of the three main strands of thought. It does not emphasize the ruling Caesar, or the ruthless moralist, or the unmoved mover. It dwells upon the tender elements in the world, which slowly and in quietness operate by love; and it finds purpose in the present immediacy of a kingdom not of this world. Love neither rules, nor is it unmoved; also it is a little oblivious as to morals. It does not look to the future; for it finds its own reward in the immediate present."[7]

---

5. Hartshorne, *Social Process*, 147.
6. Whitehead, *Religion in the Making*, 57.
7. Whitehead, *Process and Reality*, 343.

Appendix B

Stages of Knowing God

IN HIS AMBITIOUS BOOK, *How to Know God*, world-renowned author and spiritual leader Deepak Chopra assures readers that anyone can engage in the divine-human relationship—"it isn't a matter of faith, religious teaching, innate goodness, luck or some other mysterious factor," Chopra explains. "Our brains are hardwired to find God." The human nervous system has seven biological responses that correspond to seven levels of divine experience. These are shaped not by any one religion (they are shared by all faiths) but by the brain's need to take an infinite, chaotic universe and find meaning in it. *How to Know God* describes every person's quest, for, as Chopra puts it, "God is our highest instinct to know ourselves."

Chopra devotes a chapter to each of seven "visions" of God: "Protector," "Almighty," "God of Peace," "Redeemer," "Creator," "God of Miracles," and "Pure Being." In every chapter he asks and answers the same questions for the readers: "Who am I?" "How do I fit in?" "How do I find God?" The format illuminates different personality types that are attracted to these seven different visions.

Chopra's list of responses to God includes: fight or flight (a God who can save us from danger), reactive (a rule-giving God), restful awareness (a God who brings tranquility out of chaos), intuitive (a good and forgiving God), creative (God as Creator), visionary (God as exalted), and sacred (God as the source of everything). Different personalities envision God differently, says Chopra; a go-getter determined to shape his own destiny will imagine a creative God, whereas someone who feels she is just barely getting through the day will have the stage-one "fight or flight" response, envisioning a God who can rescue her. For Chopra, someone who has reached stage seven is more in tune with God than someone still at stage one.

Appendix B

Seven Ascending Stages/Understandings of God

The seven stages reflect the journey toward God, each stage affirming God's reality at that level and meeting a particular need:

Fight-or-flight response: in Stage One, God is like a parent who looks out for the safety of a child. We turn to this God because we need to survive.

Reactive response: Stage Two is the brain's creation of a personal identity. Beyond mere survival, everyone pursues the needs of an ego. We do this instinctively, and from this response a new God emerges, one who has power and might, laws and rules. We turn to this God because we need to achieve, accomplish, and compete.

Restful awareness response: The brain can be active or at rest. Stage Three is its response when wishing peace. Rest and activity alternate in every part of the brain. The divine equivalent is a God who brings peace, who enables us to find a calm center in the midst of outward chaos.

Intuitive response: the brain looks for information both within and without. Outer knowledge is objective, but inner knowledge is intuitive. In Stage Four the brain looks within for a God that is understanding and forgiving. We need God to validate the goodness of our inner world.

Creative response: the human brain can invent new things and discover new facts, a creative ability apparently coming from the unknown. We call this inspiration, and its mirror is a Creator who made the world from nothing. In Stage Five we turn to God out of our wonder at the beauty and complexity of nature.

Visionary response: the brain can directly contact "the light," a form of pure awareness that feels joyful and blessed. This contact can be bewildering; rootless in the material world, this response comes as a vision from an exalted God that delivers healing and miracles. A Stage-Six God explains why miracles can exist side by side with ordinary mundane reality.

Sacred response: the brain was born from a single fertilized cell with no brain functions. The brain senses this speck of life as its source. Stage Seven presents us with a God of pure being, one who doesn't think but just is. We need God because without a source, our existence has no foundation.

Bibliography

Alcock, John. *The Triumph of Sociobiology*. New York: Oxford University Press, 2001.
Allen, Diogenes. *Christian Belief in a Postmodern World: The Full Wealth of Conviction*. Louisville, KY: Westminster John Knox, 1989.
———. *Theology for a Troubled Believer: An Introduction to the Christian Faith*. Louisville, KY: Westminster John Knox, 2010.
Allison Jr., Dale C. *Constructing Jesus*. Grand Rapids, MI: Baker, 2010.
———. *The Historical Christ and the Theological Jesus*. Grand Rapids, MI: Eerdmans, 2009.
———. *Jesus of Nazareth: Millenarian Prophet*. Minneapolis, MN: Fortress, 1998.
Anderson, Bernhard W. *Understanding the Old Testament*. 5th ed. Upper Saddle River, NJ: Pearson, 2007.
Armstrong, Karen. *The Bible: A Biography*. New York: Grove, 2007.
———. *The Case for God*. New York: Anchor, 2010.
———. *A Short History of Myth*. New York: Canongate, 2005.
Aus, Roger David. *The Death, Burial, and Resurrection of Jesus, and the Death, Burial, and Translation of Moses in Judaic Tradition*. Lanham MD: University Press of America, 2008.
Barbour, Ian G. *Myths, Models and Paradigms: A Comparative Study in Science and Religion*. New York: Harper & Row, 1974.
———. *Nature, Human Nature, and God*. Minneapolis, MN: Fortress, 2002.
———. *Religion and Science: Historical and Contemporary Issues*. New York: HarperSanFrancisco, 1997.
Barker, Dan. *Godless*. Berkeley, CA: Ulysses, 2008.
Bauckham, Richard. *Jesus and the Eyewitnesses: The Gospels as Eyewitness Testimony*. Grand Rapids, MI: Eerdmans, 2006.
Behe, Michael. *Darwin's Black Box*. New York: Simon & Schuster, 1996.
Borg, Marcus J. *The God We Never Knew*. New York: HarperSanFrancisco, 1998.
———. *The Heart of Christianity: Rediscovering a Life of Faith*. New York: HarperSanFrancisco, 2003.
———. *Meeting Jesus Again for the First Time*. New York: HarperSanFrancisco, 1995.
———. *Reading the Bible Again for the First Time*. New York: HarperSanFrancisco, 2002.
———, and N. T. Wright. *The Meaning of Jesus: Two Visions*. New York: HarperSanFrancisco, 2000.
Boyer, Pascal. *Religion Explained: The Evolutionary Origins of Religious Thought*. New York: Basic Books, 2001.
Brierley, Michael W. "Naming a Quiet Revolution: The Panentheistic Turn in Modern Theology." In *In Whom We Live and Move and Have Our Being: Panentheistic*

Reflections on God's Presence in a Scientific World, edited by Philip Clayton and Arthur Peacocke, 1–15. Grand Rapids, MI: Eerdmans, 2004.

Buckley, Michael J. *At the Origins of Modern Atheism*. New Haven, CT: Yale University Press, 1987.

Bultmann, Rudolf. "Kerygma and Mythology." In *Kerygma and Myth*, edited by Hans Werner Bartsch, 1–44. New York: Harper & Row, 1961

Caird, G. B. *The Language and Imagery of the Bible*. Philadelphia, PA: Westminster, 1980.

Caplan, Arthur L. *The Sociobiology Debate*. New York: Harper & Row, 1978.

Caputo, John D. "Atheism, A/theology and the Postmodern Condition." In *The Cambridge Companion to Atheism*, edited by Michael Martin. Cambridge: Cambridge University Press, 2007.

Chopra, Deepak. *How to Know God*. New York: Three Rivers, 2000.

Clayton, Philip. "God Beyond Orthodoxy: Process Theology for the 21st Century," 1–16. Online: http://www.philipclayton.net/files/papers/GodBeyondOrthodoxy-r3.pdf.

———, and Arthur Peacocke. *In Whom We Live and Move and Have our Being: Panentheistic Reflections on God's Presence in a Scientific World*. Grand Rapids, MI: Eerdmans, 2004.

Collins, Robin. "Evolution and Original Sin." In *Perspectives on an Evolving Creation*, edited by Keith B. Miller, 469–501. Grand Rapids, MI: Eerdmans, 2003.

Cronon, William. "Only Connect . . ." *The American Scholar* 67 (1998) 73–80.

Crossan, John Dominic. *A Long Way from Tipperary: A Memoir*. San Francisco: HarperSanFrancisco, 2000.

Darwin, Charles. *On the Origin of Species by Means of Natural Selection*. London: John Murray, 1859.

Darwin, Francis. *Life and Letters of Charles Darwin*. New York: Appleton, 1887.

Davies, Paul. *God and the New Physics*. New York: Simon and Schuster, 1983.

Dawkins, Richard. *The Blind Watchmaker*. New York: Norton, 1986.

———. *Climbing Mount Improbable*. New York: Norton, 1996.

———. *The God Delusion*. New York: Houghton Mifflin, 2006.

———. *The Greatest Show on Earth: The Evidence for Evolution*. New York: Free Press, 2009.

———. *The Selfish Gene*. Oxford: Oxford University Press, 1976.

Dembski, William A. *Mere Creation*. Downers Grove, IL: InterVarsity, 1998.

Dennett, Daniel C. *Breaking the Spell: Religion as a Natural Phenomenon*. New York: Penguin. 2006.

———. *Darwin's Dangerous Idea: Evolution and the Meanings of Life*. New York: Simon & Schuster, 1995.

Dobzhansky, Theodosius. "Nothing in Biology Makes Sense Except in the Light of Evolution." *The American Biology Teacher* 35 (1973) 125–29. Online: http://people.delphiforums.com/lordorman/light.htm.

Edwards, Denis. *The God of Evolution: A Trinitarian Theology*. Mahwah, NJ: Paulist, 1999.

Ferngren, Gary B. *The History of Science and Religion in the Western Tradition: An Encyclopedia*. New York: Garland, 2000.

Finlay, Graeme. "*Homo divinus*: the ape that bears God's image." *Science and Christian Belief* 15 (2003) 1–34. Online: http://www.scienceandchristianbelief.org/articles/finlay.pdf.

Fischer, Dick. "In Search of the Historical Adam: Part I." *Perspectives on Science and Christian Faith* 45 (1993) 241–51. Online: http://www.asa3.org/ASA/PSCF/1993/PSCF12-93Fischer.html.
Foster, Richard J. *Celebration of Discipline: The Path to Spiritual Growth.* New York: Harper & Row, 1978.
Fox, Matthew. *On Becoming a Musical, Mystical Bear: Spirituality American Style.* Mahwah, NJ: Paulist, 1976.
———. *Original Blessing.* Santa Fe, NM: Bear & Co., 1983.
Freud, Sigmund. *The Future of an Illusion.* New York: Anchor, 1964.
Gilkey, Langdon. *Creationism on Trial.* Minneapolis, MN: Winston, 1985.
Gould, Stephen Jay. "Evolution as Fact and Theory." In *Hen's Teeth and Horse's Toes*, 253–62. New York: Norton, 1983.
———. "Nonoverlapping Magisteria." *Natural History* (March 1997) 16–22.
———. *Rocks of Ages.* New York: Ballantine, 1999.
Greene, Brian. *The Elegant Universe.* New York: Vintage, 1999.
Griffin, David Ray. *Reenchantment without Supernaturalism: A Process Philosophy of Religion.* Ithaca, NY: Cornell University Press, 2001.
Griffith-Jones, Robin. *The Four Witnesses.* New York: HarperSanFrancisco, 2000.
———. *The Gospel According to Paul.* New York: HarperSanFrancisco, 2004.
Hahn, Thich Nhat. *Living Buddha, Living Christ.* New York: Riverhead, 2007.
Ham, Ken. *The Lie: Evolution.* Green Forest, AR: Master Books, 1987.
Harris, Sam. *The End of Faith: Religion, Terror, and the Future of Reason.* New York: Norton, 2004.
———. *Letter to a Christian Nation.* New York: Knopf, 2006.
Hartshorne, Charles. *The Divine Relativity: A Social Conception of God.* New Haven, CT: Yale University Press, 1948.
———. *Man's Vision of God.* Chicago: Willett, Clark & Company, 1941.
———. *A Natural Theology for Our Time.* La Salle, IL: Open Court, 1967.
———. *Reality as Social Process.* Glencoe, IL: Free Press, 1953.
Haught, John F. *Deeper Than Darwin: The Prospect for Religion in the Age of Evolution.* Boulder, CO: Westview, 2003.
———. *God After Darwin: A Theology of Evolution.* Boulder, CO: Westview, 2000.
———. *God and the New Atheism.* Louisville, KY: Westminster John Knox, 2008.
———. *The Promise of Nature: Ecology and Cosmic Purpose.* Mahwah, NJ: Paulist, 1993.
———. *Responses to 101 Questions on God and Evolution.* Mahwah, NJ: Paulist, 2001.
———. *Science and Religion: From Conflict to Conversation.* Mahwah, NJ: Paulist, 1995.
———. *What is God?: How to Think About the Divine.* Mahwah, NJ: Paulist, 1986.
Hawking, Stephen. *A Brief History of Time.* New York: Bantam, 1988.
———, and Leonard Mlodinow. *The Grand Design.* New York: Bantam, 2010.
Helms, Randel M. *Gospel Fictions.* Amherst, NY: Prometheus, 1988.
———. *Who Wrote the Gospels?* Altadena, CA: Millennium, 1997.
Hendry, George S. *Theology of Nature.* Philadelphia, PA: Westminster, 1980.
Hick, John. *An Interpretation of Religion: Human Responses to the Transcendent.* New Haven, CT: Yale University Press, 1989.
———. *Disputed Questions in Theology and the Philosophy of Religion.* New Haven: CT: Yale University Press, 1993.
Hinde, Robert A. *Why Gods Persist: A Scientific Approach to Religion.* New York: Routledge, 1999.

Hitchens, Christopher. *God is Not Great: How Religion Poisons Everything*. Lebanon, IN: Twelve Books, 2007.
Hordern, William E. *A Layman's Guide to Protestant Theology*. Rev. ed. New York: Macmillan, 1968.
Hurd, James. "Hominids in the Garden?" In *Perspectives on an Evolving Creation*, edited by Keith B. Miller, 208–233. Grand Rapids, MI: Eerdmans, 2003.
Huxley, Julian. *Religion without Revelation*. New York: Harper, 1957.
James, William. *The Varieties of Religious Experience*. New York: Routledge, 2008.
Jantzen, Grace. *God's World, God's Body*. Philadelphia, PA: Westminster, 1984.
Johnson, Elizabeth. "Does God Play Dice?: Divine Providence and Chance." In *An Evolving Dialogue: Theological and Scientific Perspectives on Evolution*, edited by James B. Miller, 353–70. Harrisburg, PA: Trinity, 2001.
Johnson, Phillip. *Darwin on Trial*. Washington, DC: Regnery Gateway, 1991.
Küng, Hans. *Does God Exist?* Translated by Edward Quinn. New York: Doubleday, 1980.
Kurtz, Paul. *Science and Religion: Are They Compatible?* Amherst, NY: Prometheus, 2003.
Lamoureux, Denis O. *Evolutionary Creation: A Christian Approach to Evolution*. Eugene, OR: Wipf & Stock, 2008.
Larson, Edward J. *Evolution: The Remarkable History of a Scientific Theory*. New York: Modern Library, 2006.
Levine, Amy-Jill. *The Misunderstood Jew: The Church and the Scandal of the Jewish Jesus*. New York: HarperOne, 2006.
———, and Marc Zvi Brettler. *The Jewish Annotated New Testament*. New York: Oxford University Press, 2011.
Livingstone, David N. *Darwin's Forgotten Defenders: The Encounter between Evangelical Theology and Evolutionary Thought*. Grand Rapids, MI: Eerdmans, 1967.
Loftus, John W. *The Christian Delusion*. Amherst, NY: Prometheus, 2010.
———. *Why I Became an Atheist*. Amherst, NY: Prometheus, 2008.
Mackie, J. L. *The Miracle of Theism: Arguments for and against the Existence of God*. Oxford: Clarendon, 1982.
McGrath, Alister E. *Christian Theology: An Introduction*. 5th ed. Malden, MA: Wiley-Blackwell, 2011.
———. *Dawkins' God: Genes, Memes and the Meaning of Life*. Oxford: Blackwell, 2004.
McFague, Sallie. *The Body of God: an Ecological Theology*. Minneapolis, MN: Fortress, 1993.
McKibben, Bill. *The End of Nature*. New York: Random House, 1989.
Meier, J. P. *A Marginal Jew: Rethinking the Historical Jesus*. 3 vols. New York: Doubleday, 1991–2001.
Miller, Kenneth R. *Finding Darwin's God: A Scientist's Search for Common Ground Between God and Evolution*. New York: Perennial, 1999.
Miller, M. P. "Midrash." In *The Interpreter's Dictionary of the Bible*. Sup. vol., 593–97. Nashville, TN: Abingdon, 1976.
Moltmann, Jürgen. *God in Creation: A New Theology of Creation and the Spirit of God*. Minneapolis, MN: Fortress, 1993.
———. "God's Kenosis in the Creation and the Consummation of the World." In *The Work of Love: Creation as Kenosis*, edited by John Polkinghorne, 137–51. Grand Rapids, MI: Eerdmans, 2001.

Moore, James R. *The Post-Darwinian Controversies*. New York: Cambridge University Press, 1979.
Murphy, George L. *The Cosmos in the Light of the Cross*. Harrisburg, PA: Trinity, 2003.
Murphy, Nancey. *Reconciling Theology and Science*. Kitchener, Ontario: Pandora Press, 1997.
Noll, Mark A., and David Livingstone. "Charles Hodge and B. B. Warfield on Science, the Bible, Evolution, and Darwinism." In *Perspectives on an Evolving Creation*, edited by Keith B. Miller, 61–71. Grand Rapids, MI: Eerdmans, 2003
Peacocke, Arthur. "Biological Evolution—A Positive Theological Appraisal." In *Evolutionary and Molecular Biology: Scientific Perspectives on Divine Action*, edited by R. J. Russell et al., 357–76. Vatican City: Vatican Observatory, 1998.
———. *Theology for a Scientific Age: Being and Becoming—Natural, Divine, and Human*. Minneapolis, MN: Fortress, 1993.
Pinker, Steven. *The Blank Slate: The Modern Denial of Human Nature*. New York: Viking, 2002.
Polkinghorne, John. *Belief in God in an Age of Science*. New Haven, CT: Yale University Press, 1998.
———. *One World: The Interaction of Science and Theology*. Princeton, NJ: Princeton University Press, 1987.
———. *Quarks, Chaos and Christianity: Questions to Science and Religion*. New York: Crossroad, 1996.
Price, Peter. *Biological Evolution*. Fort Worth, TX: Saunders College Publishing, 1995.
Rice, Alan W. "The Cosmology of Modern Science." In *Building a Christian World View*, edited by W. Andrew Hoffecker, 2:71–111. Phillipsburg, NJ: Presbyterian and Reformed, 1988.
Robinson, John A. T. *Honest to God*. Philadelphia, PA: Westminster, 1963.
———. *Jesus and His Coming*. 2nd ed. Philadelphia, PA: Westminster, 1979.
Rolston, Holmes. "Does Nature Need to be Redeemed?" *Zygon* 29 (1994) 205–29.
Rose, Michael R. *Darwin's Spectre: Evolutionary Biology in the Modern World*. Princeton, NJ: Princeton University Press, 1998.
Ruse, Michael. *Can a Darwinian be a Christian?* Cambridge: Cambridge University Press, 2001.
Russell, Bertrand. *Why I Am Not a Christian*. New York: Simon & Schuster, 1957.
Sagan, Carl. *Cosmos*. New York: Random House, 1980.
———. *The Demon-Haunted World: Science as a Candle in the Dark*. New York: Random House, 1995.
Sanders, E. P. *Jesus and Judaism*. Philadelphia, PA: Fortress, 1985.
———. "Jesus: His Religious Type." *Reflections* 87 (1992) 4–12.
Schneider, Robert J. "Science and Faith: Perspectives on Christianity and Science." No pages. Online: http://community.berea.edu/scienceandfaith/default.asp.
Schulweis, Harold M. *For Those Who Can't Believe*. New York: HarperPerennial, 1995.
Shermer, Michael. *How We Believe: Science, Skepticism, and the Search for God*. New York: Freeman, 2000.
———. *Why People Believe Weird Things*. New York: Freeman, 1997.
Singer, Peter. *The Expanding Circle: Ethics and Sociobiology*. New York: Farrar, Straus & Giroux, 1981.
Smith, Huston. *Why Religion Matters*. San Francisco: HarperSanFrancisco, 2001.
Spong, John Shelby. *Eternal Life: A New Vision*. New York: HarperOne, 2009.

———. *Liberating the Gospels: Reading the Bible with Jewish Eyes.* New York: HarperSanFrancisco, 1997.
———. *Resurrection: Myth or Reality?* New York: HarperSanFrancisco, 1994.
———. *The Sins of Scripture.* New York: HarperOne, 2006.
———. *Why Christianity Must Change or Die.* New York: HarperOne, 1999.
Steiner, George. *Language and Silence.* London: Faber, 1967.
Stenger, Victor J. *God: The Failed Hypothesis. How Science Shows that God Does Not Exist.* Amherst, NY: Prometheus, 2007.
———. *Has Science Found God?: The Latest Results in the Search for Purpose in the Universe.* Amherst, NY: Prometheus, 2003.
Suchocki, Marjorie. *God, Christ, Church: A Practical Guide to Process Theology.* Rev. ed. New York: Crossroad, 1989.
———. "What is Process Theology?" 1–24. Online: http://www.processandfaith.org/sites/default/files/pdfs/What_Is_Process_Theology.pdf.
Swimme, Brian, and Thomas Berry. *The Universe Story.* New York: HarperSanFrancisco, 1992.
Swinburne, Richard. *The Existence of God.* Oxford: Clarendon, 1979.
———. *Is There a God?* Rev. ed. Oxford: Oxford University Press, 2010.
Tattersall, Ian. *Becoming Human: Evolution and Human Uniqueness.* New York: Harcourt Brace and Co., 1998.
Teilhard de Chardin, Pierre. *Christianity and Evolution.* Translated by René Hague. New York: Harcourt Brace and Co., 1969.
Valantasis, Richard, et al. *The Gospels and Christian Life in History and Practice.* Lanham, MD: Rowman & Littlefield, 2009.
Vande Kappelle, Robert P. *Into Thin Places.* Eugene, OR: Resource Publications, 2010.
Van Huyssteen, J. Wentzel Vrede. *Encyclopedia of Science and Religion.* 2 vols. New York: Macmillan, 2003.
Van Till, Howard J. "The Fully Gifted Creation." In *Three Views on Creation and Evolution*, edited by J. P. Moreland and John Mark Reynolds, 161–247. Grand Rapids, MI: Zondervan, 1999.
———. *Portraits of Creation: Biblical and Scientific Perspectives on the World's Formation.* Grand Rapids, MI: Eerdmans, 1990.
Walls, Andrew F. *The Missionary Movement in Christian History: Studies in the Transmission of Faith.* Maryknoll, NY: Orbis, 1996.
Whitehead, Alfred North. *Process and Reality.* Rev. ed. New York: Free Press, 1978.
———. *Religion in the Making.* New York: Fordham University Press, 1996.
———. *Science and the Modern World.* New York: Free Press, 1967.
Williams, Patricia A. *Doing without Adam and Eve: Sociobiology and Original Sin.* Minneapolis, MN: Fortress, 2001.
Wilson, E. O. *On Human Nature.* Cambridge, MA: Harvard University Press, 1978.
Witham, Larry A. *By Design: Science and the Search for God.* San Francisco: Encounter, 2003.
———. *Where Darwin Meets the Bible: Creationists and Evolutionists in America.* New York: Oxford University Press, 2002.
Wolpert, Lewis. *Six Impossible Things Before Breakfast: The Evolutionary Origins of Belief.* New York: Norton, 2006.
Wright, Robert. *The Moral Animal: The New Science of Evolutionary Psychology.* New York: Pantheon, 1994.

Subject/Name Index

Abraham, 68, 71, 72–73, 162
accommodation, principle of, xxx, 49, 171–72, 195
Adam, 30, 45, 47, 189, 193, 194, 195, 197, 208
   original sin and, 208–12
Adams, John, xx–xxi
adoptionism, 108
adventure, 80–81, 174, 236, 237, 238, 239, 243
afterlife, xi, xxv, xxvi, xxvii, 10, 23–28, 86, 113, 136, 145, 227
agnosticism, xxiv
Ahaz (king), 21
Akiba (rabbi), 66
allegory, allegorical, 22, 44, 49, 65, 130
Allen, Diogenes, 76n3
Allison, Dale, 125
Anderson, Bernhard W., xv
Anselm of Canterbury, 30, 47
anthropology, 3, 7, 8, 9, 59
Antiochus Epiphanes (ruler), 20
anti-Semitism, 121, 132–34, 226
apocalypticism, 6, 22, 25, 27, 122, 123, 125, 142, 221
apologetics, 13, 15, 19
apophatic tradition (unknowing), x, 37–40, 46–52, 54, 242
Apostles Creed, 29
Aquinas, Thomas, 54, 169, 171, 200
   view of the soul, 204–6, 207
Aristotle, 27, 90, 171, 200, 204, 205, 207
Arius, 46–47
Armageddon, 142, 143
Armstrong, Karen, x, xii, xv
astronomy, 59, 161, 171
Athanasius (bishop), 32, 46–47

atheism, atheists, xxiv, 39, 40, 52, 53, 54, 57, 64, 75, 77, 79, 98, 151, 182, 219
   new atheism, 40, 54
atonement theology, 30, 35, 47, 101–2, 112
Augustine (bishop), 48–49, 54, 93, 94, 204, 207, 233
   creation and, 93–95
   models of God, 48–49
   original sin and, 210
   predestination and, 14
   principle of accommodation, xxx, 49, 171
   science and, 49
   soul and, 204
   theistic evolution, 93–94, 233–34
Aulen, Gustav, 112
Aus, Roger David, 131

Babylonian Exile, 24–25, 111–12, 115, 121, 129
Bacon, Francis, 170, 171
Barbour, Ian G., xv, 152, 156, 158
Baronius, Cardinal, 169
Barth, Karl, 13–14, 75
Bauckham, Richard, 106n3
Behe, Michael, 223–24
belief, beliefs, xii, xiii, xviii, xxvi, 4, 6, 10, 12, 13, 31, 35, 39, 42, 43–44, 45–46, 47, 52, 60, 74, 96, 111, 118, 159, 183, 225, 241, 242, 243
   assessment of, 157
   See also Outsider Test for Belief
Berry, Thomas, x
Bible, biblical, xxiii, xxvi–xxvii, xxviii, xxix, 3, 4, 6, 7, 8, 10, 16, 22, 38, 43, 49, 57, 61, 63, 64, 69, 71, 85,

255

Subject/Name Index

Bible, biblical–continued
    97, 105–16, 128, 134, 169, 172, 173, 181, 194, 216, 218, 222–23, 226
  authority of, 92, 169, 170, 173
  authorship, 105–7, 220–21
  biblical theology, 7, 8
  biblical studies, 5, 8, 87, 220
  concept of salvation in, 28
  creation and, 67–68, 90, 97, 219
  evolution and, 182
  God and, 3, 8, 69, 74
  inspiration of, 7, 67–69, 97, 106, 169, 173
  interpretation (exegesis), xxvi–xxviii, 20–22, 97, 170, 171, 208
  miracles and, 64–66
  morality and, 74–75
  myth and, 39, 40
  narrative framework of, xxvii, 112
  purpose of, 172–73
  role of, xviii–xix
  science and, 169–73
  soul and, 198–99
  See also inerrancy; literalism, biblical; New Testament; Old Testament; postcritical understanding; sacrament, Bible as; scripture; scripture, sacredness of; story theology; Wisdom literature
Big Bang, 98, 161, 173, 182
biology, xxxi, 9, 99, 149, 150, 161, 164, 166, 167, 168, 182, 186, 197, 200, 217, 219, 227–32
Boehme, Jacob, x
Bonhoeffer, Dietrich, xii, 87–88, 223
Book of Nature, xxx, 97, 170, 182, 185, 193
Book of Scripture, xxx, 170
Borg, Marcus, x, xii, xv, 30, 84–86, 120, 126, 130
boundary questions, 166, 219
brain. *See* mind/body relationship
Brierley, Michael, 245
Bryan, William Jennings, 188
Buddhism, 13, 38

Bultmann, Rudolph, xii, 87
Bunyan, John, xii

Caird, G. B., 123n7
Calvin, John, xxx, 14, 97, 169, 171
Calvinism (Reformed Theology), 6, 7, 8, 32, 97
Caputo, John D., 53–54
Catholicism. *See* Roman Catholicism
chaos theory, 161
Chautauqua Institution, xii, 8
Chopra, Deepak, xv, 89n27, 247–48
Christendom, 71, 119, 227
Christianity, Christian, x, xix, xxi, xxiii, xxix, 7, 8, 9–11, 13–15, 16–17, 18, 23–24, 26, 27, 35, 38, 39, 40, 41, 43, 44, 46, 57, 61, 71, 83, 84, 88, 90, 95, 96, 105, 107, 113, 114, 118, 119, 122, 124, 134, 140, 141, 149, 160, 169, 173, 174, 193, 194, 198, 201, 204, 208, 210, 220, 221, 222, 223, 241, 242, 246
  Bible and, 130, 218–19, 222
  changing nature of, 31–32
  Christian life, 10, 27, 36, 84, 86, 113, 114, 169
  Confessions of, xi
  dissent and, 73
  early, xxiii, 6, 18, 22, 26, 31, 46, 106n3, 110, 111, 113, 119, 122, 123, 125, 127, 131, 141, 142, 149, 218, 219, 221
  evolution and, xxxi, 97–98, 181–83, 189, 193–95, 200–202, 213–32, 236
  in America, 181–83
  Judaism and, xiii, xxvi, xxvii, xxviii, 19, 24, 42, 69, 107, 110, 117, 132–34
  miracles and, 18
  missionary nature of, 13, 31
  other religions and, 13
  religionless, xii, 87–88
  science and, 91, 182–83, 223
  unity, 32–34
  See also apophatic tradition

Subject/Name Index

Christology, 14–15, 48, 107–10, 117–18, 246
circle, circular model, xxv, 58–59
Collins, Robin, 197
conscience, xi, 33, 57, 69, 69–73
consciousness, 203–4, 238
Constantine (emperor), 46, 47
Copernicus/Copernican, 14, 169, 171, 181
corporate personality, 23–24
cosmic story, 161–63
cosmogony, 91
cosmology, 3, 7, 8, 9, 150, 160, 167, 168, 172, 201, 212, 234
  models of, 95
covenant, 20, 63, 66, 73, 160
creation
  creatio continua (continuous creation), 100, 185, 233, 234, 240, 242
  doctrine of, xv, xxvi, xxxi, 3, 50, 86, 90–103, 169, 183, 208, 215, 219, 227
  evolution and, 92–98, 193–95, 217–18, 236
  ex nihilo, 76–77, 244
  stories of, 115, 149, 150, 160, 189, 193, 194, 195, 216
creation spirituality, 84n20
creationism, "creation science," xxxi, 39, 91–92, 183, 208
credo, 44, 45
creeds, 29, 90, 117, 120, 141, 144, 222, 226, 227
critical understanding, xxiii–xxiv, 12–34
Cronon, William, 174
Crossan, John Dominic, xii, 125, 130, 131
Cyril of Jerusalem (bishop), x, 45

Damasio, Antonio, 206
Dana, James, 96, 97
Daniel (author/prophet), 20, 21, 25, 220
Dante Alighieri, 27
Daoism, 37, 38

Darwin, Charles, xiii, xvi, xxvi, xxix, 93, 96, 99, 149, 150, 151, 155, 186, 187, 188, 189, 202, 213, 214–17, 220, 230, 231, 232, 233, 234
Darwinism, Darwinian, 96, 102, 150, 198, 200, 201, 209, 210, 224, 236
  consciousness and, 203
  design and, 213–32
  social, 214, 216
Dawkins, Richard, xiii, xx, 40, 54, 151, 152, 183, 218, 219, 225, 228–31
D'Costa, Gavin, 15–16
Dead Sea Scrolls, 22, 41, 221
deduction, 156
deism, 15
demythologization, xii, 87
Dennett, Daniel, 151, 152, 183, 218, 219
Denys the Areopagite (Pseudo-Dionysius), x, 50–52
Derrida, Jacques, 52
Descartes, 203
design, xxxi, 90, 91, 96, 213–34
  See also order; teleology
Dillard, Annie, x
Dobzhansky, Theodosius, xxvi, 95
Dodd, C. H., 124
dogmatism, xiii
doubt, 35
dualism, xxxi, 60, 64, 75, 84n20, 90, 168, 198, 199, 236
Dyson, Freeman, 239

Easter. *See* resurrection
Eastern Orthodoxy, 47, 95
Eckhart, Meister, x, 53, 145
Edwards, Denis, 98
Einstein, Albert, xxvi, 96, 200
elegance, 179–80
ellipse, elliptical model, xxv–xxvi, 58–59
Enlightenment, xix, xx, 3, 10, 15, 27, 53, 134, 149, 220
entropy, 161, 162–63
epistemology, 7, 8, 9
eschatology, xvii, 5–6, 19, 26, 27, 117
  Jesus and, 121–28

257

Subject/Name Index

eternal life. *See* afterlife
ethics/morality, 7, 8, 9, 24, 42, 53, 65, 67, 71, 159, 205, 214, 215, 227, 241, 245
   God's will and, 75
   Kierkegaard's ethical stage, 70, 71
   of biblical heroes, 68–69
   of God, 225–26
Eucharist, 51, 160
Evagrius of Pontus, x, 48
evangelicals. *See* Protestant, evangelicals
evil, 4, 46, 90, 94–95, 101, 112, 121, 159, 199, 210, 211, 212, 216, 221, 240, 245
evolution, xiii, xv, xxvi, xxx, xxxi, 40, 94, 96, 97, 99, 102, 150, 151, 152, 154, 155, 161, 173, 182, 183, 193, 194, 201, 209, 211, 213, 217, 219, 232, 234, 235, 236, 237, 238, 239, 242, 245
   against design, 227–32
   as theory, 186–87
   biological evolution, 186–92, 232
   cosmic evolution, 184–85, 242
   macroevolution, 187–88
   microevolution, 187, 188
   theistic, 92–99, 150
   See also cosmic story; Modern Synthesis
exclusivism, 10, 13
exegesis, 44
existential, existentialism, 70, 83, 241
experience, human, xviii, xix, xxiv, 12, 78, 79, 80, 83, 120, 125, 141, 156, 157, 242
eye: imperfect design, 229
Ezekiel (prophet), 24, 69, 121, 143

faith, xxv, xxvi, 3, 4, 5, 9, 10, 11, 12, 18, 35–36, 39, 43, 46, 57, 58, 59, 64, 65, 66, 70, 71–72, 153, 208, 241–43, 247
   journey of, ix, xxiii–xxiv, xxv, 89
   leap of, 71, 241
   reason and, xiii, xxv, 18, 39, 59, 65, 241

   See also postcritical understanding (mature faith)
Feuerbach, Ludwig, 40
Finlay, Graeme, 197
Fischer, Dick, 194–95
forgiveness, 113, 121
   of sins, 31, 114
Foster, Richard, 16
Fox, George, x
Fox, Matthew, x, xv, 84n20
framework hypothesis, 92
Francis of Assisi, x
freedom/free will, 24, 94, 98, 196, 203, 237
Freud, Sigmund, 40, 78
fundamentalism, xvii, xix, 14, 39, 40, 54, 64, 126, 218, 222, 235

Gadamer, Hans-Georg, 78–79
Galileo Galilei, 170, 171
Gandhi, Mahatma, 30, 176
Garden of Eden, 3, 114
Gardner, Howard, 36
God, x, xi, xxi–xxii, xxiv, xxv, xxvi, xxviii, xxx, xxxii, 7, 8, 10, 11, 14, 15, 16–17, 22, 24, 28, 29, 35, 36, 39, 40, 43, 46, 47, 49, 50–52, 53, 57, 58–59, 60, 61, 66, 67, 70, 71, 72, 74–89, 105, 111, 112, 113, 114, 115, 116, 121, 126, 130, 132, 136, 145, 149, 150, 151, 152, 161, 168, 182, 183, 206, 215, 217, 223, 225–26, 227, 232, 234, 236, 237, 239, 244, 245
   as creator, 28, 46, 76–77, 85, 90–103, 184, 195, 211, 225, 233, 238, 240, 244, 247, 248
   as Ground of Being, xii, 86, 88
   as mystery, 79–83, 87
   as personal, xxvi, 15, 74, 77, 83, 85, 87, 88, 174
   as "The Real," 15
   as Totally Other, 75
   attributes of, xn4, 3, 23, 38, 64, 83, 226
   covenantal understanding of, 63
   doctrine of, xv

Subject/Name Index

existence of, xvii, xxix–xxx, 15, 38, 40, 57, 61, 70, 78, 153, 183, 215–16, 225, 227
experience of, x, xi, xviii, 11, 78, 79, 80, 82–83, 86, 116, 247
faith in, 18
images of, 48–49, 75, 83–84, 85, 146
inadequate (too small) views of, x, 174
knowledge of, 11, 47, 247–48
love of, xxxi, 23, 72, 85, 99–100, 101, 113, 143, 196, 211, 225, 237, 238, 239, 245, 246
models of, xxv–xxvii, 48, 58, 75, 75–79, 83–87, 98, 247–48
morality of, 75, 225–27
prayer and, 16–17, 61–64
promise and, 232–34
suffering and, 101–2
unknowability of, 47, 48, 51
See also apophatic tradition; Bible, God and; panentheism; theism (supernatural)
"God of the Gaps," 94, 223, 225, 227
goosebumps, 228
gospels, xxiii, xxvi, xxvii, xxviii, 29, 41, 43, 106–7, 111, 115, 119, 125, 129, 130, 131, 133, 136–37, 142, 221, 222
Gould, Stephen Jay, 187, 228
Goulder, Michael D., 131
grace, 14, 168
Gray, Asa, 93–94, 96, 97
Griffin, David Ray, 76
Gundry, Robert, 132

haggadah, xxvii, xxviii, 131, 133, 138
Hahn, Thich Nhat, xv
Ham, Ken, 183, 208
Harris, Sam, 40, 54
Hartshorne, Charles, 245, 246
Hasidim, 20
Haught, John F., xv, 77–78, 81–82, 83, 99, 102, 150, 151, 152, 153, 201, 202, 211, 233–34, 240
Hawking, Stephen, 179n11

heaven, xi, 4, 6, 23–27, 28, 60, 61, 77, 219, 227
Heidegger, Martin, 79
hell, xi, 4, 6, 13, 23–28, 60, 215, 219, 226, 227
Hellenism, Hellenization, 20, 26, 44, 135
Helmholtz, Hermann von, 229
Hendry, George S., xvi
Herod (king), 22, 133
Heschel, Abraham, 65
Hick, John, xii, xv, 13–16
hierarchy of explanations, 151, 152, 217
hierarchy of sciences, 164–68, 217, 219, 232
Hildegard of Bingen, x
Hinduism, 18, 38
Hitchens, Christopher, 40
Hodge, Charles, 171
Holocaust, 27, 226
Holy Spirit, 34, 35, 41, 46, 84, 85, 86, 97, 108–9, 113, 114, 127, 136, 141, 160, 169, 171, 233
  Spirit model, xxvi, 84–86
homosexuality, 33, 226
Hooker, Joseph, 230
humanism, 27, 70, 134
Hume, David, 18, 215
Hurd, James, 195
hypothetico-deductive method, 156, 168

ichneumon wasp, 230–31
image of God (*imago dei*), xxxi, 48, 59, 83, 189, 193, 195, 196–97, 206, 216
incarnation, 107–10
induction, 156, 170
inerrancy (biblical), xvii, 97, 169–70, 193, 217, 218
inspiration. *See* Bible, inspiration of
intellect (understanding), 48–49
Intelligent Design, 97, 99, 183, 223
Intertestamental Period, 22, 24, 25
Isaac (patriarch), 68, 72
Isaiah (prophet), 21, 109, 121, 124, 128, 220

259

Subject/Name Index

Islam, 13, 38, 40, 42, 71, 174, 182, 222
   dissent and, 73
Israel, 73

Jacob (patriarch), 68, 73
James, William, 120, 128
Jantzen, Grace, 245
Jeans, James, 161
Jefferson, Thomas, xx
Jerome, Saint, 43
Jesus Christ, x–xi, xviii, xxiv, xxvi,
   xxviii, xxix, 4, 21–22, 28, 32,
   35, 39, 41–43, 46–47, 61, 88, 90,
   107, 108, 109, 111, 112–14, 115,
   117, 130, 132, 136, 137, 139,
   143, 145, 160–61, 169, 172, 196,
   197, 208, 211, 246
   as prophet, 127, 128
   as Savior, 28–31, 196, 225
   birth of, 21–22, 107, 130, 137
   eschatology and, 121–28, 142
   faith in, 18, 43–44
   images of, 120, 141
   incarnation of, 46–47
   Jewishness of, xxvii, xxviii, 117–28
   passion of, 29–31, 42, 68, 85, 101–2,
      119, 122, 142, 143, 144
   prayer and, 61
   predestination and, 13–15
   self-understanding, 118, 126–27
   titles of, 107–10, 119, 141
   transfiguration of, 131
   See also Christology; incarnation;
      resurrection
Job, 65, 68, 69, 72
John the Baptist, 118, 121, 125
Johnson, Elizabeth, 99
Johnson, Phillip, 183
Judaism, Jewish, xii, xix, xxvii, xxviii,
   17, 18, 19, 22, 25, 41, 57, 71,
   110, 128, 129, 132, 133, 135,
   145, 174, 198, 221, 222
   dissent and, 73
   eschatological beliefs, 26, 41,
      121–28, 142
   rabbinic, rabbinical, 26, 41, 53
   views of body, 198
   views of spirit, 84
   See also Christianity, Judaism and;
      Jesus Christ, Jewishness of; New
      Testament, Jewishness of
Julian of Norwich, x

kataphatic, x
kenosis, 100, 101
Kepler, Johannes, 59
Kierkegaard, Søren, x, 63, 70–72,
   241–42
King Jr., Martin Luther, 30, 176
kingdom of God, xxvii, 26, 27, 28, 43,
   121, 122, 124, 125, 126, 127,
   128, 142, 145, 246
Kingsley, Charles, 98
Küng, Hans, 236

Latourette, Kenneth Scott, 5
Lewis, C. S., 6, 117
limbo, 27
Lindsay, T. M., 170
literalism, biblical, xvii, xxviii, xxxi, 6,
   10, 11, 12, 21, 31, 40, 45, 49,
   64–65, 67–69, 74, 87, 97, 114,
   115, 118, 131, 137, 153, 154,
   174, 181, 193, 194, 217, 218,
   235. *See also* accommodation,
   principle of
Loftus, John W., xxiv
logos, xiii, xxv, 36–37, 39, 52
Logos Christology, 47
Lonergan, Bernard, 78
love, xiii, 24, 34, 49, 54, 60, 61–62, 100,
   101, 143, 155, 174, 196, 237,
   238, 243, 245, 246
   analogy of, 49
   experience of, x–xi, xiii, 100
Luther, Martin, 3

Maccabees, 20, 25, 26
Madison, James, xx–xxi
Malthus, Thomas, 213
Marcion, 135
Marx, Karl, 40, 78
Mass, 38
Maximus the Confessor, x, 47, 52

Subject/Name Index

Mayr, Ernst, 151
McCosh, James, 97
McFague, Sallie, 245
McGrath, Alistair, 15, 28
McKibben, Bill, xvi
McLaren, Brian, xii, xvii, xv
memory, 48
Mendel, Menahem (rabbi), 64
Merton, Thomas, x
messiah, 41, 42, 126, 142
Metzger, Bruce, xv, 5
Michelangelo, 64
midrash, midrashic, xxviii, 21, 22, 41, 43, 44, 129, 130, 144
Mill, John Stuart, 75
Miller, Kenneth, 231–32
mind/body relationship, 202–7, 245
miqra, 41, 42, 44, 51
miracles, xxv, 18–19, 43, 57, 64–66, 75, 127, 131, 137, 178, 215, 222, 248
Modern Synthesis, 95, 187
Moltmann, Jürgen, 76–77, 100–101
monks, monasticism, 48
Moore, Aubrey, 96
morality. *See* ethics
Mormonism, 18
Morris, Henry, 208
Moses, 22, 42, 51, 64, 65, 73, 106, 111, 126, 129, 130, 131, 171, 220
Muhammad, 42, 222
Murphy, George, 101
Murphy, Nancey, xvi
music, 39, 68
Muslim. *See* Islam
mystery, sense of, 18, 44, 77, 78–83, 144, 145
mystic, mystical, mysticism, 82, 87, 88, 99, 126, 139, 158, 219
myth, mythology, xii, 36–37, 39, 45, 52, 78, 87, 159–61
mythos, xiii, xxv, 36–37, 39

natural selection, 93–94, 96, 98, 150, 151, 182, 187, 198, 200, 213–14, 224
natural theology, 97, 214

nature, laws of, 18, 91, 94, 96, 100, 162, 216, 217
  See also Book of Nature
Nazism, 27
Neanderthals, 191–92
neuroscience, 198, 199
new atheism. *See* atheism
New Testament, xxiv, xxviii, 31, 41, 43, 102, 107, 112, 113, 117, 119, 120, 134, 141, 198, 208, 209, 221, 222, 226
  afterlife and, 27–28
  canonical status, 31–32
  doctrine of creation, 90
  eschatology and, 125
  faith and, 44
  interpretations of the cross, 30–31
  Jewishness of, xxviii, 130–37
  rhetorical nature of, 221
Newton, Isaac, 184
Newtonian mechanics, 187
Nietzsche, Friedrich, 40, 78
nonreductive physicalism (emergent realism), xxxi, 165–66, 168, 199–200, 217
Nouwen, Henri, x

Old Testament (Hebrew Bible), 43–44, 74, 83, 110, 111, 113, 115, 120, 127, 128, 129, 131, 133–34, 198, 209, 222, 225, 226
  doctrine of creation, 90
order, organization, 200–202, 216, 233, 239
Origen of Alexandria, x, 44, 226
original sin, xxxi, 150, 208–12
Orr, James, 96, 170
Otto, Rudolf, 78, 79
Outsider Test for Faith, xxiv, xxv, 12, 13, 18

Paley, William, 214–15
panentheism, xxvi, xxxi, 76–83, 102, 105, 237, 244, 245
Pascal, Blaise, x, 241
Paul, Saint, x, 12, 22, 26–27, 30, 41, 43, 62, 100, 102, 107–9, 122, 128,

Subject/Name Index

Paul, Saint–continued
    138, 139, 141, 143, 145, 196,
    198, 204, 209, 221
    eschatology, 126, 198
    love, 100
    original sin, 209
    prayer, 62
    resurrection of Jesus, 136, 140
    resurrection of the body, 198
Peacocke, Arthur, xxx, 77, 98, 99, 167
Pentateuch, 87, 220
Pentecost, 131, 141, 160
Peter, Saint, 130, 138, 143
pesher, 22, 41, 42
Pharaoh (ruler), 22, 23, 68, 111, 131
Pharisees, 26
Phillips, J. B., x
philosophy, *philosophia*, 44, 45, 50
physics, xxx, xxxi, 52, 93, 101, 163, 164,
    165, 167, 178, 232
Plato, 90, 203, 204, 207
Plotinus, 50, 64
pluralism. *See* religious pluralism
Polkinghorne, John, 98, 99, 101
Popper, Karl, 204
positivism, 165
postcritical understanding (mature
    faith), xxiv–xxv, xxvi, 10–11, 59,
    114, 116, 222
    the Bible and, 10–11, 114–16
postmodernism, xvii, 52–54
prayer, xxv, 16–17, 35, 48, 57, 61–64, 75
precritical understanding (Precritical
    Paradigm), xxiii, xxv, 9–10, 35,
    59, 114, 118
predestination, 13–16
Presbyterian Church (U.S.A.), 5, 32–34
Princeton Theological Seminary, xii,
    xvi, 5, 6, 12, 97
process theology, xxvi, 78, 87, 238–40
    ethics, 245
    evil, 240, 245
    God in, 76n3, 238–40, 244–46
    sin, 240
    tenets of, 244–46

prophets, prophecy, x, xxv, 19–22, 30,
    41, 42, 69, 126, 127, 128, 134,
    177
promise, 3, 162, 174, 212, 133–34
Protestantism, 218, 222
    evangelicals, 14, 28, 71, 95, 102,
    123, 126, 217, 218, 222
providence, 97, 150, 234, 236
purgatory, 27

Qur'an, 42, 182, 222

Rahner, Karl, x, 78
rapture of believers, 27
reason, xxvi, 24, 37, 38, 45, 48, 52, 53,
    59, 66, 242
    role of, xviii, xix, 54, 72
reductionism, xxv, 19, 59, 163, 166–67,
    174, 198, 199
Reformation, Protestant, xvii, 32, 101,
    169, 222
Reformed Theology. *See* Calvinism
religion, xvii, xxi–xxii, 17, 36, 37, 51,
    52, 53, 57, 72, 80, 81, 82, 88,
    156, 165, 176, 222, 234, 241, 247
    assessment of, xx–xxi, 40
    evolution of, xix–xx
    role of, xvii, xxi–xxii, xxvi, 17, 37,
    52, 53, 80, 88
    science and, xiii, xv, xviii–xxxi, 18,
    64, 90–103, 149–59, 169, 173,
    174–80, 181–83, 193–95, 223,
    235–38
    spirituality and, xix–xxii, 8
    See also accommodation, principle
    of
religious experience, 158–59
    See also experience, human
religious extremism, 71–72
religious pluralism, 10, 13, 16, 58
remythologization, xxviii
resurrection, xxvi, xxvii–xxviii, 25–26,
    28, 126
    of Jesus, xxvii–xxviii, 18, 26, 30, 38,
    107, 108, 112, 113, 115, 118,
    120, 124, 136–45, 222
    of the dead, 25–26, 123, 125, 143

Subject/Name Index

revelation, xv, 7, 47, 67–69, 73, 75, 86, 143, 145, 170, 215, 218, 222, 242
Revelation, book of, 25, 27, 110, 123, 221
Ricoeur, Paul, 78
ritual, 37, 45–46, 78, 156, 159
Robinson, John A. T. (bishop), xii, 122
Rolston, Holmes, 101–2
Roman Catholicism, 201, 222
Ruse, Michael, xvi, 94

Sabbath, 17, 92, 108, 137, 226
sacrament, 45
    Bible as, 114, 116
Sagan, Carl, 174, 218–19
salvation, xxv, 4, 6, 13, 15, 23, 58, 113, 118, 136, 149, 168, 169, 172, 197, 212, 218
    doctrine of, 7, 28–31, 212
Sanders, E. P., 122
Schleiermacher, Friedrich, x
Schneider, Robert J., xvi, 101
Schulweis, Harold (rabbi), xv, 57, 58, 59, 60, 65, 67, 69, 73, 75
Schweitzer, Albert, x
science, xxvii, 10, 49, 52, 81, 90, 91, 149, 152, 153, 155, 156, 166, 168, 169, 171, 172, 174, 183, 187, 218, 220, 222, 223, 232, 234
    hierarchy of, 164–68
    methods of, 155–57, 175–80
    mystery and, 81–82
    provisionality of, 172, 176
    See religion, science and
scientism (scientific materialism), xxviii, 54, 91, 153, 154, 183
Scopes trial, 188
scripture (biblical), xi, xii, xiii, xxvi, xxviii, xxx, 6, 12, 22, 33, 35, 37, 38, 42, 44–45, 48, 49, 51, 65, 92, 97, 105–16, 128, 144, 156, 161, 169, 171, 208, 214, 222–23, 242
    role of, xviii, xix
    sacredness of, 69, 114
    See also accommodation, principle of; Bible; Book of Scripture; New Testament; Old Testament

Seleucids, 20, 25
Sellars, Roy Wood, 165–66
Seneca, 27
Sheol, 23
Shermer, Michael, 156
sin, xxxi, 4, 14, 28, 32, 58, 70, 86, 112, 113, 168, 208, 210, 226, 240
    doctrine of, 29, 30, 31, 86, 208
    See also original sin
Skinner, B. F., 81
Smith, Huston, xv, xxii
Smith, Joseph, 18
sociobiology, 210
Socrates, 54, 71
soul, xxxi, 23, 24, 25, 197–202, 204–6, 207
    biblical view of, 198–99
    models for, 199
Spinoza, Baruch, 204
Spirit, Holy. *See* Holy Spirit
spirituality. *See* religion
Spong, John Shelby (bishop), xi, xiii, xv, 61, 75, 83, 88, 129, 130, 131, 142
Steiner, George, 39
Stevens, Wallace, 58
stewardship, 197
story theology, 110–14, 157, 159–61
Strauss, David Frederich, 87
Suchocki, Marjorie, 245

Talmud, 129
Tatersall, Ian, 54
Teilhard de Chardin, Pierre, x, 95, 185, 210, 212
teleology, xxxi, 161, 163
    See also design; order
temple, 41, 85, 111, 122, 132, 143
temple theology, 31
Ten Commandments, 108
Tertullian, xxx, 170
theistic evolution. *See* evolution, theistic
theism (supernatural), xi–xii, xiii, xxiv, 15, 17, 19n5, 58, 62, 74–77, 82, 83, 87–88, 100, 145, 154, 225, 225n9, 227n13, 235, 242, 244
theodicy, 100

263

Subject/Name Index

theology, theologians, xvii, xxvi, xxx, 7, 8, 9, 38, 39, 40, 51, 54, 58, 66, 74, 87, 96, 97, 98, 99, 100, 110, 111, 113, 121, 150, 151, 154, 163, 167, 168, 169, 195, 217, 218, 221, 232, 242, 246
   liturgy and, 51
   sources of, xviii–xix
   See also Bible, biblical theology; natural theology
Tillich, Paul, x, xii, 54, 63, 78, 88
Torah, 41, 54, 129, 132, 223
tradition: role of, xviii
Trinity, 49, 50, 88, 98, 120
truth, xxvi, 8, 18, 52, 54, 59, 78, 80, 82, 223
typology, typological, 22

unity. *See* Christianity, unity of
unknowing. *See* apophatic tradition

Van Till, Howard, 98
Vattimo, Gianni, 53
verification principle. *See* positivism
vestigial organs, 228–30
Virgil, 27
vitalism, vital force, xxxi, 200

Walsch, Neale Donald, xxi–xxii
Warfield, B. B., 97
Wellhausen, Julius, 87
Wesley, John, x
Wesleyan Quadrilateral, xviii
Westminster Shorter Catechism, xviii, 242
Whitehead, Alfred North, 76, 78, 80, 87, 99, 152, 239, 245, 246
wilderness, 111
Williams, Patricia, 209, 210
Williams, Robyn, 231
Wisdom literature, x
Wood, Robert W., 178
Woodmorappe, John, 194
Woolman, John, x
worldview, 4, 7, 9, 95, 219
   biblical, 220–21
worship, 16–17, 64, 92, 122, 220

Wright, N. T., 125

Young Earth Creationism, 97, 182, 183, 193, 194, 208
   See also Intelligent Design

Zoroaster, 24
Zoroastrianism, 24–25

www.ingramcontent.com/pod-product-compliance
Lightning Source LLC
Chambersburg PA
CBHW070338230426
43663CB00011B/2367